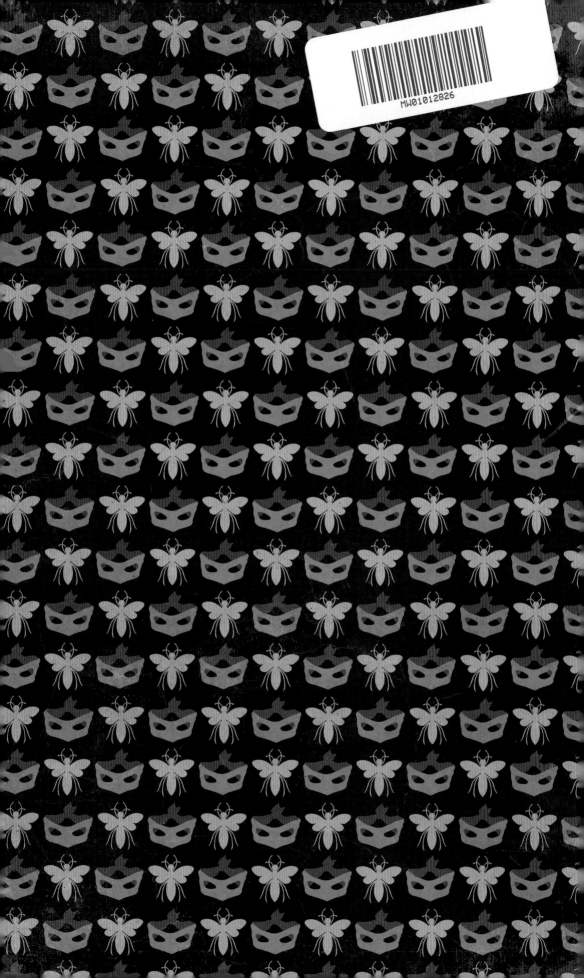

THE LONE RANGER® GREEN HORNET®

CHAMPIONS OF JUSTICE

DYNAMITE®

Nick Barrucci, CEO / Publisher
Juan Collado, President / COO
Joe Rybandt, Executive Editor
Matt Idelson, Senior Editor
Anthony Marques, Assistant Editor
Kevin Ketner, Editorial Assistant
Jason Ullmeyer, Art Director
Geoff Harkins, Senior Graphic Designer
Cathleen Heard, Graphic Designer
Alexis Persson, Production Artist
Chris Caniano, Digital Associate
Rachel Kilbury, Digital Assistant
Brandon Dante Primavera, V.P. of IT and Operations
Rich Young, Director of Business Development
Alan Payne, V.P. of Sales and Marketing
Keith Davidsen, Marketing Director
Pat O'Connell, Sales Manager

First Printing
1 2 3 4 5 6 7 8 9 10

ISBN10: 1-5241-0294-6

ISBN13: 978-1-5241-0294-4

Online at **www.DYNAMITE.com**
On Facebook **/Dynamitecomics**
On Instagram **/Dynamitecomics**
On Tumblr **dynamitecomics.tumblr.com**
On Twitter **@dynamitecomics**
On YouTube **/Dynamitecomics**

For information regarding press, media rights, foreign rights, licensing, promotions, and advertising e-mail: marketing@dynamite.com

WRITTEN BY
MICHAEL USLAN
ART BY
GIOVANNI TIMPANO
COLOR BY
PETE PANTAZIS
LETTERS BY
TROY PETERI
COVER BY
JOHN CASSADAY
COVER COLOR BY
JUNE CHUNG

EXECUTIVE EDITOR
JOSEPH RYBANDT

ASSOCIATE EDITOR
ANTHONY MARQUES

COLLECTION DESIGN
ALEXIS PERSSON

Special thanks to
David Grace at
Green Hornet, Inc.

Special thanks to
Alex Ward and
Steve Behling.

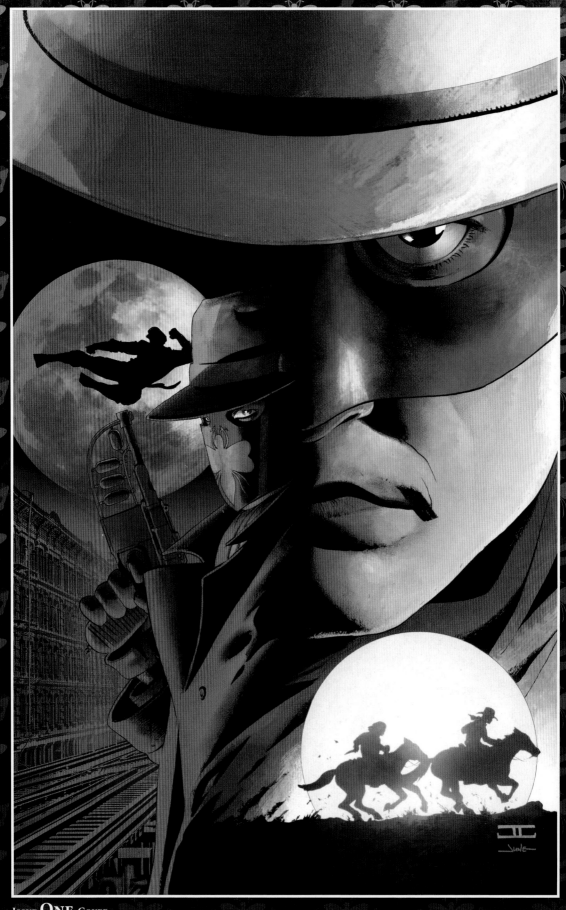

ISSUE ONE COVER

ART BY JOHN CASSADAY COLORS BY JUNE CHUNG

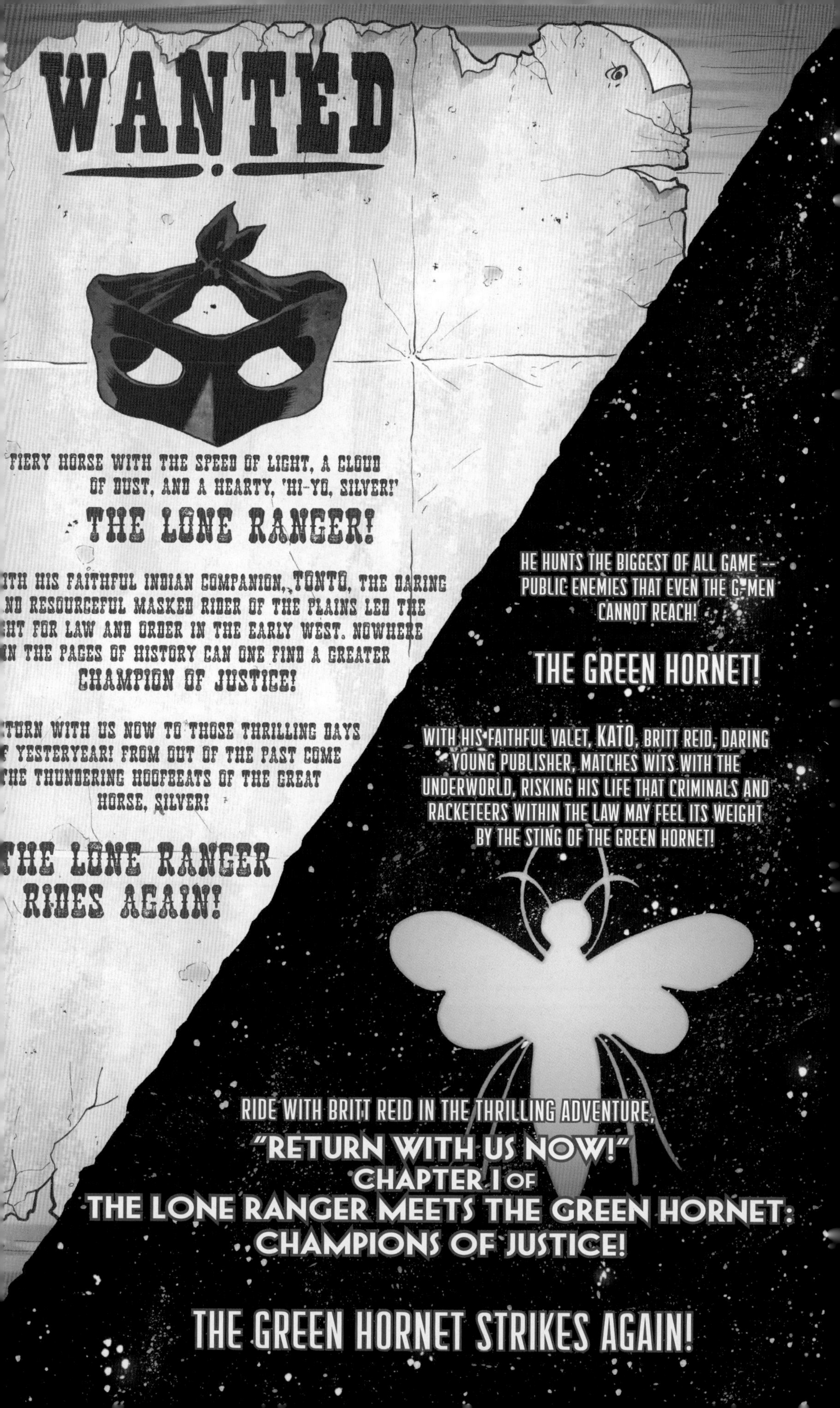
WANTED
FIERY HORSE WITH THE SPEED OF LIGHT, A CLOUD OF DUST, AND A HEARTY, 'HI-YO, SILVER!'
THE LONE RANGER!
ITH HIS FAITHFUL INDIAN COMPANION, TONTO, THE DARING ND RESOURCEFUL MASKED RIDER OF THE PLAINS LED THE HT FOR LAW AND ORDER IN THE EARLY WEST. NOWHERE IN THE PAGES OF HISTORY CAN ONE FIND A GREATER CHAMPION OF JUSTICE!
TURN WITH US NOW TO THOSE THRILLING DAYS YESTERYEAR! FROM OUT OF THE PAST COME THE THUNDERING HOOFBEATS OF THE GREAT HORSE, SILVER!
THE LONE RANGER RIDES AGAIN!
HE HUNTS THE BIGGEST OF ALL GAME -- PUBLIC ENEMIES THAT EVEN THE G-MEN CANNOT REACH!
THE GREEN HORNET!
WITH HIS FAITHFUL VALET, KATO, BRITT REID, DARING YOUNG PUBLISHER, MATCHES WITS WITH THE UNDERWORLD, RISKING HIS LIFE THAT CRIMINALS AND RACKETEERS WITHIN THE LAW MAY FEEL ITS WEIGHT BY THE STING OF THE GREEN HORNET!
RIDE WITH BRITT REID IN THE THRILLING ADVENTURE,
"RETURN WITH US NOW!"
CHAPTER I OF
THE LONE RANGER MEETS THE GREEN HORNET:
CHAMPIONS OF JUSTICE!
THE GREEN HORNET STRIKES AGAIN!

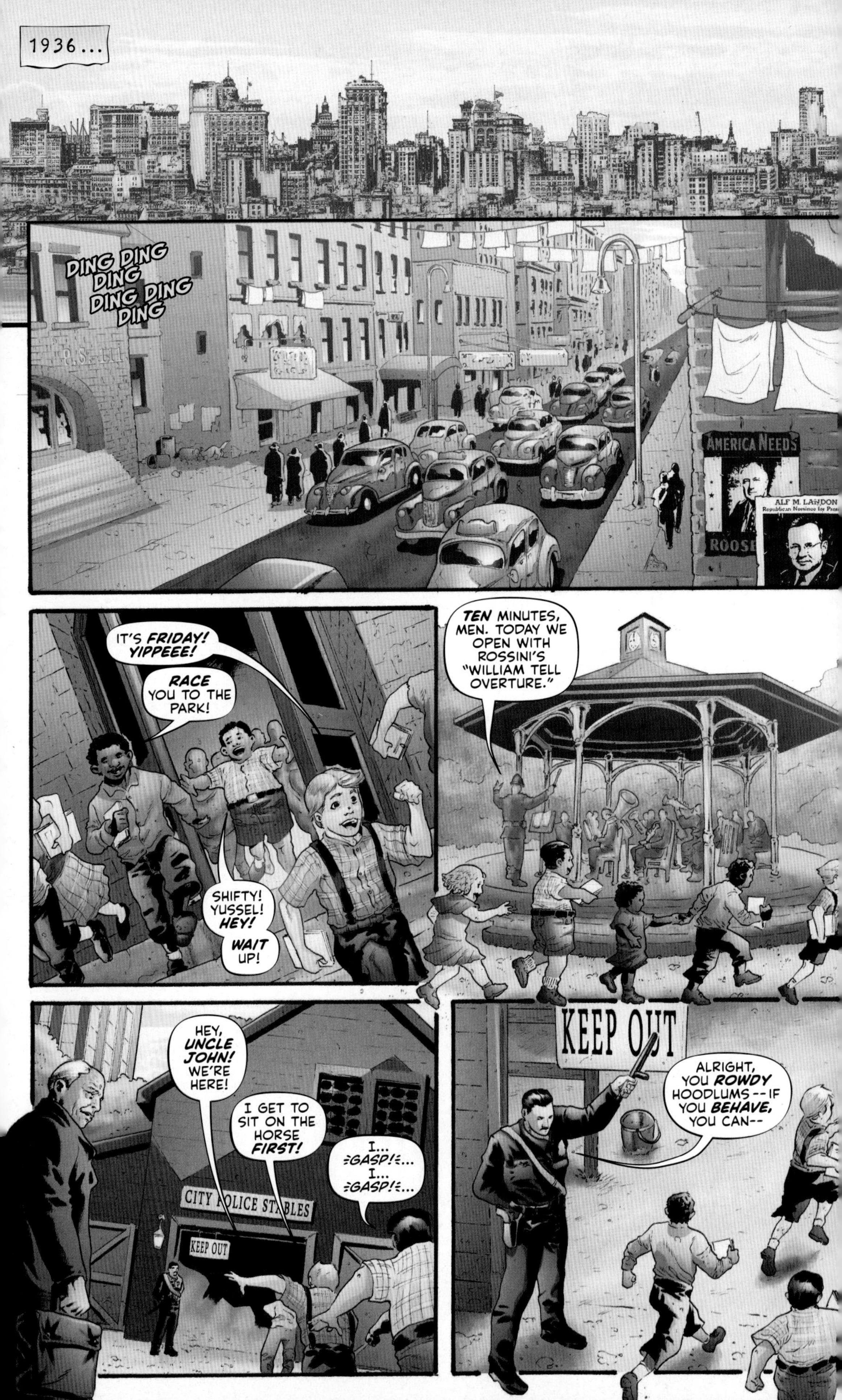
1936...
DING DING DING DING DING DING
AMERICA NEEDS ROOSE
ALF M. LANDON Republican Nominee for Presi
IT'S FRIDAY! YIPPEEE!
RACE YOU TO THE PARK!
SHIFTY! YUSSEL! HEY!
WAIT UP!
TEN MINUTES, MEN. TODAY WE OPEN WITH ROSSINI'S "WILLIAM TELL OVERTURE."
HEY, UNCLE JOHN! WE'RE HERE!
I GET TO SIT ON THE HORSE FIRST!
I... GASP!... I... GASP!...
CITY POLICE STABLES
KEEP OUT
KEEP OUT
ALRIGHT, YOU ROWDY HOODLUMS--IF YOU BEHAVE, YOU CAN--

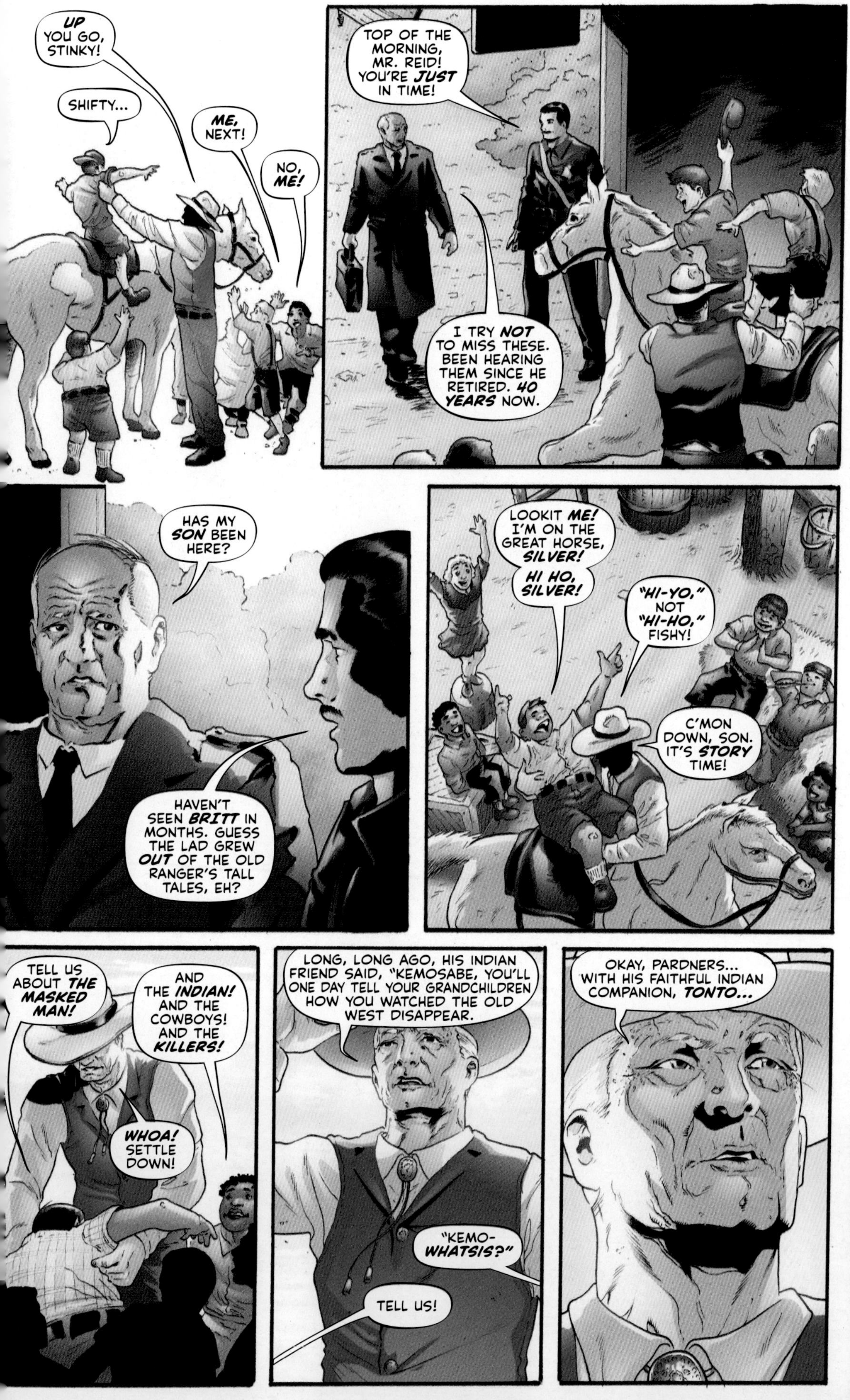

UP YOU GO, STINKY!
SHIFTY...
ME, NEXT!
NO, ME!
TOP OF THE MORNING, MR. REID! YOU'RE JUST IN TIME!
I TRY NOT TO MISS THESE. BEEN HEARING THEM SINCE HE RETIRED. 40 YEARS NOW.
HAS MY SON BEEN HERE?
HAVEN'T SEEN BRITT IN MONTHS. GUESS THE LAD GREW OUT OF THE OLD RANGER'S TALL TALES, EH?
LOOKIT ME! I'M ON THE GREAT HORSE, SILVER!
HI HO, SILVER!
"HI-YO," NOT "HI-HO," FISHY!
C'MON DOWN, SON. IT'S STORY TIME!
TELL US ABOUT THE MASKED MAN!
AND THE INDIAN! AND THE COWBOYS! AND THE KILLERS!
WHOA! SETTLE DOWN!
LONG, LONG AGO, HIS INDIAN FRIEND SAID, "KEMOSABE, YOU'LL ONE DAY TELL YOUR GRANDCHILDREN HOW YOU WATCHED THE OLD WEST DISAPPEAR.
"KEMO-WHATSIS?"
TELL US!
OKAY, PARDNERS... WITH HIS FAITHFUL INDIAN COMPANION, TONTO...

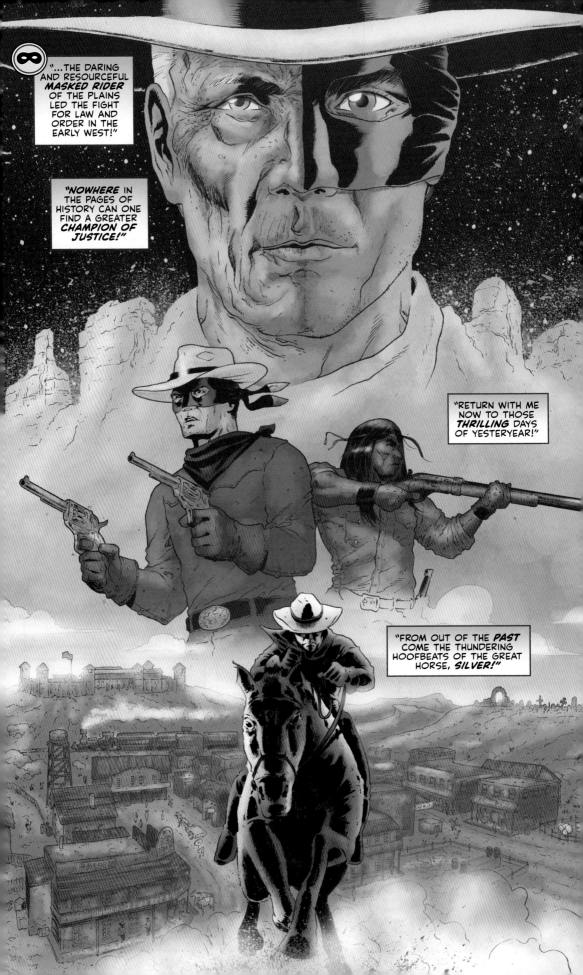

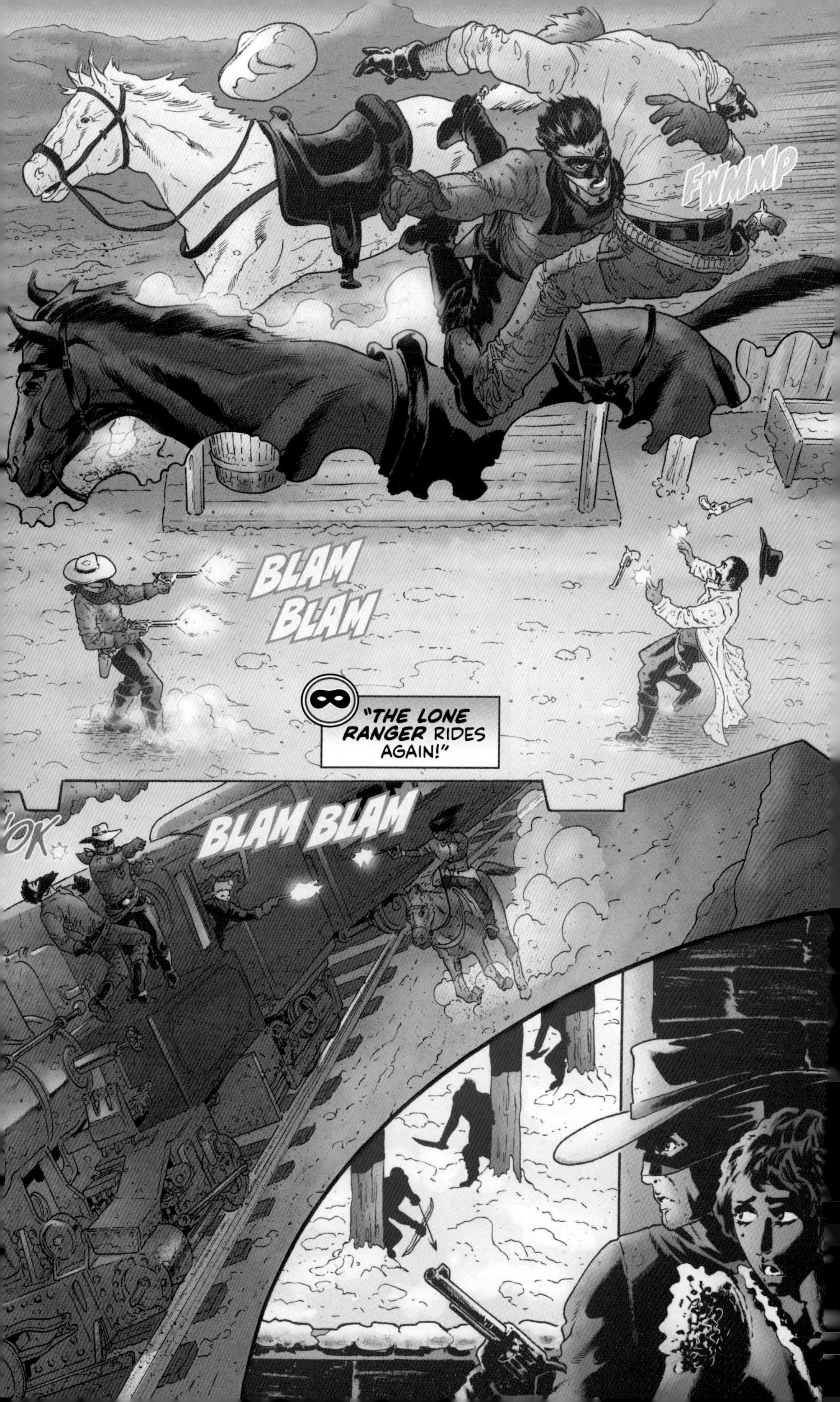

FWMMP
BLAM
BLAM
"THE LONE RANGER RIDES AGAIN!"
BLAM BLAM

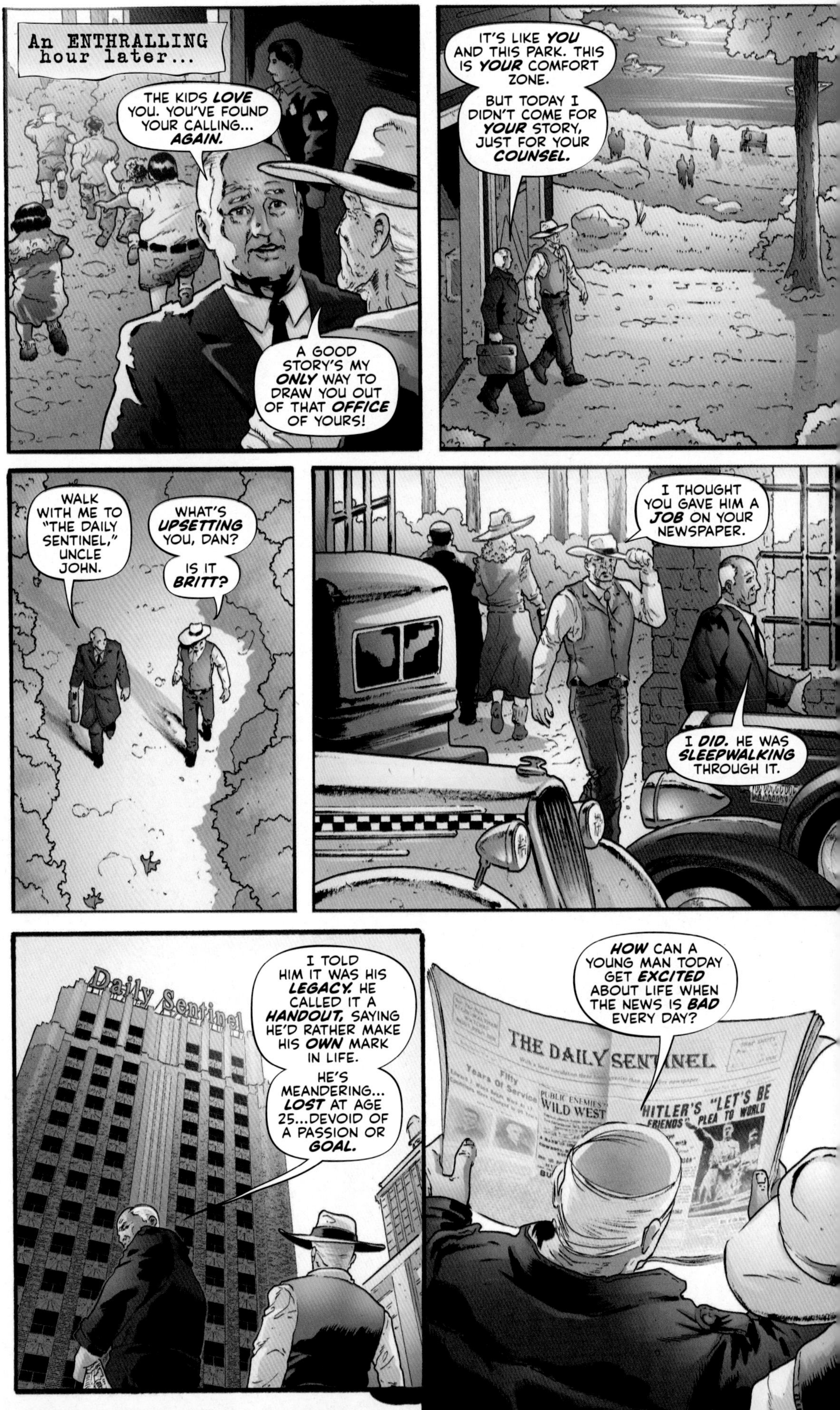
An ENTHRALLING hour later...
THE KIDS LOVE YOU. YOU'VE FOUND YOUR CALLING... AGAIN.
A GOOD STORY'S MY ONLY WAY TO DRAW YOU OUT OF THAT OFFICE OF YOURS!
IT'S LIKE YOU AND THIS PARK. THIS IS YOUR COMFORT ZONE.
BUT TODAY I DIDN'T COME FOR YOUR STORY, JUST FOR YOUR COUNSEL.
WALK WITH ME TO "THE DAILY SENTINEL," UNCLE JOHN.
WHAT'S UPSETTING YOU, DAN?
IS IT BRITT?
I THOUGHT YOU GAVE HIM A JOB ON YOUR NEWSPAPER.
I DID. HE WAS SLEEPWALKING THROUGH IT.
Daily Sentinel
I TOLD HIM IT WAS HIS LEGACY. HE CALLED IT A HANDOUT, SAYING HE'D RATHER MAKE HIS OWN MARK IN LIFE.
HE'S MEANDERING... LOST AT AGE 25...DEVOID OF A PASSION OR GOAL.
HOW CAN A YOUNG MAN TODAY GET EXCITED ABOUT LIFE WHEN THE NEWS IS BAD EVERY DAY?
THE DAILY SENTINEL
Fifty Years of Service
PUBLIC ENEMIES
WILD WEST
HITLER'S "LET'S BE FRIENDS" PLEA TO WORLD

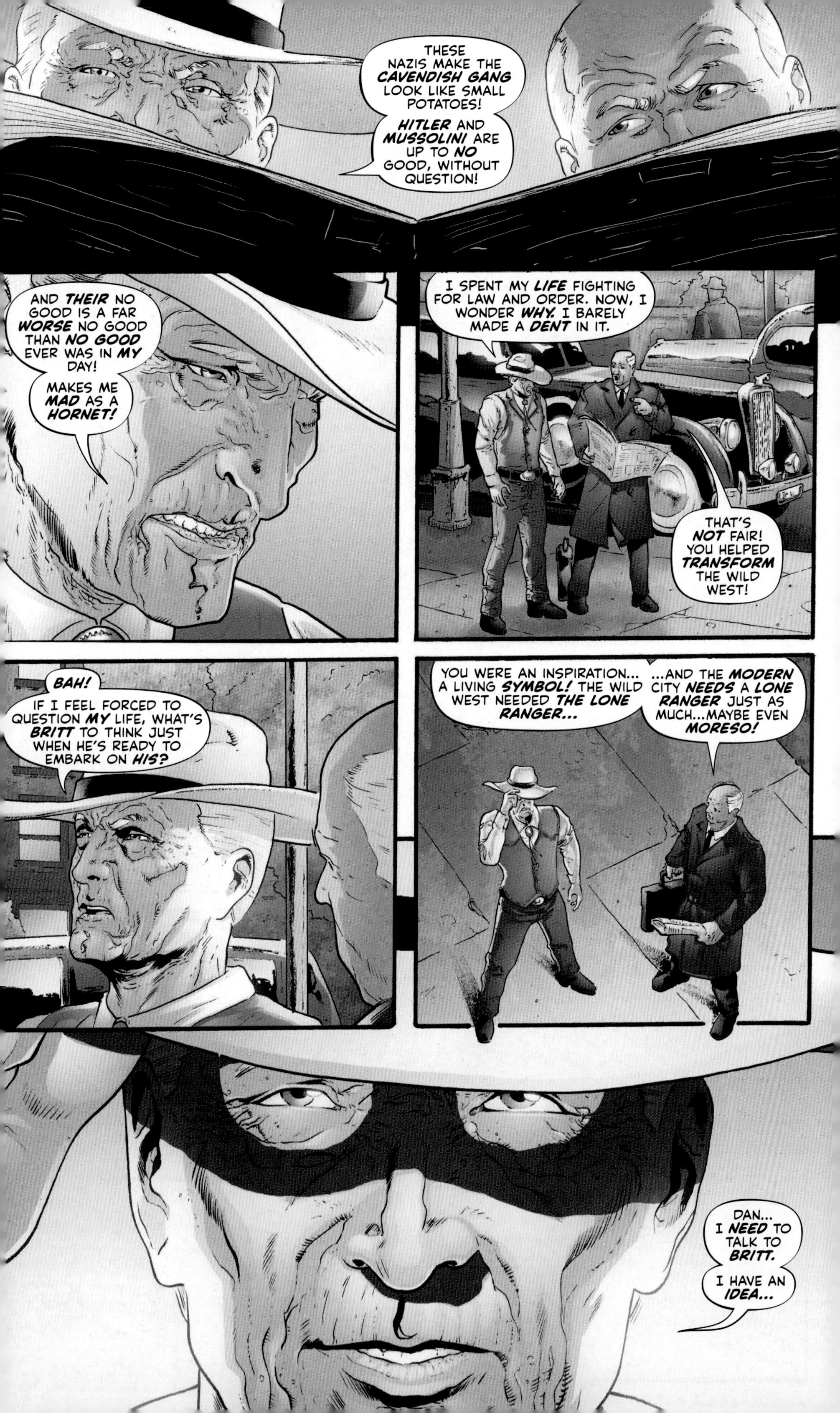

THESE NAZIS MAKE THE CAVENDISH GANG LOOK LIKE SMALL POTATOES!
HITLER AND MUSSOLINI ARE UP TO NO GOOD, WITHOUT QUESTION!
AND THEIR NO GOOD IS A FAR WORSE NO GOOD THAN NO GOOD EVER WAS IN MY DAY!
MAKES ME MAD AS A HORNET!
I SPENT MY LIFE FIGHTING FOR LAW AND ORDER. NOW, I WONDER WHY. I BARELY MADE A DENT IN IT.
THAT'S NOT FAIR! YOU HELPED TRANSFORM THE WILD WEST!
BAH!
IF I FEEL FORCED TO QUESTION MY LIFE, WHAT'S BRITT TO THINK JUST WHEN HE'S READY TO EMBARK ON HIS?
YOU WERE AN INSPIRATION... A LIVING SYMBOL! THE WILD WEST NEEDED THE LONE RANGER...
...AND THE MODERN CITY NEEDS A LONE RANGER JUST AS MUCH...MAYBE EVEN MORESO!
DAN... I NEED TO TALK TO BRITT.
I HAVE AN IDEA...

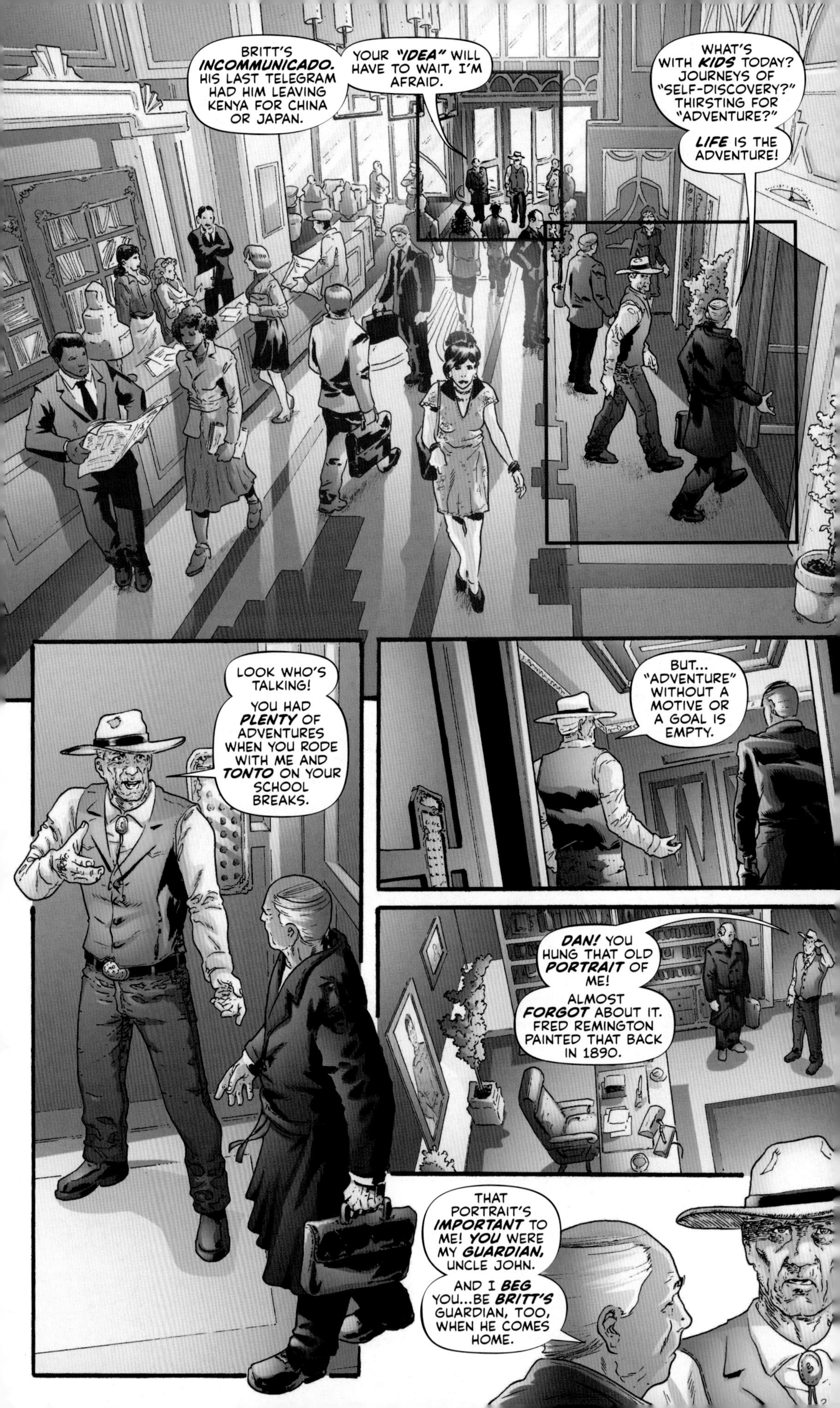
BRITT'S *INCOMMUNICADO.* HIS LAST TELEGRAM HAD HIM LEAVING KENYA FOR CHINA OR JAPAN.
YOUR *"IDEA"* WILL HAVE TO WAIT, I'M AFRAID.
WHAT'S WITH *KIDS* TODAY? JOURNEYS OF "SELF-DISCOVERY?" THIRSTING FOR "ADVENTURE?"
LIFE IS THE ADVENTURE!
LOOK WHO'S TALKING!
YOU HAD *PLENTY* OF ADVENTURES WHEN YOU RODE WITH ME AND *TONTO* ON YOUR SCHOOL BREAKS.
BUT... "ADVENTURE" WITHOUT A MOTIVE OR A GOAL IS EMPTY.
DAN! YOU HUNG THAT OLD *PORTRAIT* OF ME!
ALMOST *FORGOT* ABOUT IT. FRED REMINGTON PAINTED THAT BACK IN 1890.
THAT PORTRAIT'S *IMPORTANT* TO ME! *YOU* WERE MY *GUARDIAN,* UNCLE JOHN.
AND I *BEG* YOU...BE *BRITT'S* GUARDIAN, TOO, WHEN HE COMES HOME.

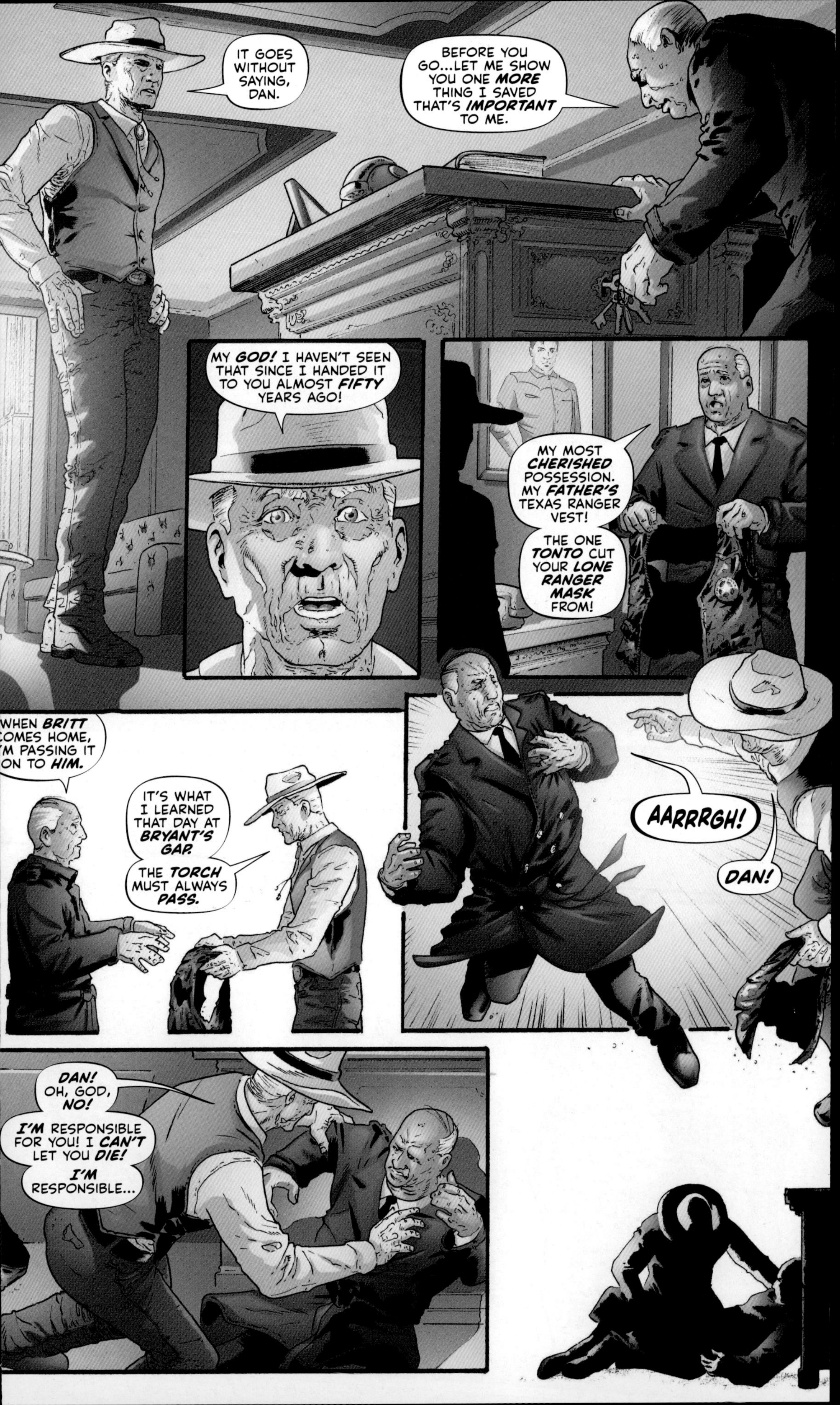
IT GOES WITHOUT SAYING, DAN.
BEFORE YOU GO...LET ME SHOW YOU ONE MORE THING I SAVED THAT'S IMPORTANT TO ME.
MY GOD! I HAVEN'T SEEN THAT SINCE I HANDED IT TO YOU ALMOST FIFTY YEARS AGO!
MY MOST CHERISHED POSSESSION. MY FATHER'S TEXAS RANGER VEST!
THE ONE TONTO CUT YOUR LONE RANGER MASK FROM!
WHEN BRITT COMES HOME, I'M PASSING IT ON TO HIM.
IT'S WHAT I LEARNED THAT DAY AT BRYANT'S GAP.
THE TORCH MUST ALWAYS PASS.
AARRRGH!
DAN!
DAN! OH, GOD, NO!
I'M RESPONSIBLE FOR YOU! I CAN'T LET YOU DIE!
I'M RESPONSIBLE...

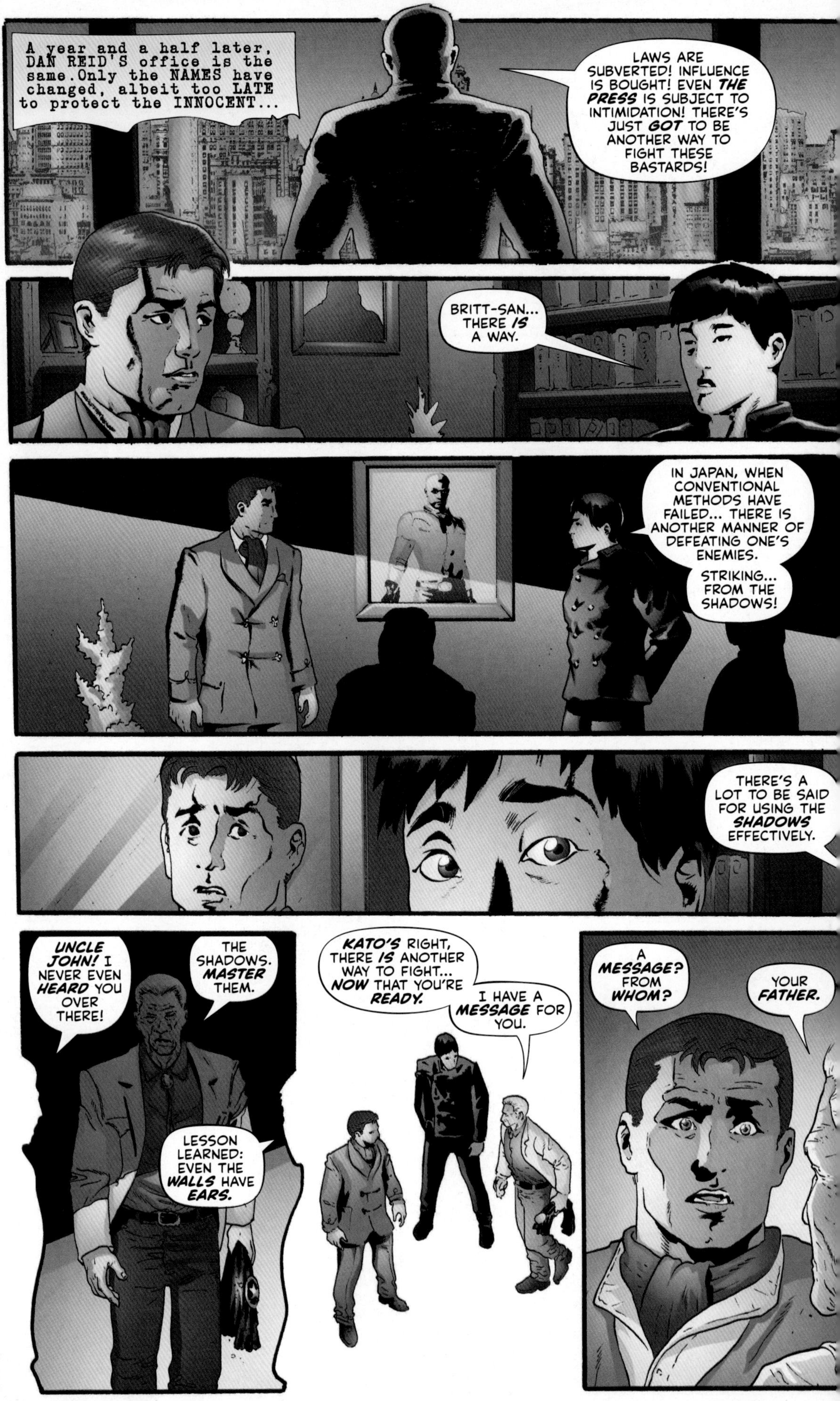

A year and a half later, DAN REID'S office is the same. Only the NAMES have changed, albeit too LATE to protect the INNOCENT...
LAWS ARE SUBVERTED! INFLUENCE IS BOUGHT! EVEN THE PRESS IS SUBJECT TO INTIMIDATION! THERE'S JUST GOT TO BE ANOTHER WAY TO FIGHT THESE BASTARDS!
BRITT-SAN... THERE IS A WAY.
IN JAPAN, WHEN CONVENTIONAL METHODS HAVE FAILED... THERE IS ANOTHER MANNER OF DEFEATING ONE'S ENEMIES.
STRIKING... FROM THE SHADOWS!
THERE'S A LOT TO BE SAID FOR USING THE SHADOWS EFFECTIVELY.
UNCLE JOHN! I NEVER EVEN HEARD YOU OVER THERE!
THE SHADOWS. MASTER THEM.
LESSON LEARNED: EVEN THE WALLS HAVE EARS.
KATO'S RIGHT, THERE IS ANOTHER WAY TO FIGHT... NOW THAT YOU'RE READY.
I HAVE A MESSAGE FOR YOU.
A MESSAGE? FROM WHOM?
YOUR FATHER.

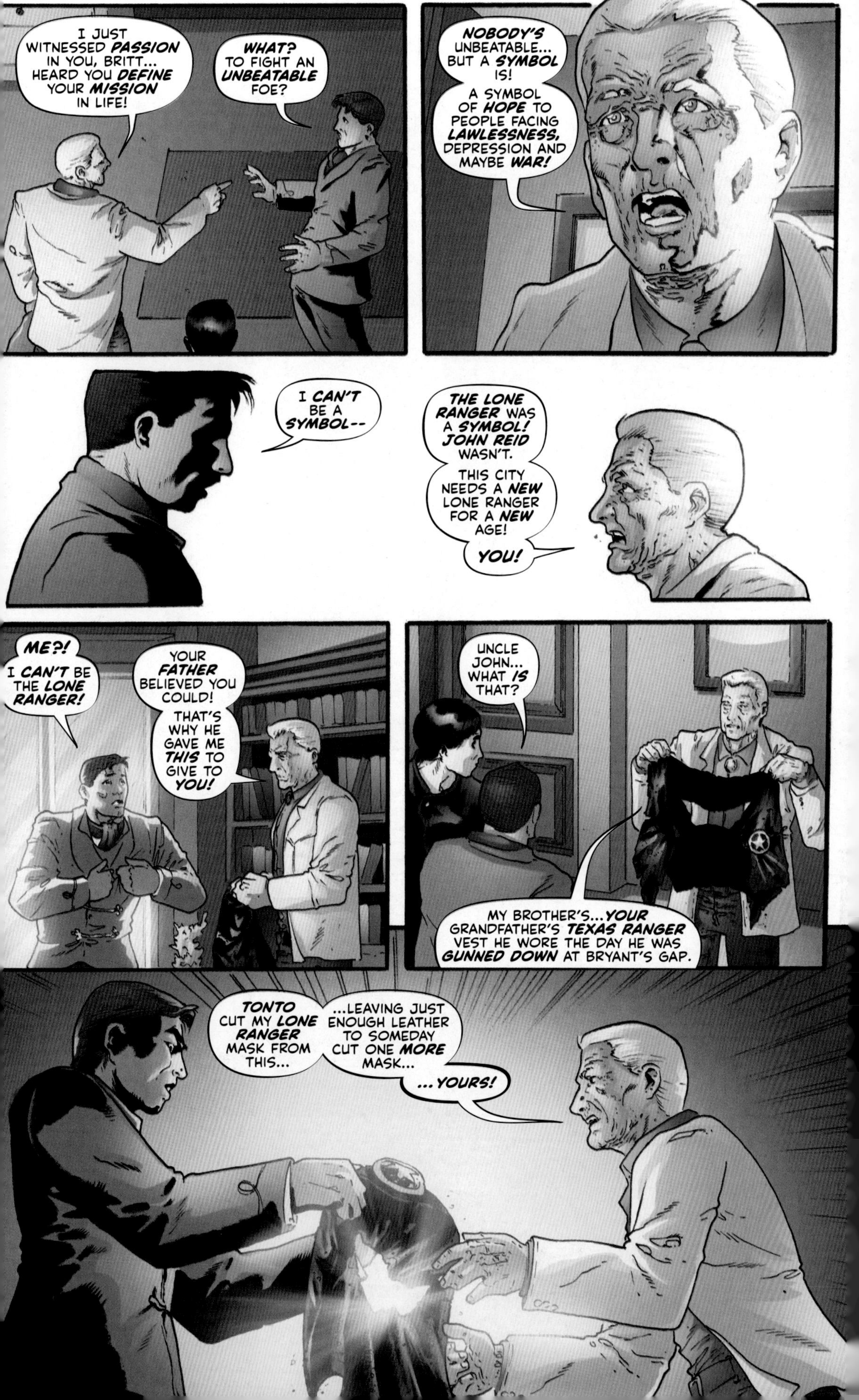
I JUST WITNESSED PASSION IN YOU, BRITT... HEARD YOU DEFINE YOUR MISSION IN LIFE!
WHAT? TO FIGHT AN UNBEATABLE FOE?
NOBODY'S UNBEATABLE... BUT A SYMBOL IS!
A SYMBOL OF HOPE TO PEOPLE FACING LAWLESSNESS, DEPRESSION AND MAYBE WAR!
I CAN'T BE A SYMBOL--
THE LONE RANGER WAS A SYMBOL! JOHN REID WASN'T.
THIS CITY NEEDS A NEW LONE RANGER FOR A NEW AGE!
YOU!
ME?!
I CAN'T BE THE LONE RANGER!
YOUR FATHER BELIEVED YOU COULD!
THAT'S WHY HE GAVE ME THIS TO GIVE TO YOU!
UNCLE JOHN... WHAT IS THAT?
MY BROTHER'S...YOUR GRANDFATHER'S TEXAS RANGER VEST HE WORE THE DAY HE WAS GUNNED DOWN AT BRYANT'S GAP.
TONTO CUT MY LONE RANGER MASK FROM THIS...
...LEAVING JUST ENOUGH LEATHER TO SOMEDAY CUT ONE MORE MASK...
...YOURS!

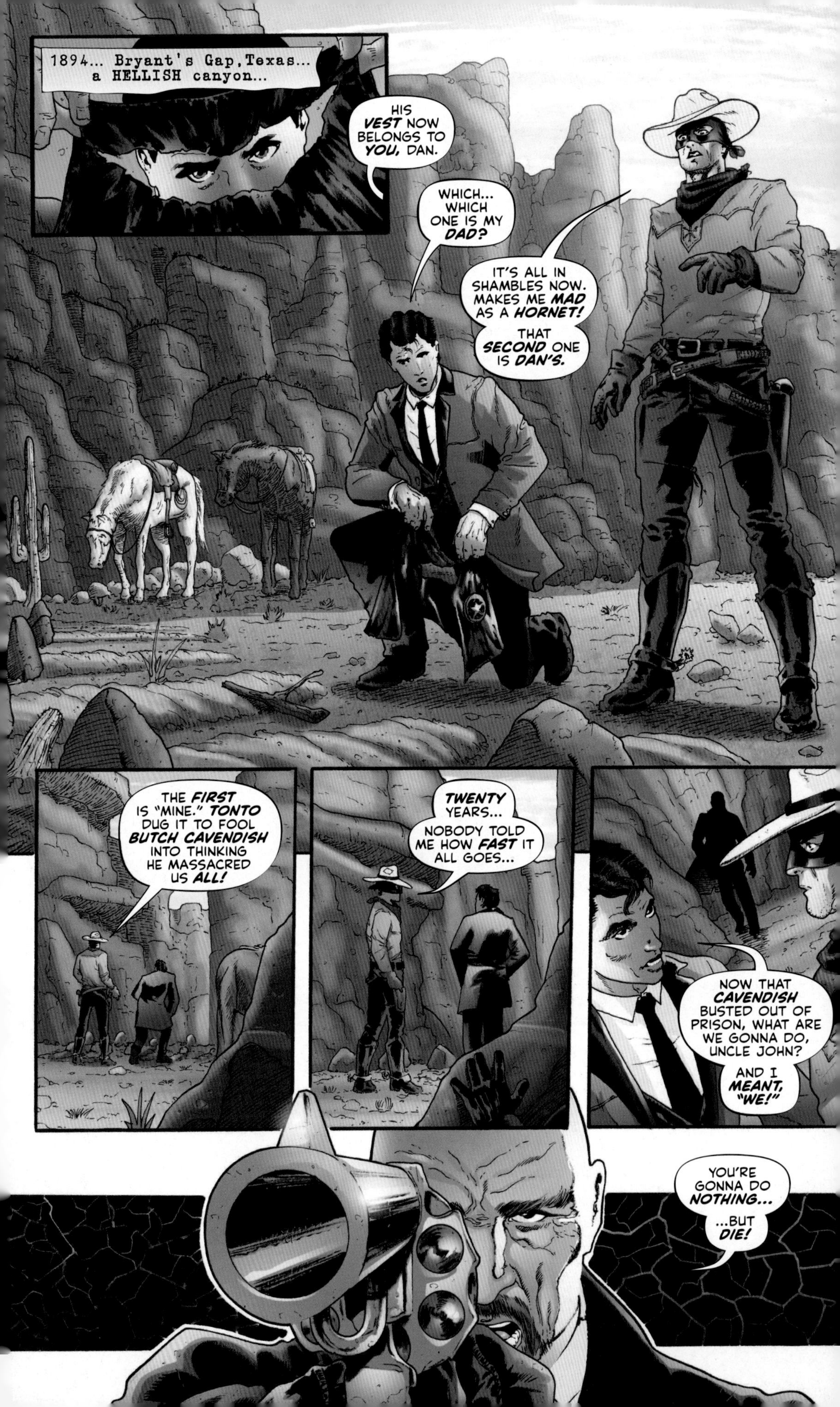

1894... Bryant's Gap, Texas... a HELLISH canyon...
HIS VEST NOW BELONGS TO YOU, DAN.
WHICH... WHICH ONE IS MY DAD?
IT'S ALL IN SHAMBLES NOW. MAKES ME MAD AS A HORNET!
THAT SECOND ONE IS DAN'S.
THE FIRST IS "MINE." TONTO DUG IT TO FOOL BUTCH CAVENDISH INTO THINKING HE MASSACRED US ALL!
TWENTY YEARS...
NOBODY TOLD ME HOW FAST IT ALL GOES...
NOW THAT CAVENDISH BUSTED OUT OF PRISON, WHAT ARE WE GONNA DO, UNCLE JOHN?
AND I MEANT, "WE!"
YOU'RE GONNA DO NOTHING...
...BUT DIE!

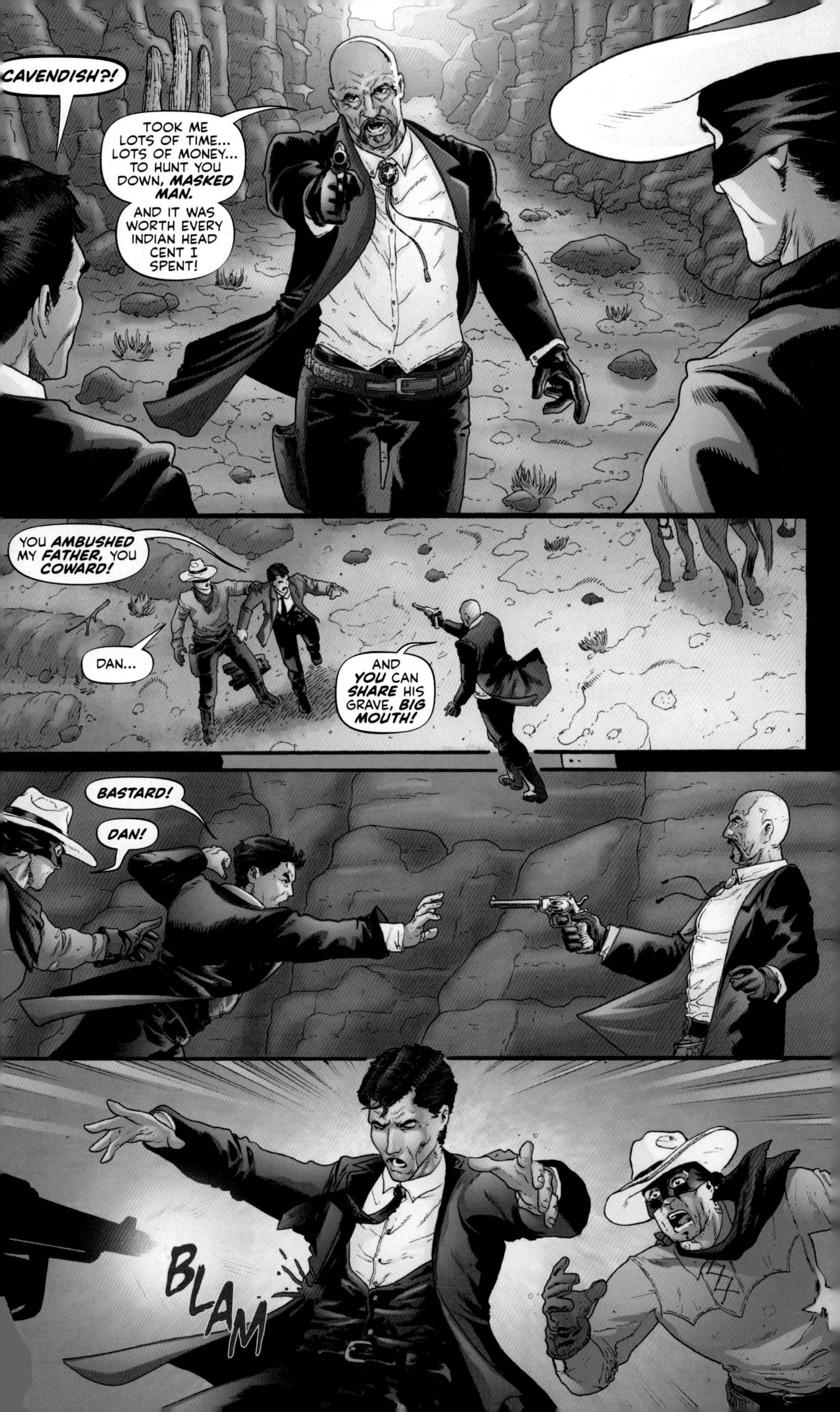
CAVENDISH?!
TOOK ME LOTS OF TIME... LOTS OF MONEY... TO HUNT YOU DOWN, MASKED MAN.
AND IT WAS WORTH EVERY INDIAN HEAD CENT I SPENT!
YOU AMBUSHED MY FATHER, YOU COWARD!
DAN...
AND YOU CAN SHARE HIS GRAVE, BIG MOUTH!
BASTARD!
DAN!
BLAM

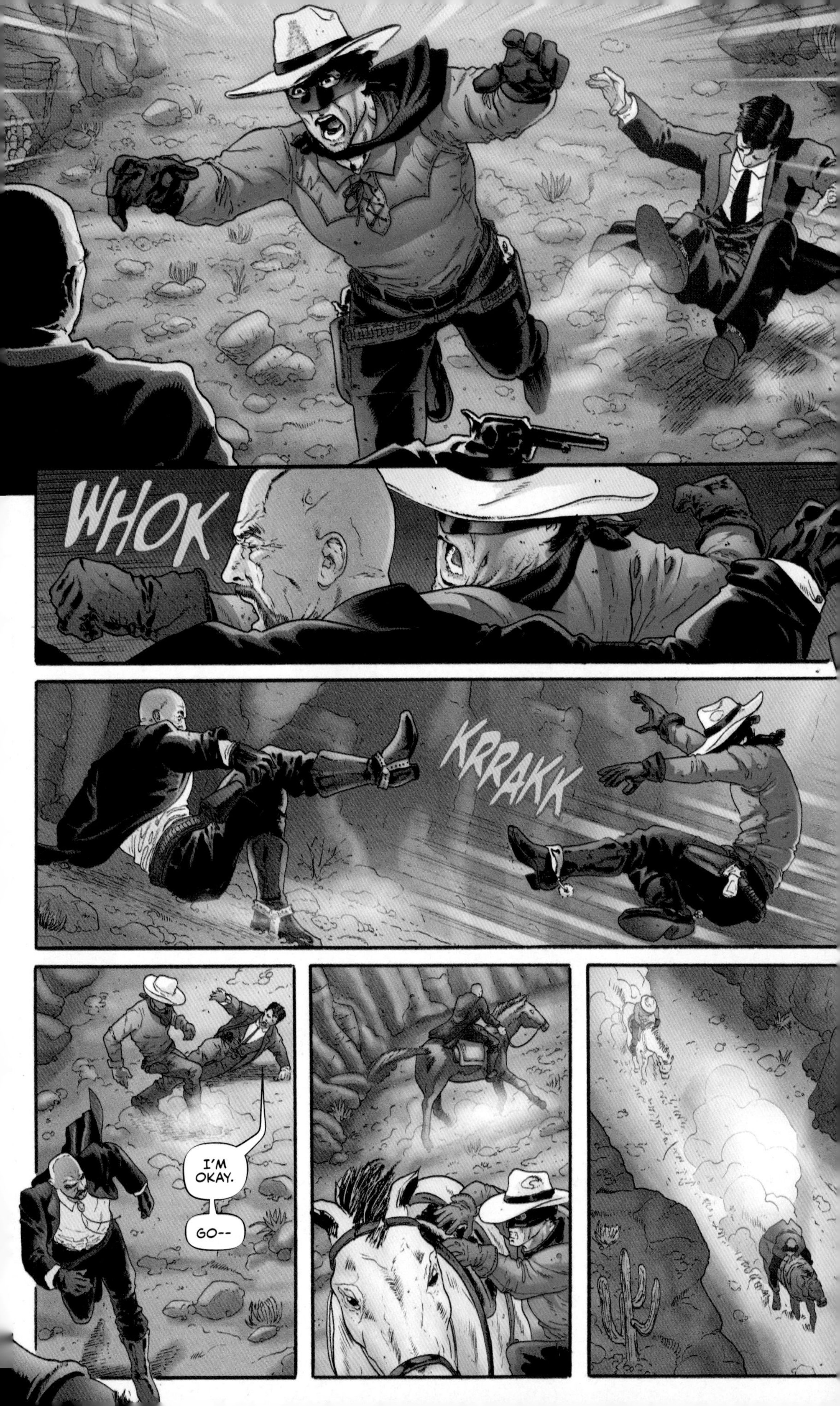
WHOK
KRRAKK
I'M OKAY.
GO--

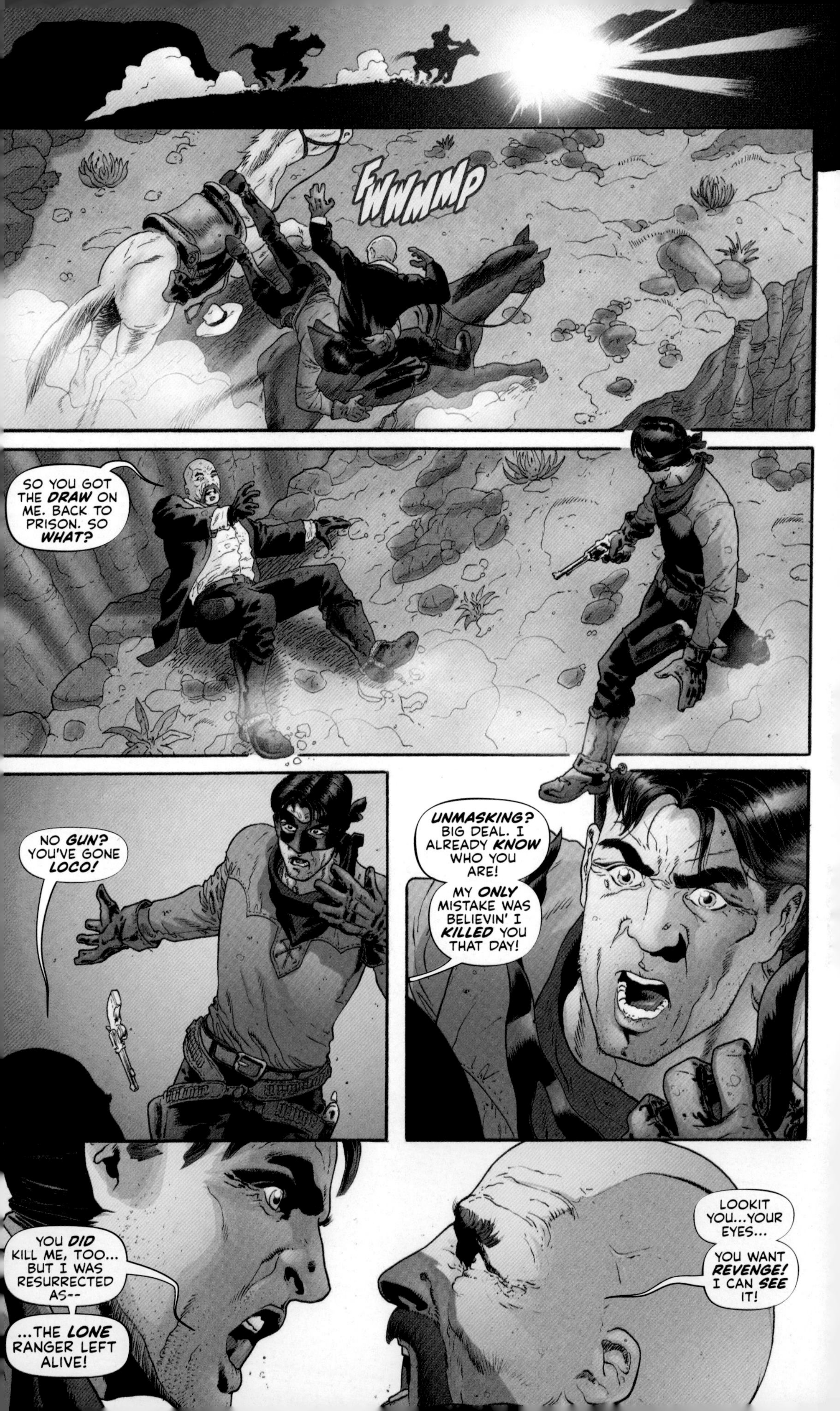
FWWMMP
SO YOU GOT THE DRAW ON ME. BACK TO PRISON. SO WHAT?
NO GUN? YOU'VE GONE LOCO!
UNMASKING? BIG DEAL. I ALREADY KNOW WHO YOU ARE!
MY ONLY MISTAKE WAS BELIEVIN' I KILLED YOU THAT DAY!
YOU DID KILL ME, TOO... BUT I WAS RESURRECTED AS--
...THE LONE RANGER LEFT ALIVE!
LOOKIT YOU...YOUR EYES...
YOU WANT REVENGE! I CAN SEE IT!

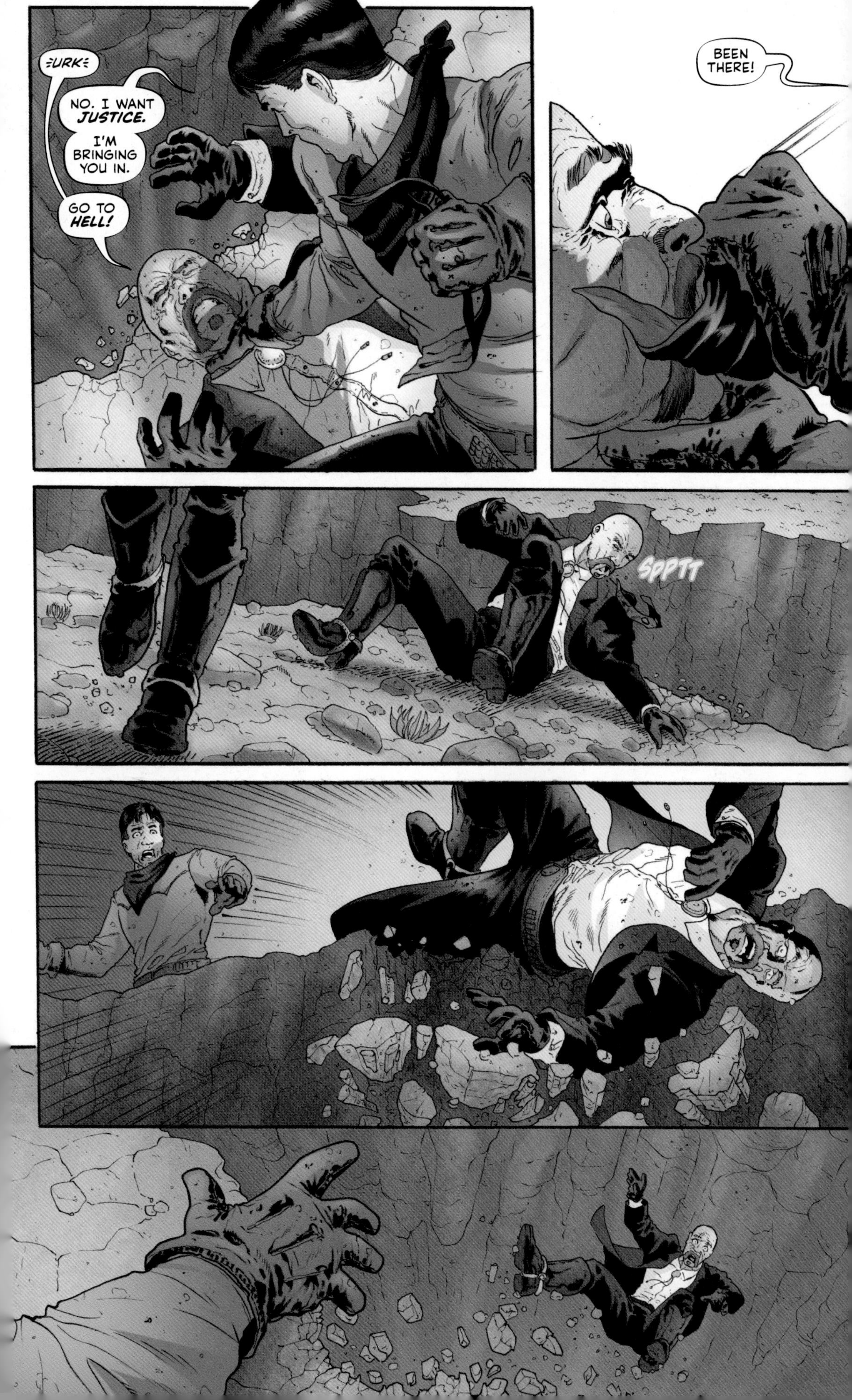

=URK=
NO. I WANT JUSTICE.
I'M BRINGING YOU IN.
GO TO HELL!
BEEN THERE!
SPPTT

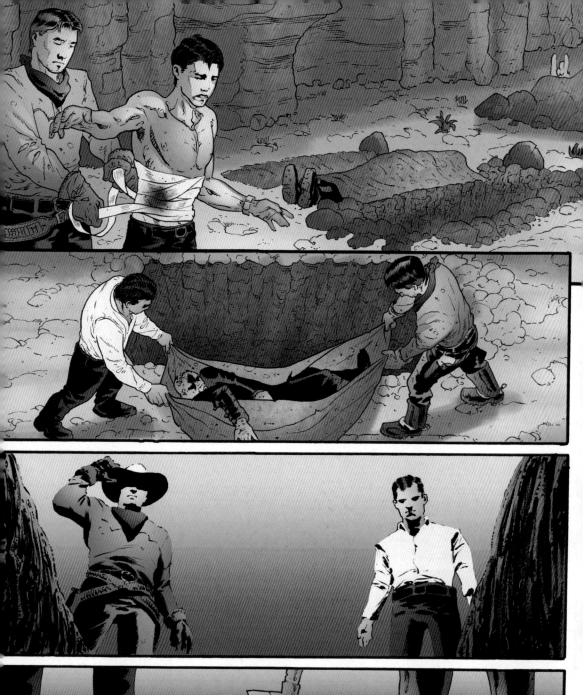

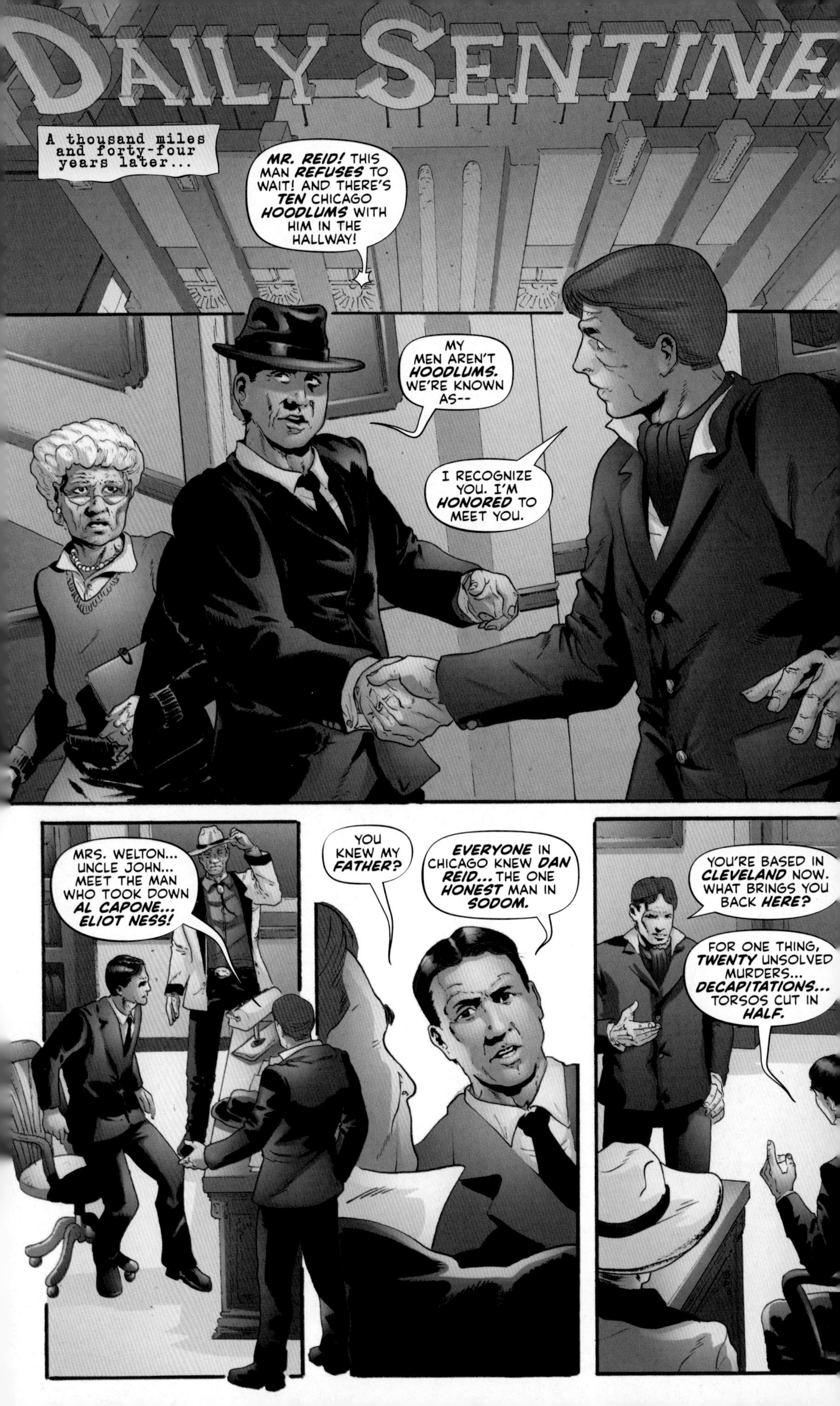
DAILY SENTINE
A thousand miles and forty-four years later...
MR. REID! THIS MAN REFUSES TO WAIT! AND THERE'S TEN CHICAGO HOODLUMS WITH HIM IN THE HALLWAY!
MY MEN AREN'T HOODLUMS. WE'RE KNOWN AS--
I RECOGNIZE YOU. I'M HONORED TO MEET YOU.
MRS. WELTON... UNCLE JOHN... MEET THE MAN WHO TOOK DOWN AL CAPONE... ELIOT NESS!
YOU KNEW MY FATHER?
EVERYONE IN CHICAGO KNEW DAN REID... THE ONE HONEST MAN IN SODOM.
YOU'RE BASED IN CLEVELAND NOW. WHAT BRINGS YOU BACK HERE?
FOR ONE THING, TWENTY UNSOLVED MURDERS... DECAPITATIONS... TORSOS CUT IN HALF.

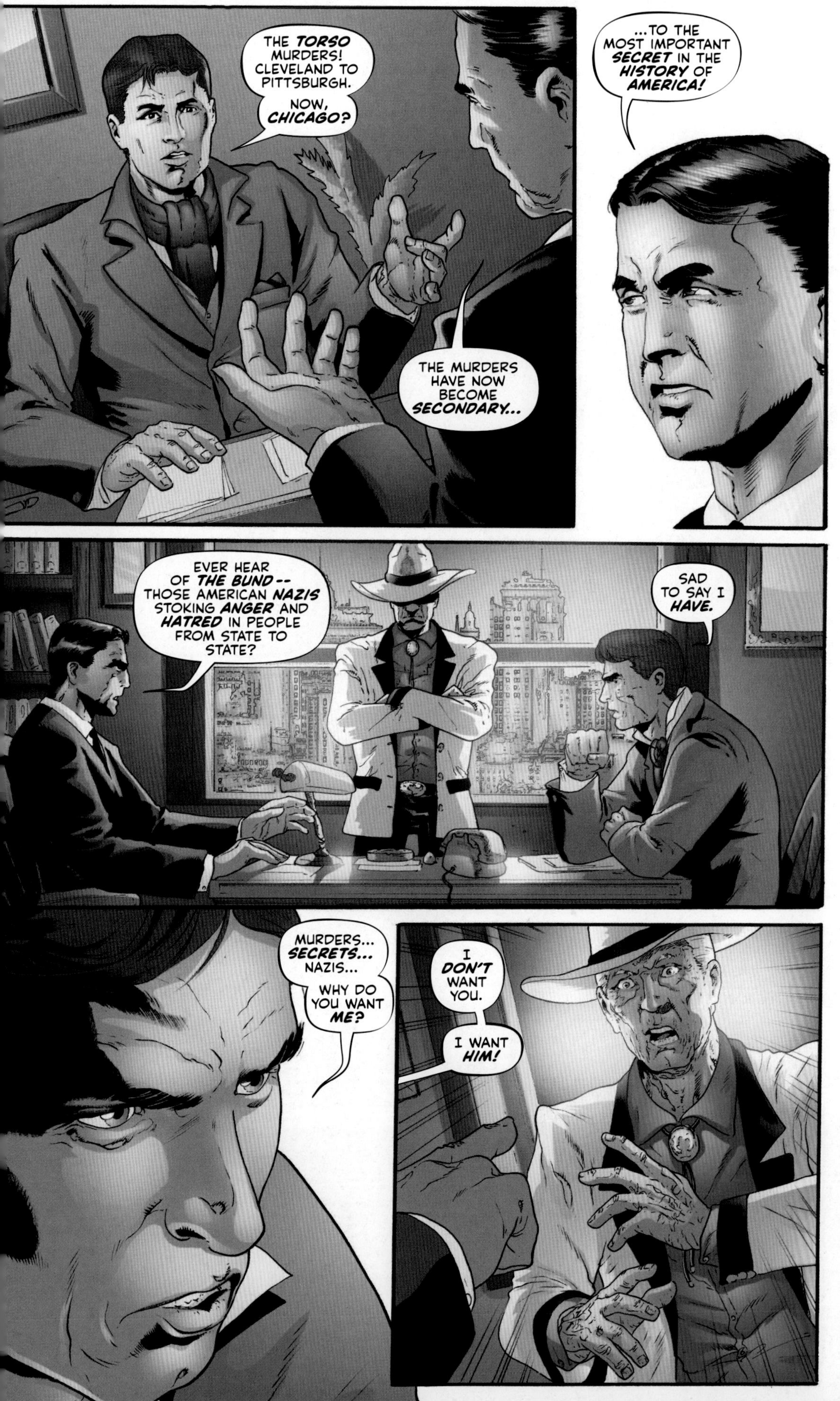
THE TORSO MURDERS! CLEVELAND TO PITTSBURGH.
NOW, CHICAGO?
THE MURDERS HAVE NOW BECOME SECONDARY...
...TO THE MOST IMPORTANT SECRET IN THE HISTORY OF AMERICA!
EVER HEAR OF THE BUND-- THOSE AMERICAN NAZIS STOKING ANGER AND HATRED IN PEOPLE FROM STATE TO STATE?
SAD TO SAY I HAVE.
MURDERS... SECRETS... NAZIS...
WHY DO YOU WANT ME?
I DON'T WANT YOU.
I WANT HIM!

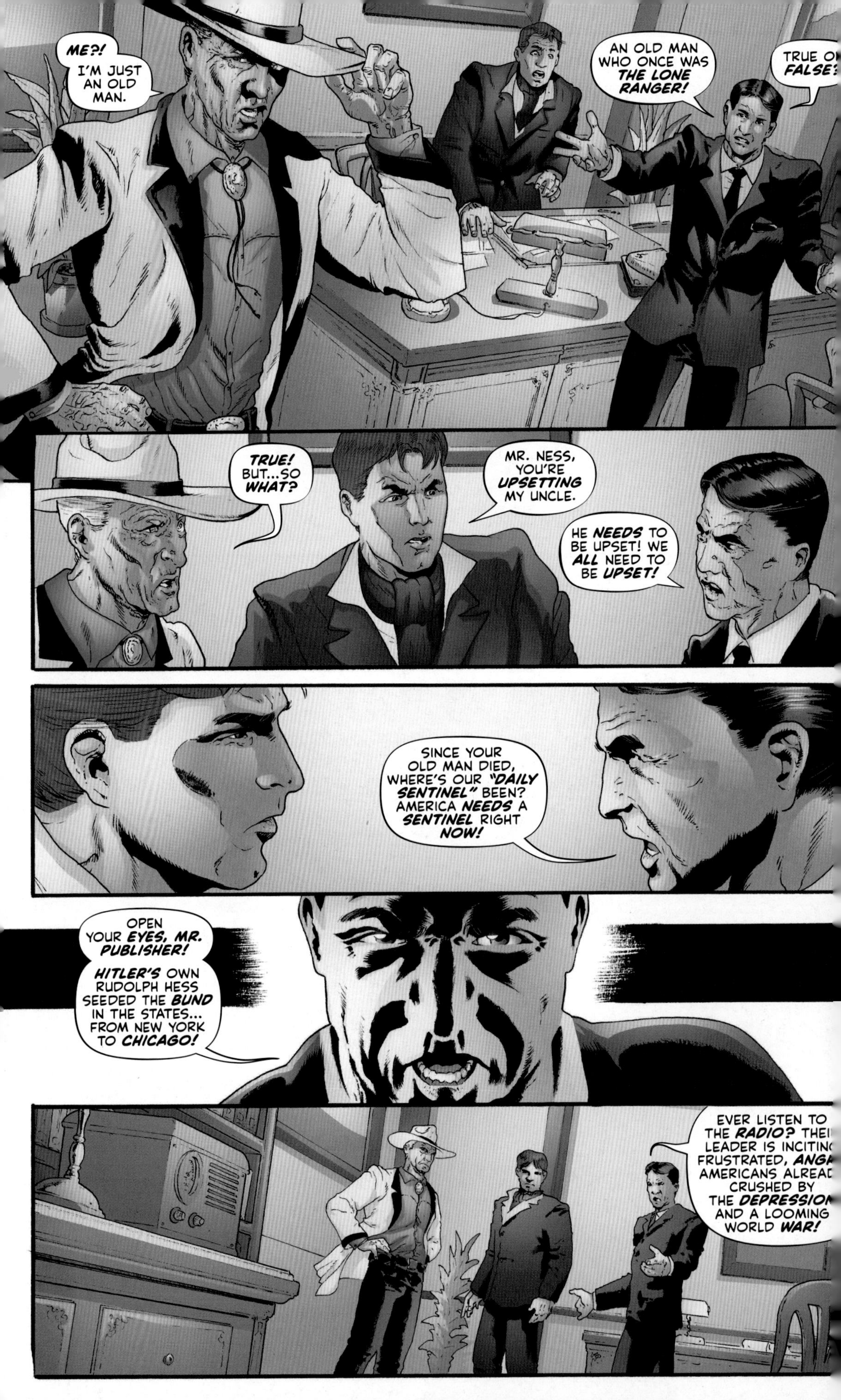

ME?! I'M JUST AN OLD MAN.
AN OLD MAN WHO ONCE WAS THE LONE RANGER!
TRUE OR FALSE?
TRUE! BUT...SO WHAT?
MR. NESS, YOU'RE UPSETTING MY UNCLE.
HE NEEDS TO BE UPSET! WE ALL NEED TO BE UPSET!
SINCE YOUR OLD MAN DIED, WHERE'S OUR "DAILY SENTINEL" BEEN? AMERICA NEEDS A SENTINEL RIGHT NOW!
OPEN YOUR EYES, MR. PUBLISHER!
HITLER'S OWN RUDOLPH HESS SEEDED THE BUND IN THE STATES... FROM NEW YORK TO CHICAGO!
EVER LISTEN TO THE RADIO? THEI LEADER IS INCITIN FRUSTRATED, ANG AMERICANS ALREA CRUSHED BY THE DEPRESSION AND A LOOMING WORLD WAR!

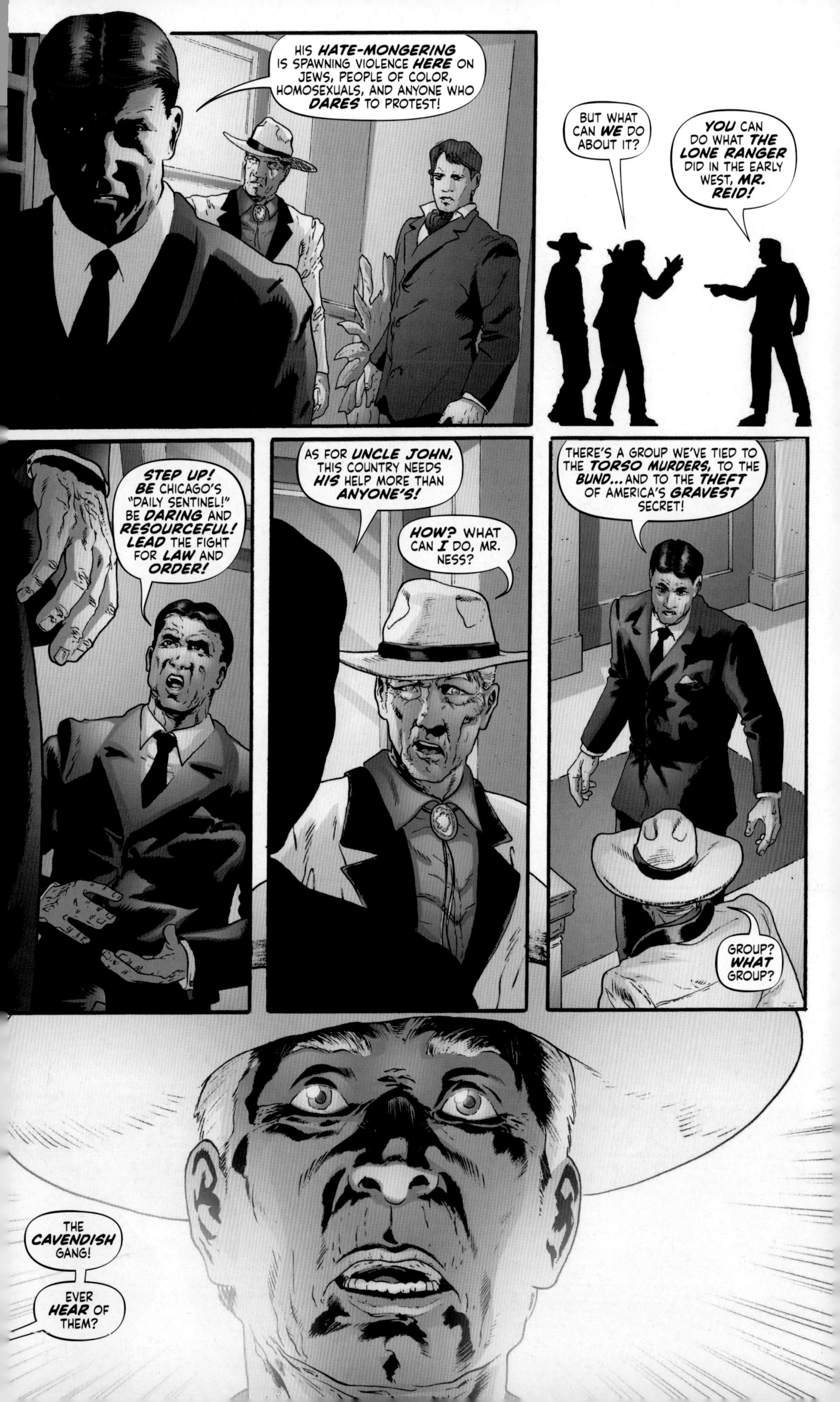

HIS HATE-MONGERING IS SPAWNING VIOLENCE HERE ON JEWS, PEOPLE OF COLOR, HOMOSEXUALS, AND ANYONE WHO DARES TO PROTEST!
BUT WHAT CAN WE DO ABOUT IT?
YOU CAN DO WHAT THE LONE RANGER DID IN THE EARLY WEST, MR. REID!
STEP UP! BE CHICAGO'S "DAILY SENTINEL!" BE DARING AND RESOURCEFUL! LEAD THE FIGHT FOR LAW AND ORDER!
AS FOR UNCLE JOHN, THIS COUNTRY NEEDS HIS HELP MORE THAN ANYONE'S!
HOW? WHAT CAN I DO, MR. NESS?
THERE'S A GROUP WE'VE TIED TO THE TORSO MURDERS, TO THE BUND... AND TO THE THEFT OF AMERICA'S GRAVEST SECRET!
GROUP? WHAT GROUP?
THE CAVENDISH GANG!
EVER HEAR OF THEM?

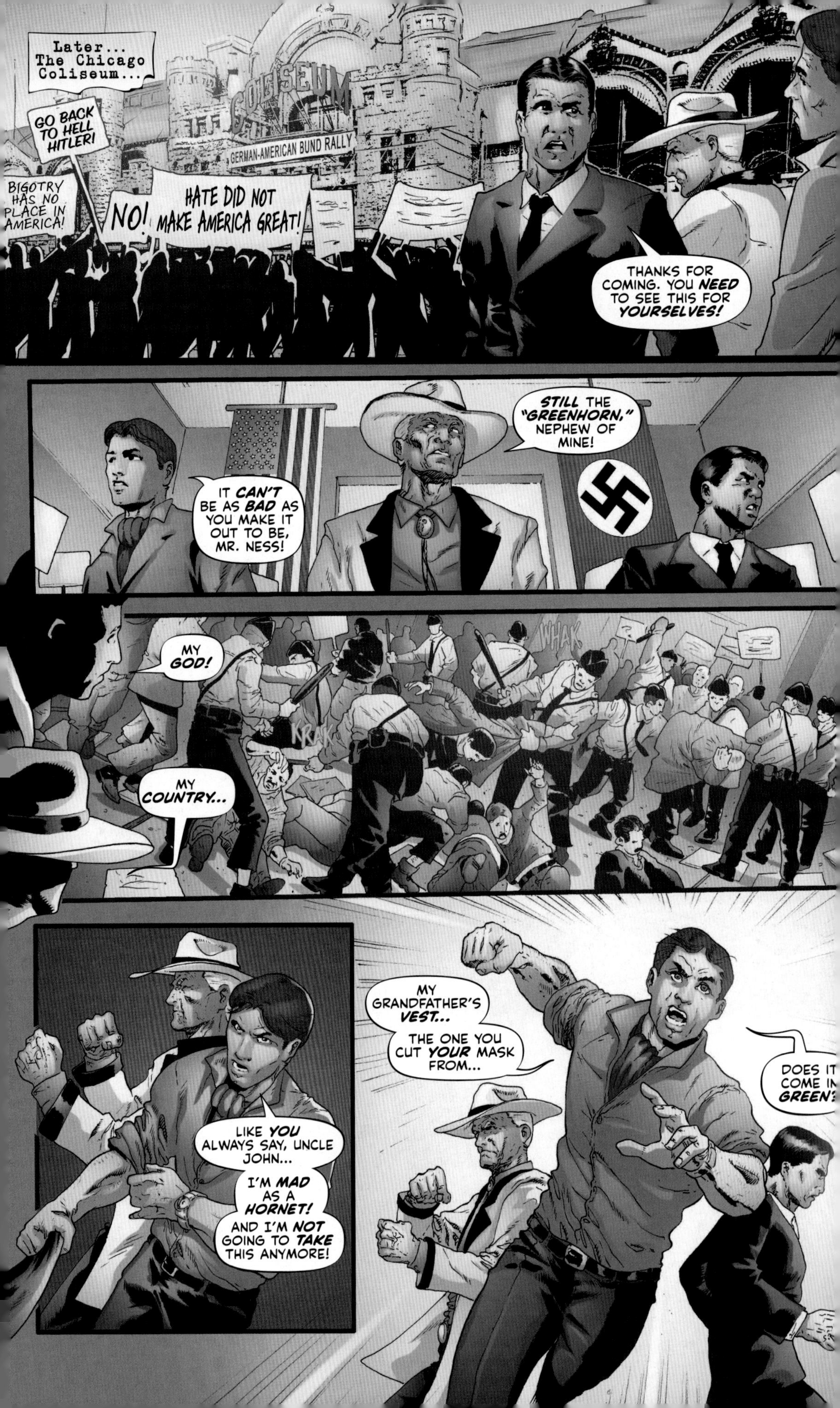
Later... The Chicago Coliseum...
COLISEUM
GERMAN-AMERICAN BUND RALLY
GO BACK TO HELL HITLER!
BIGOTRY HAS NO PLACE IN AMERICA!
NO!
HATE DID NOT MAKE AMERICA GREAT!
THANKS FOR COMING. YOU NEED TO SEE THIS FOR YOURSELVES!
STILL THE "GREENHORN," NEPHEW OF MINE!
IT CAN'T BE AS BAD AS YOU MAKE IT OUT TO BE, MR. NESS!
MY GOD!
WHAK
KRAK
MY COUNTRY...
LIKE YOU ALWAYS SAY, UNCLE JOHN...
I'M MAD AS A HORNET!
AND I'M NOT GOING TO TAKE THIS ANYMORE!
MY GRANDFATHER'S VEST...
THE ONE YOU CUT YOUR MASK FROM...
DOES IT COME IN GREEN?

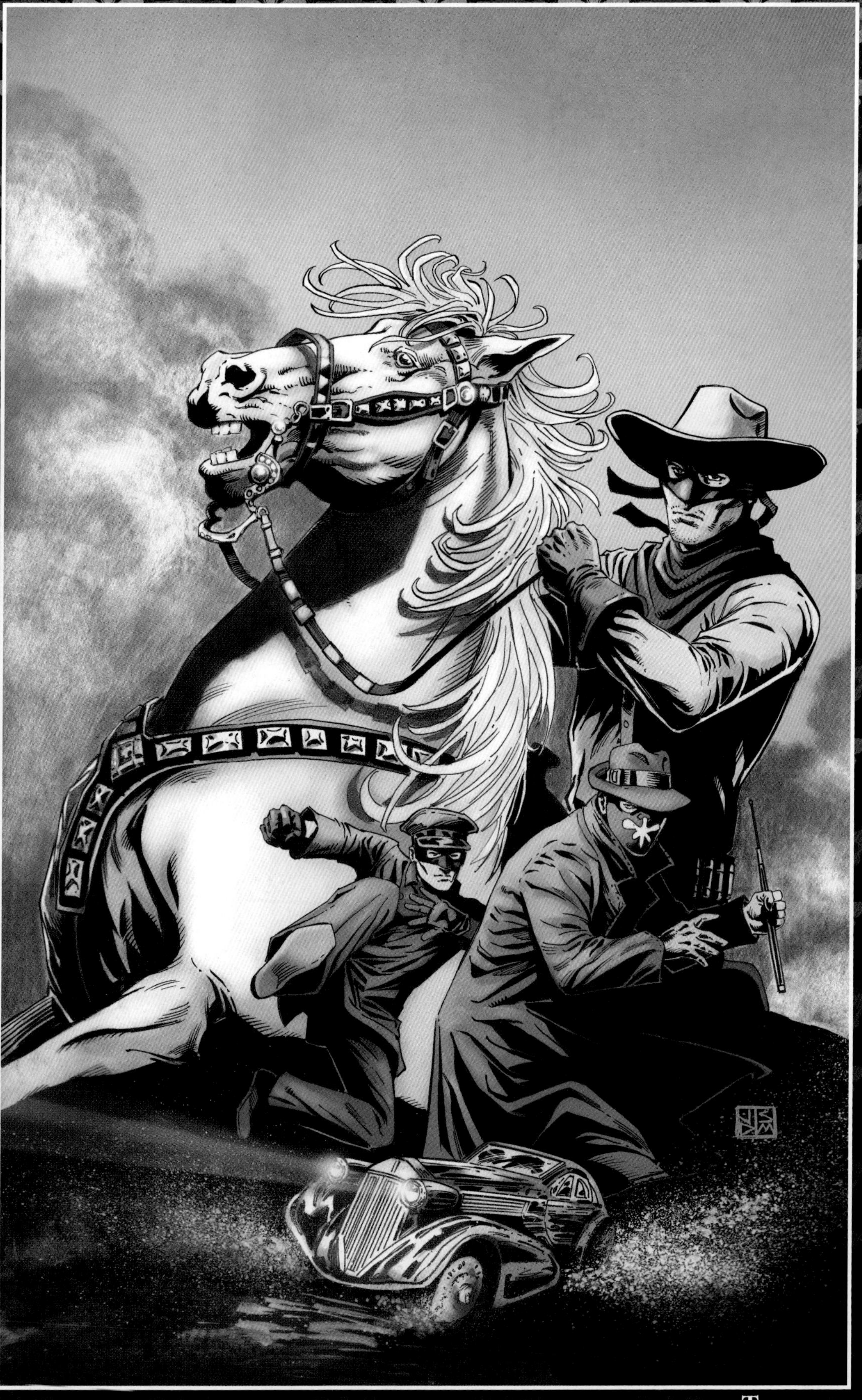

Issue TWO Cover

Art by JAN DUURSEMA Colors by SIAN MANDRAKE

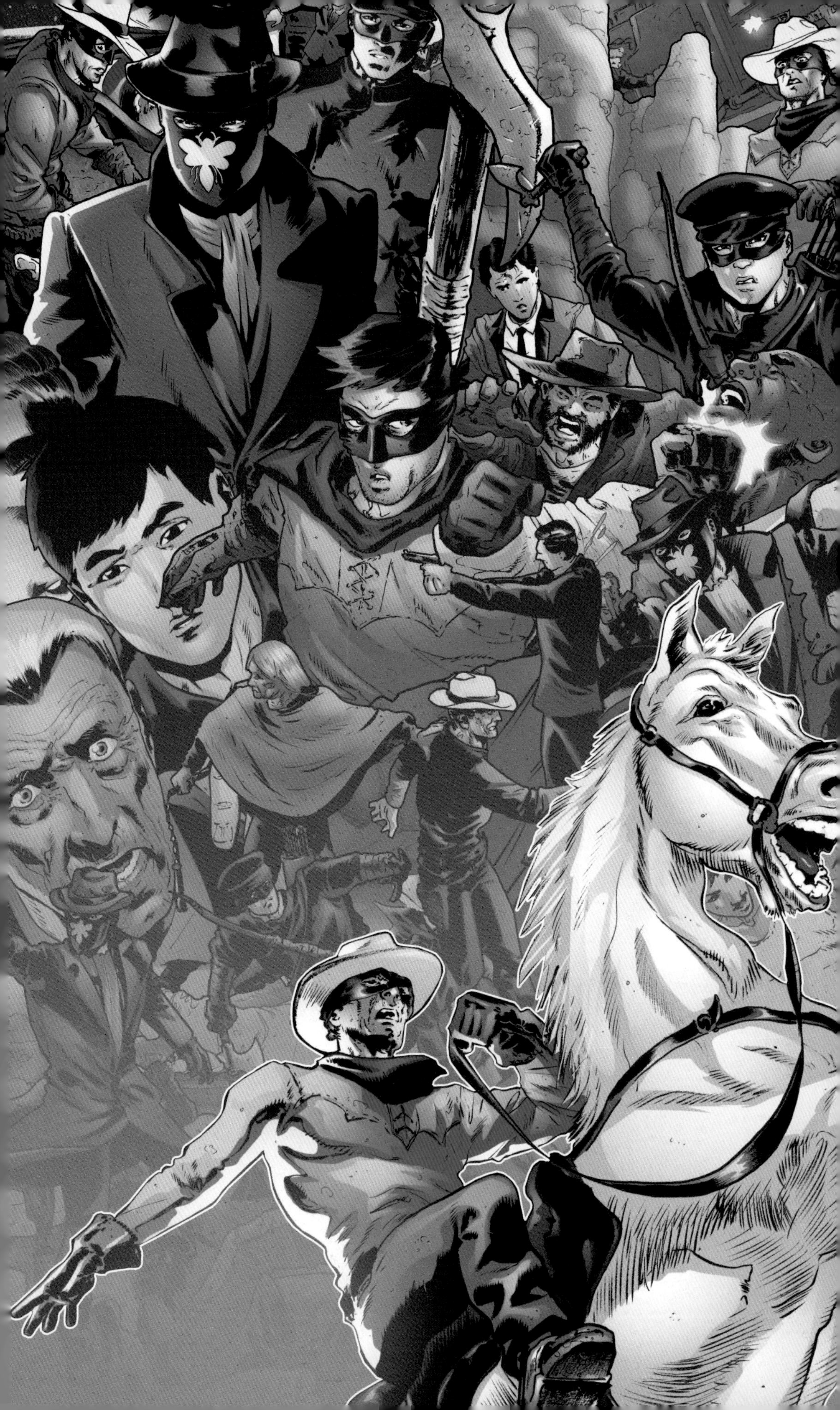

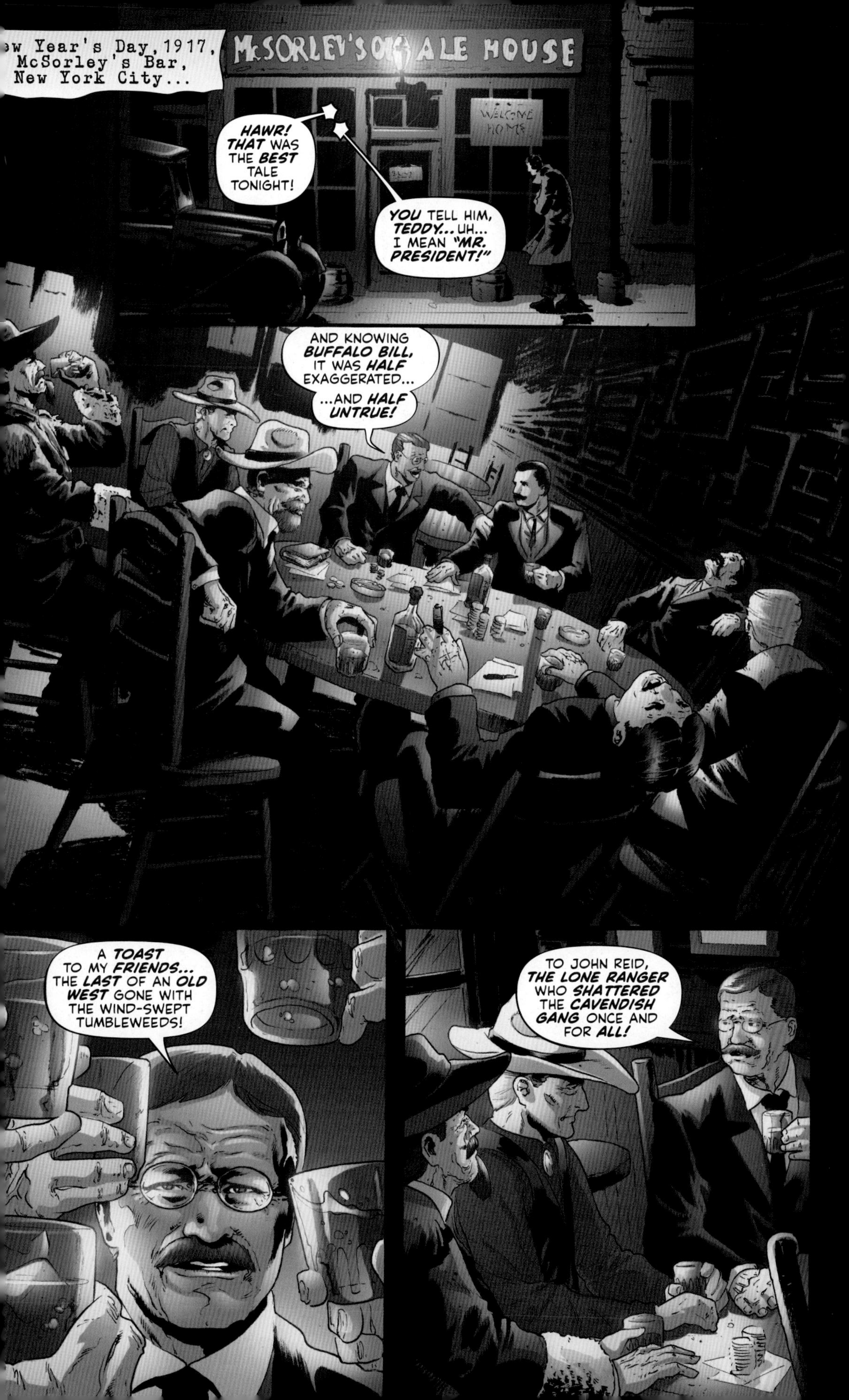
ew Year's Day, 1917, McSorley's Bar, New York City...
McSORLEY'S ... ALE HOUSE
WELCOME HOME
HAWR! THAT WAS THE BEST TALE TONIGHT!
YOU TELL HIM, TEDDY... UH... I MEAN "MR. PRESIDENT!"
AND KNOWING BUFFALO BILL, IT WAS HALF EXAGGERATED...
...AND HALF UNTRUE!
A TOAST TO MY FRIENDS... THE LAST OF AN OLD WEST GONE WITH THE WIND-SWEPT TUMBLEWEEDS!
TO JOHN REID, THE LONE RANGER WHO SHATTERED THE CAVENDISH GANG ONCE AND FOR ALL!

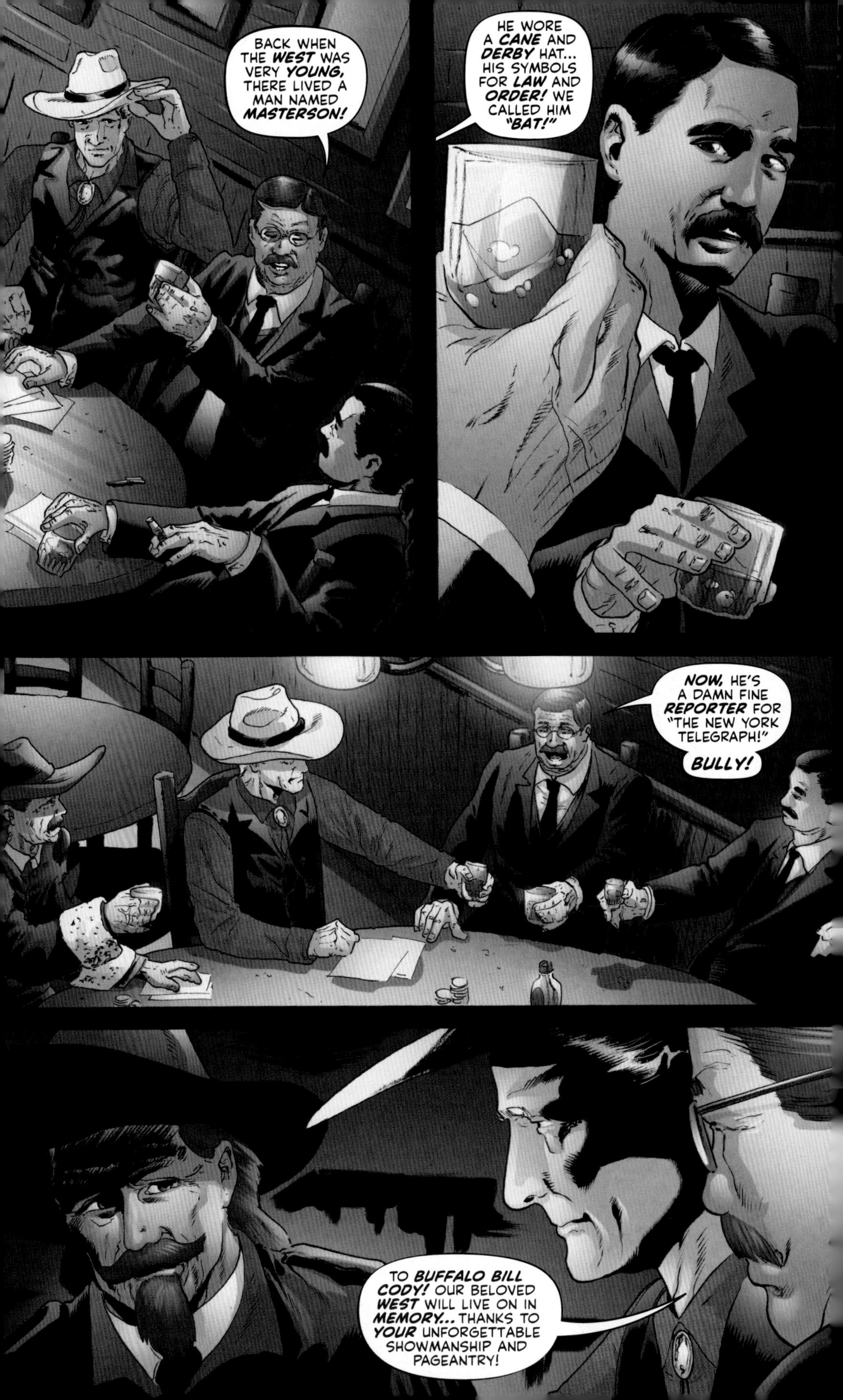
BACK WHEN THE WEST WAS VERY YOUNG, THERE LIVED A MAN NAMED MASTERSON!
HE WORE A CANE AND DERBY HAT... HIS SYMBOLS FOR LAW AND ORDER! WE CALLED HIM "BAT!"
NOW, HE'S A DAMN FINE REPORTER FOR "THE NEW YORK TELEGRAPH!"
BULLY!
TO BUFFALO BILL CODY! OUR BELOVED WEST WILL LIVE ON IN MEMORY... THANKS TO YOUR UNFORGETTABLE SHOWMANSHIP AND PAGEANTRY!

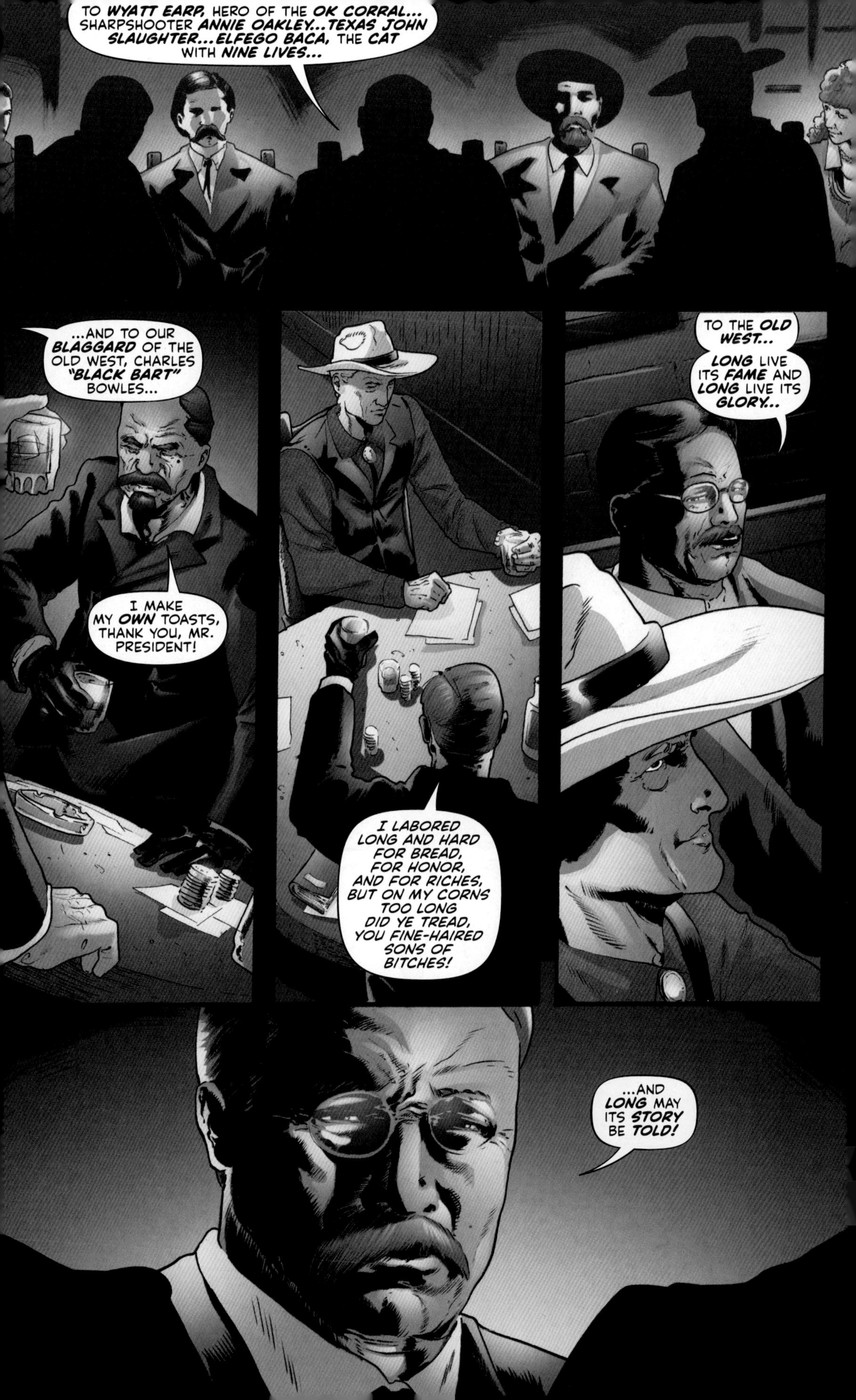
TO WYATT EARP, HERO OF THE OK CORRAL... SHARPSHOOTER ANNIE OAKLEY...TEXAS JOHN SLAUGHTER...ELFEGO BACA, THE CAT WITH NINE LIVES...
...AND TO OUR BLAGGARD OF THE OLD WEST, CHARLES "BLACK BART" BOWLES...
I MAKE MY OWN TOASTS, THANK YOU, MR. PRESIDENT!
I LABORED LONG AND HARD FOR BREAD, FOR HONOR, AND FOR RICHES, BUT ON MY CORNS TOO LONG DID YE TREAD, YOU FINE-HAIRED SONS OF BITCHES!
TO THE OLD WEST...
LONG LIVE ITS FAME AND LONG LIVE ITS GLORY...
...AND LONG MAY ITS STORY BE TOLD!

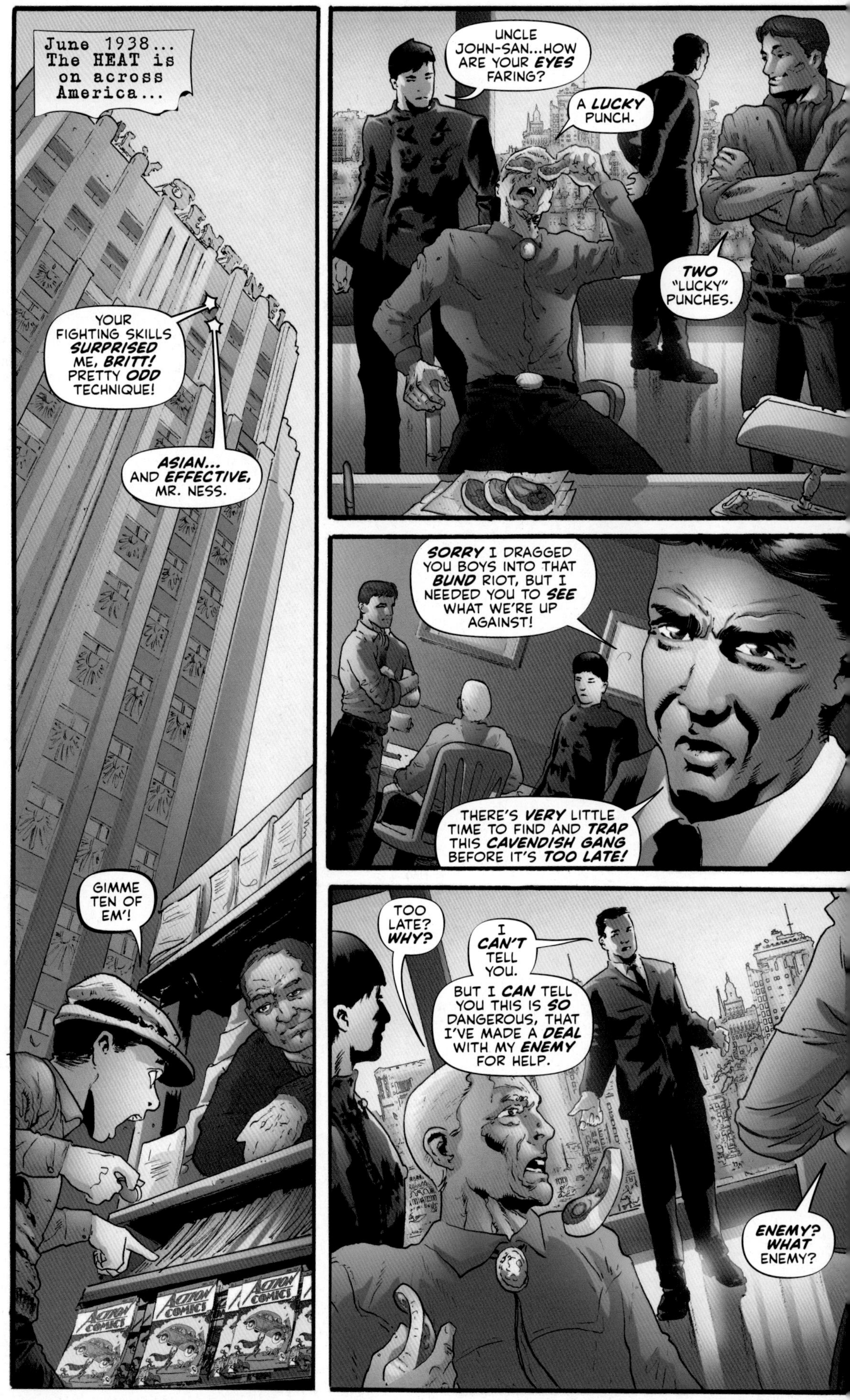
June 1938... The HEAT is on across America...
YOUR FIGHTING SKILLS SURPRISED ME, BRITT! PRETTY ODD TECHNIQUE!
ASIAN... AND EFFECTIVE, MR. NESS.
GIMME TEN OF EM'!
ACTION COMICS
UNCLE JOHN-SAN...HOW ARE YOUR EYES FARING?
A LUCKY PUNCH.
TWO "LUCKY" PUNCHES.
SORRY I DRAGGED YOU BOYS INTO THAT BUND RIOT, BUT I NEEDED YOU TO SEE WHAT WE'RE UP AGAINST!
THERE'S VERY LITTLE TIME TO FIND AND TRAP THIS CAVENDISH GANG BEFORE IT'S TOO LATE!
TOO LATE? WHY?
I CAN'T TELL YOU.
BUT I CAN TELL YOU THIS IS SO DANGEROUS, THAT I'VE MADE A DEAL WITH MY ENEMY FOR HELP.
ENEMY? WHAT ENEMY?

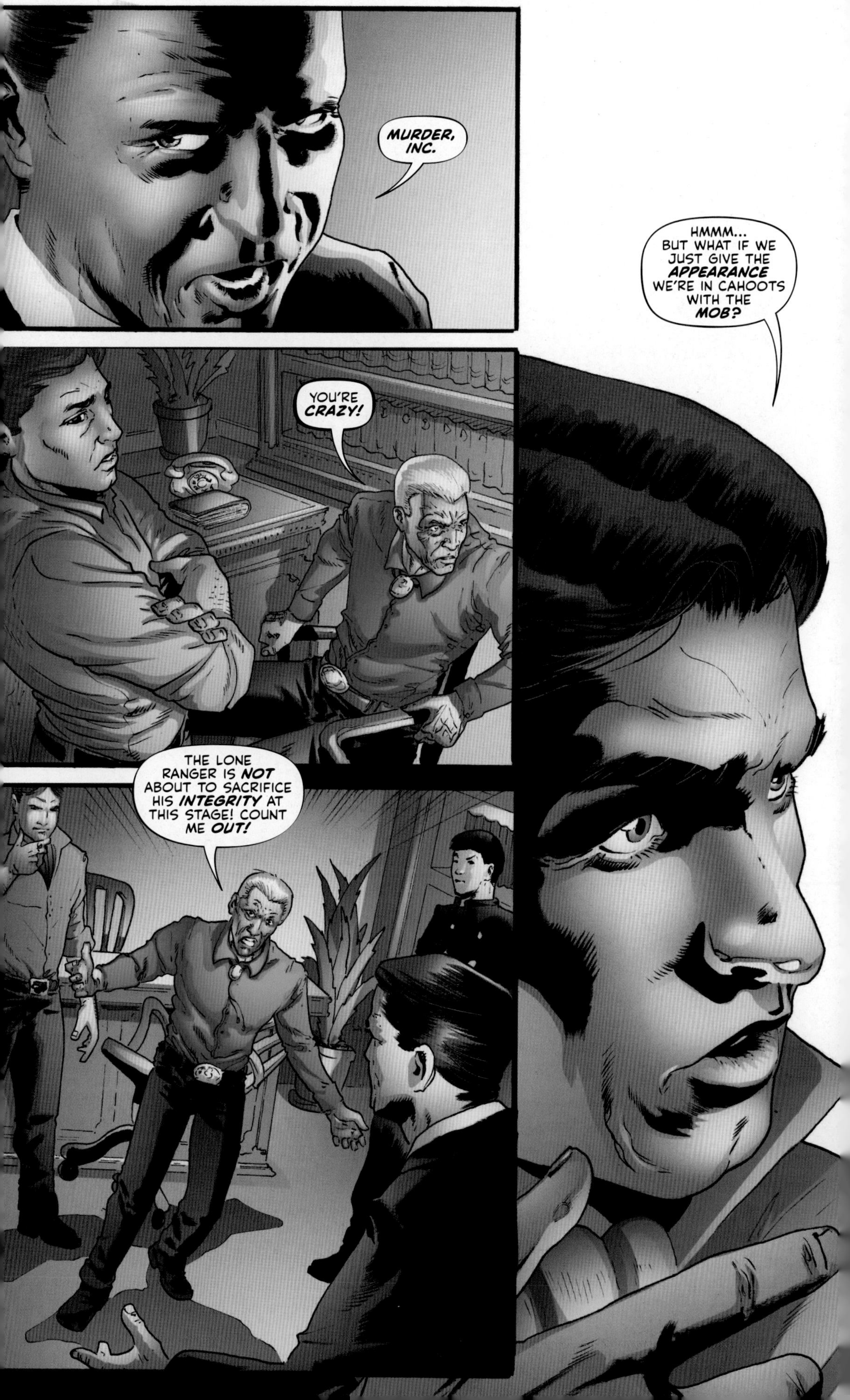
MURDER, INC.
HMMM... BUT WHAT IF WE JUST GIVE THE APPEARANCE WE'RE IN CAHOOTS WITH THE MOB?
YOU'RE CRAZY!
THE LONE RANGER IS NOT ABOUT TO SACRIFICE HIS INTEGRITY AT THIS STAGE! COUNT ME OUT!

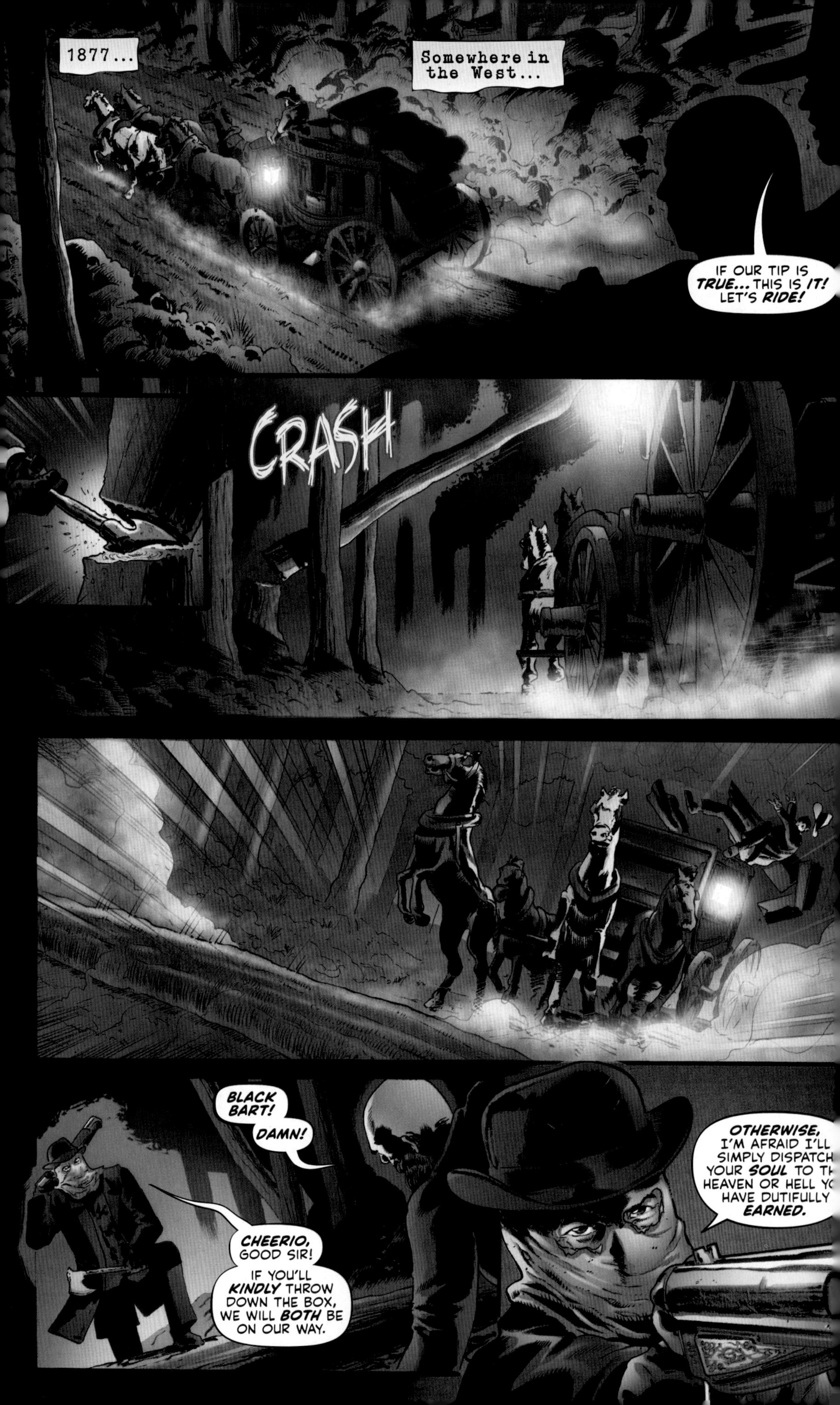
1877...
Somewhere in the West...
IF OUR TIP IS TRUE... THIS IS IT! LET'S RIDE!
CRASH
BLACK BART!
DAMN!
CHEERIO, GOOD SIR!
IF YOU'LL KINDLY THROW DOWN THE BOX, WE WILL BOTH BE ON OUR WAY.
OTHERWISE, I'M AFRAID I'LL SIMPLY DISPATCH YOUR SOUL TO TH HEAVEN OR HELL YO HAVE DUTIFULLY EARNED.

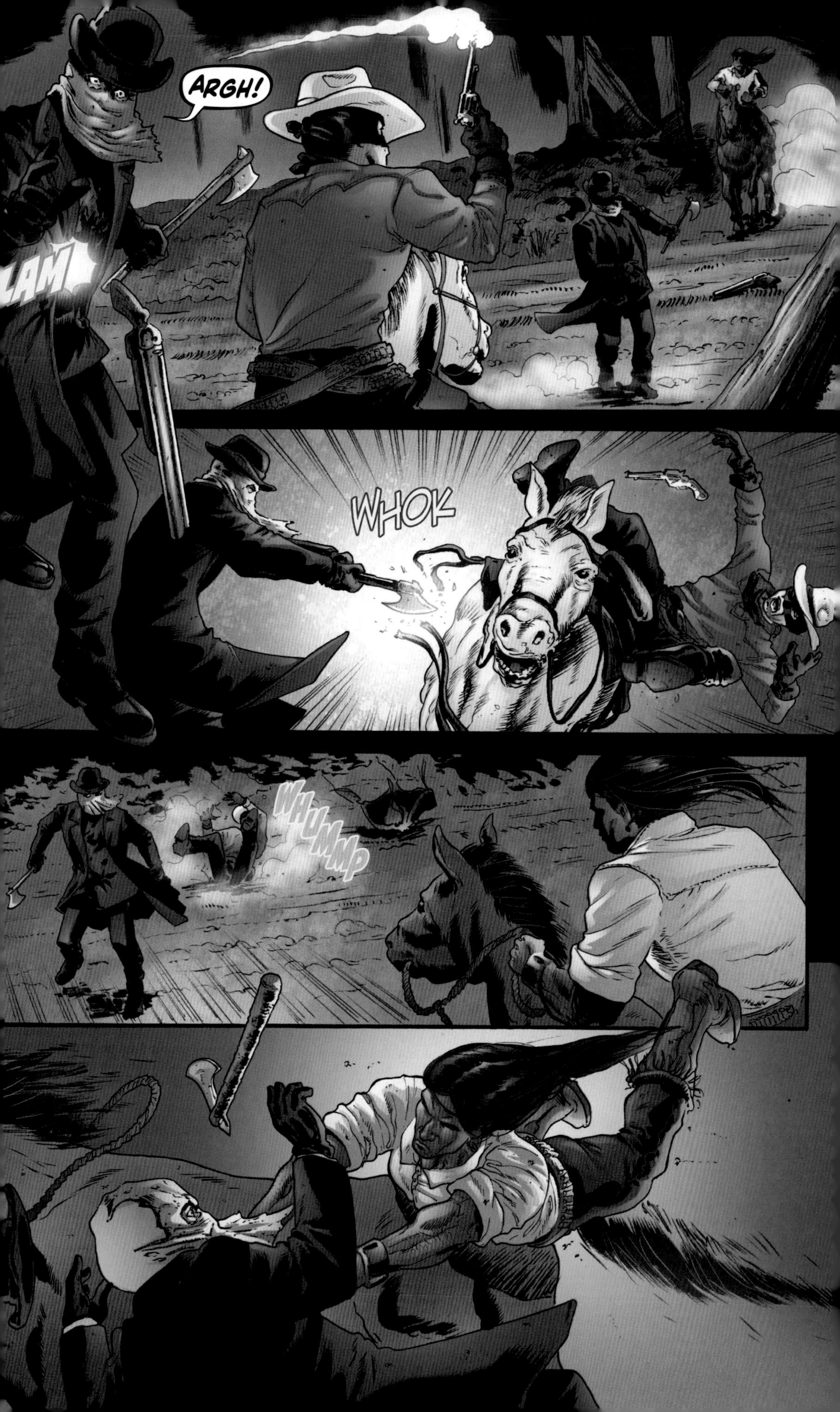

ARGH!
LAM!
WHOK
WHUMMP

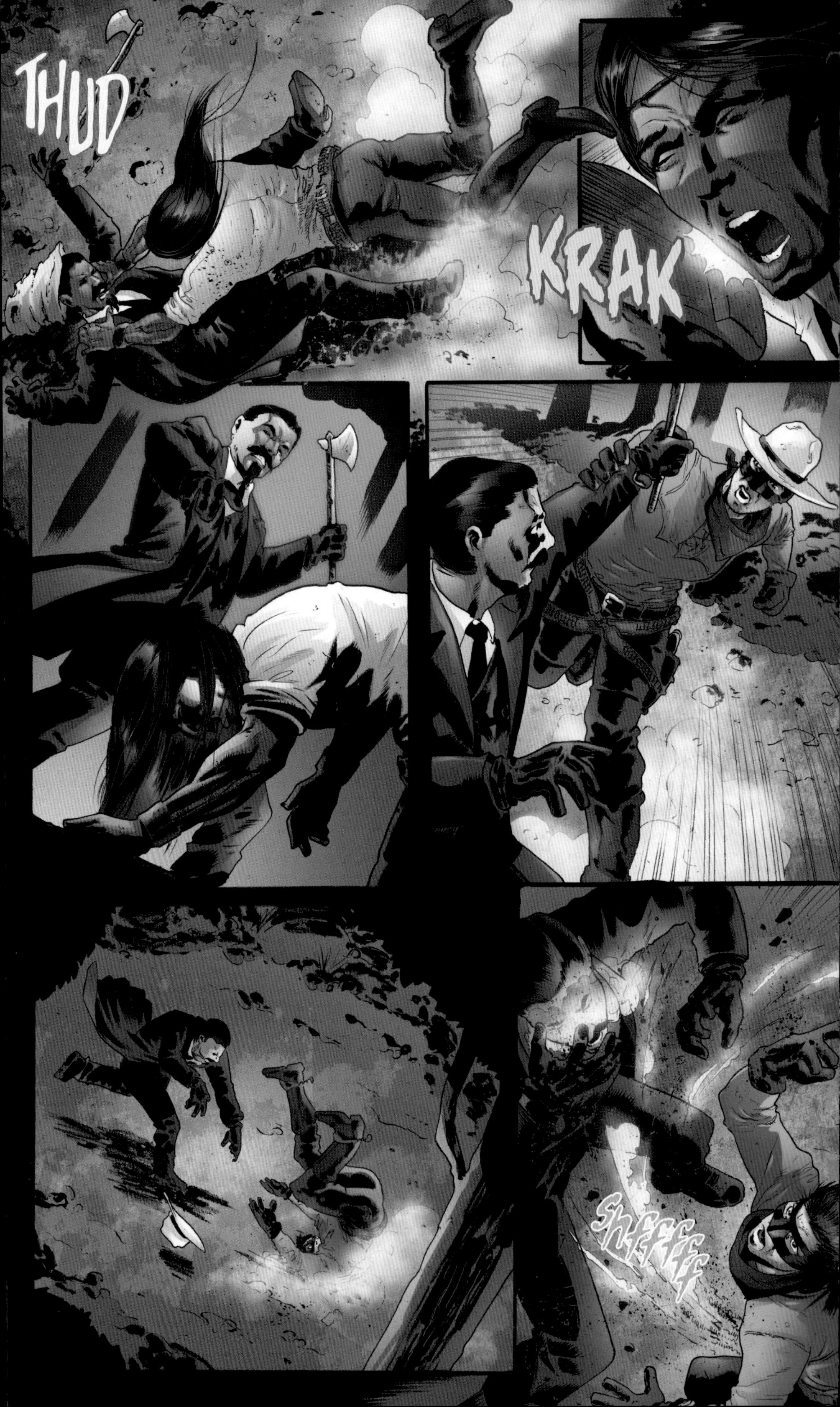
THUD
KRAK

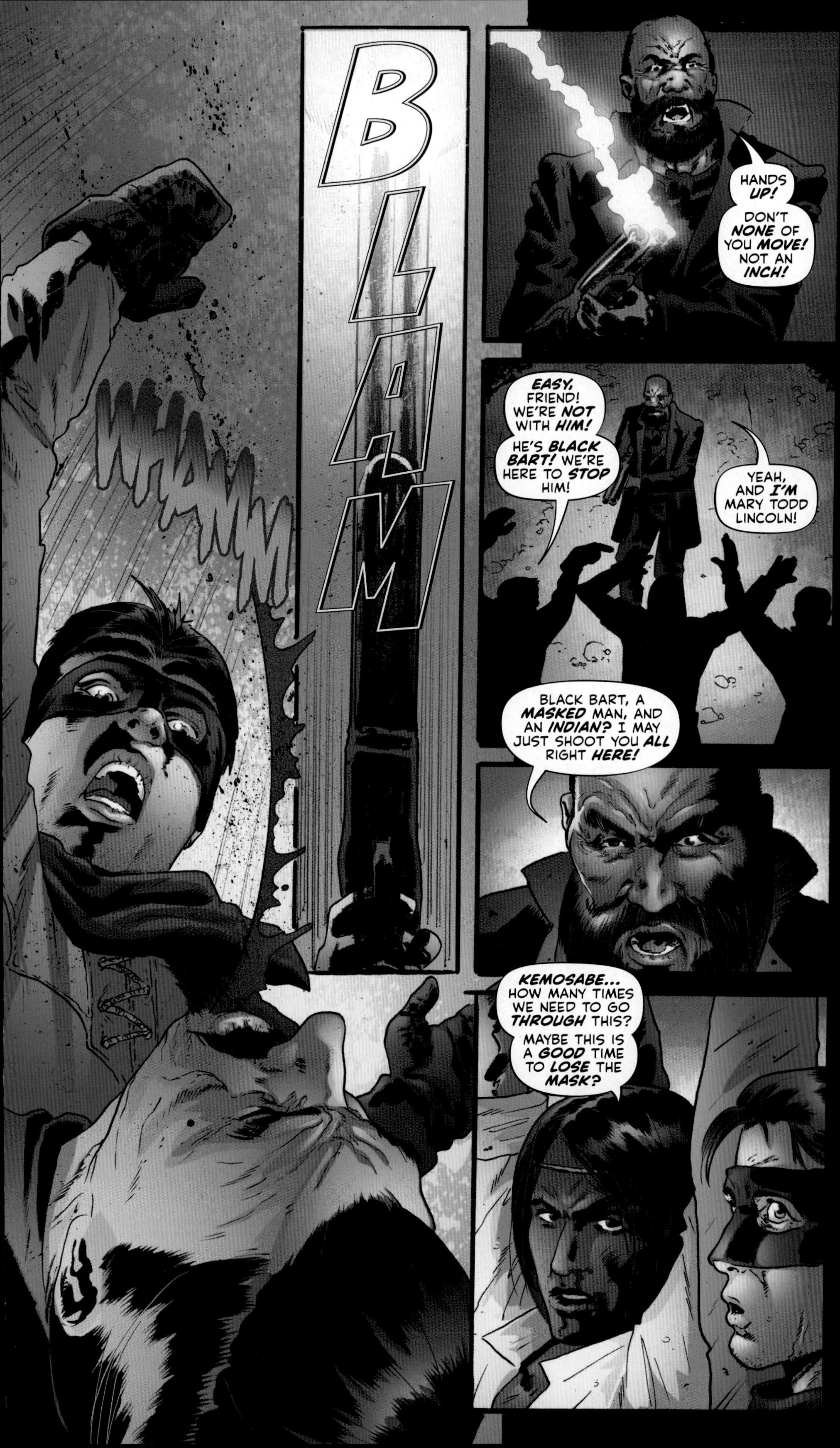
BLAM
HANDS UP! DON'T NONE OF YOU MOVE! NOT AN INCH!
EASY, FRIEND! WE'RE NOT WITH HIM!
HE'S BLACK BART! WE'RE HERE TO STOP HIM!
YEAH, AND I'M MARY TODD LINCOLN!
BLACK BART, A MASKED MAN, AND AN INDIAN? I MAY JUST SHOOT YOU ALL RIGHT HERE!
WHAM
KEMOSABE... HOW MANY TIMES WE NEED TO GO THROUGH THIS?
MAYBE THIS IS A GOOD TIME TO LOSE THE MASK?

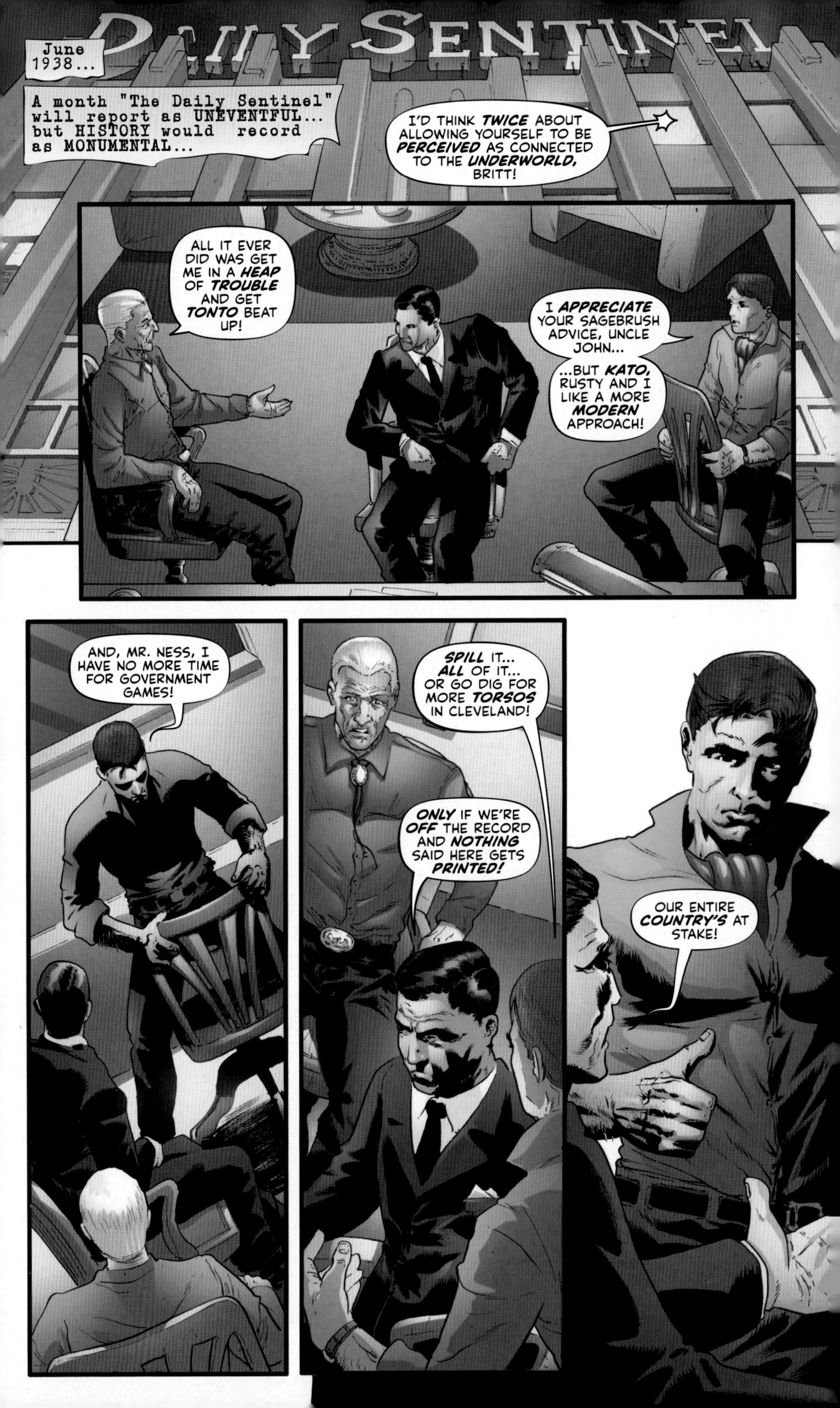

DAILY SENTINEL
June 1938...
A month "The Daily Sentinel" will report as UNEVENTFUL... but HISTORY would record as MONUMENTAL...
I'D THINK TWICE ABOUT ALLOWING YOURSELF TO BE PERCEIVED AS CONNECTED TO THE UNDERWORLD, BRITT!
ALL IT EVER DID WAS GET ME IN A HEAP OF TROUBLE AND GET TONTO BEAT UP!
I APPRECIATE YOUR SAGEBRUSH ADVICE, UNCLE JOHN...
...BUT KATO, RUSTY AND I LIKE A MORE MODERN APPROACH!
AND, MR. NESS, I HAVE NO MORE TIME FOR GOVERNMENT GAMES!
SPILL IT... ALL OF IT... OR GO DIG FOR MORE TORSOS IN CLEVELAND!
ONLY IF WE'RE OFF THE RECORD AND NOTHING SAID HERE GETS PRINTED!
OUR ENTIRE COUNTRY'S AT STAKE!

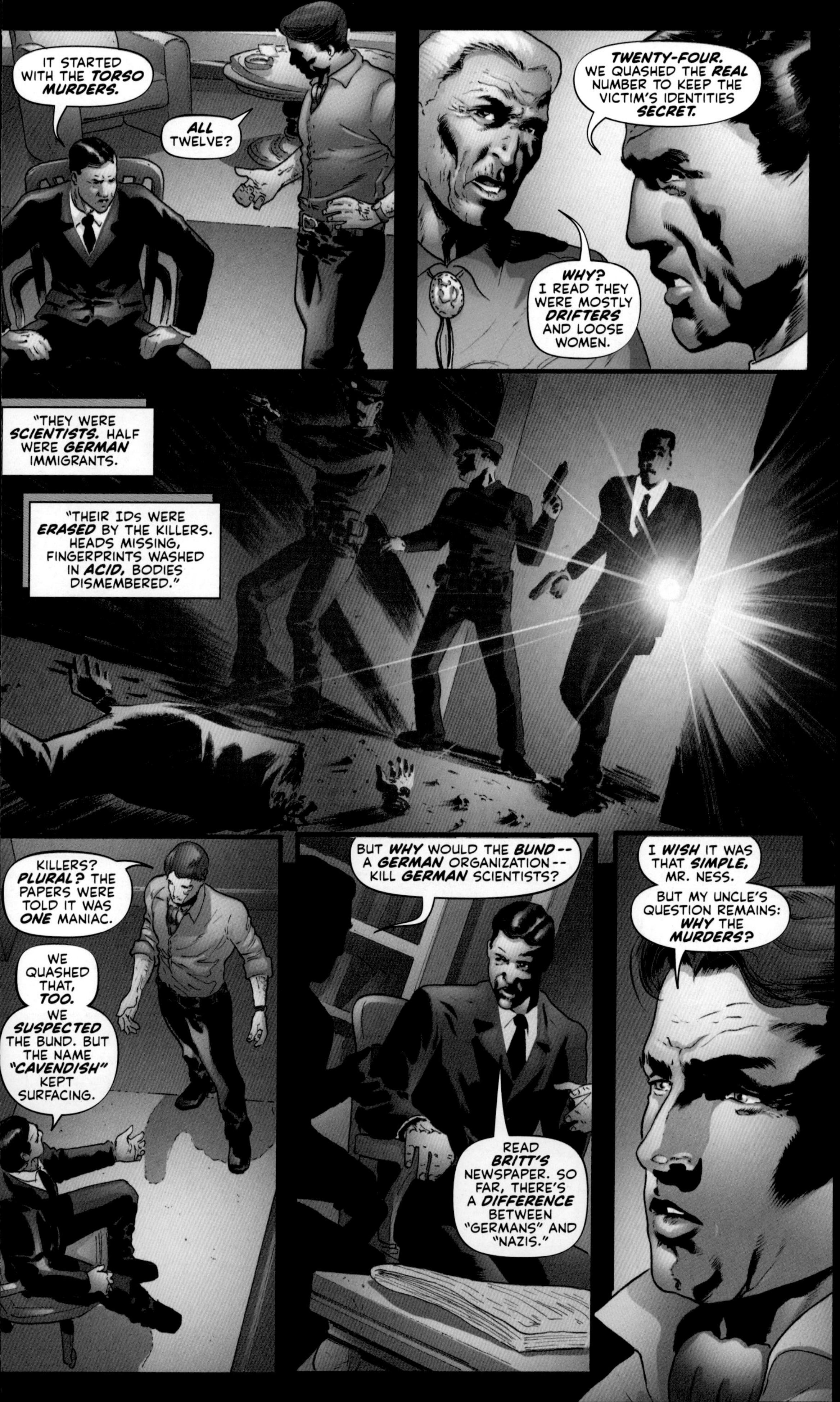
IT STARTED WITH THE TORSO MURDERS.
ALL TWELVE?
TWENTY-FOUR. WE QUASHED THE REAL NUMBER TO KEEP THE VICTIM'S IDENTITIES SECRET.
WHY? I READ THEY WERE MOSTLY DRIFTERS AND LOOSE WOMEN.
"THEY WERE SCIENTISTS. HALF WERE GERMAN IMMIGRANTS.
"THEIR IDs WERE ERASED BY THE KILLERS. HEADS MISSING, FINGERPRINTS WASHED IN ACID, BODIES DISMEMBERED."
KILLERS? PLURAL? THE PAPERS WERE TOLD IT WAS ONE MANIAC.
WE QUASHED THAT, TOO. WE SUSPECTED THE BUND. BUT THE NAME "CAVENDISH" KEPT SURFACING.
BUT WHY WOULD THE BUND -- A GERMAN ORGANIZATION -- KILL GERMAN SCIENTISTS?
READ BRITT'S NEWSPAPER. SO FAR, THERE'S A DIFFERENCE BETWEEN "GERMANS" AND "NAZIS."
I WISH IT WAS THAT SIMPLE, MR. NESS.
BUT MY UNCLE'S QUESTION REMAINS: WHY THE MURDERS?

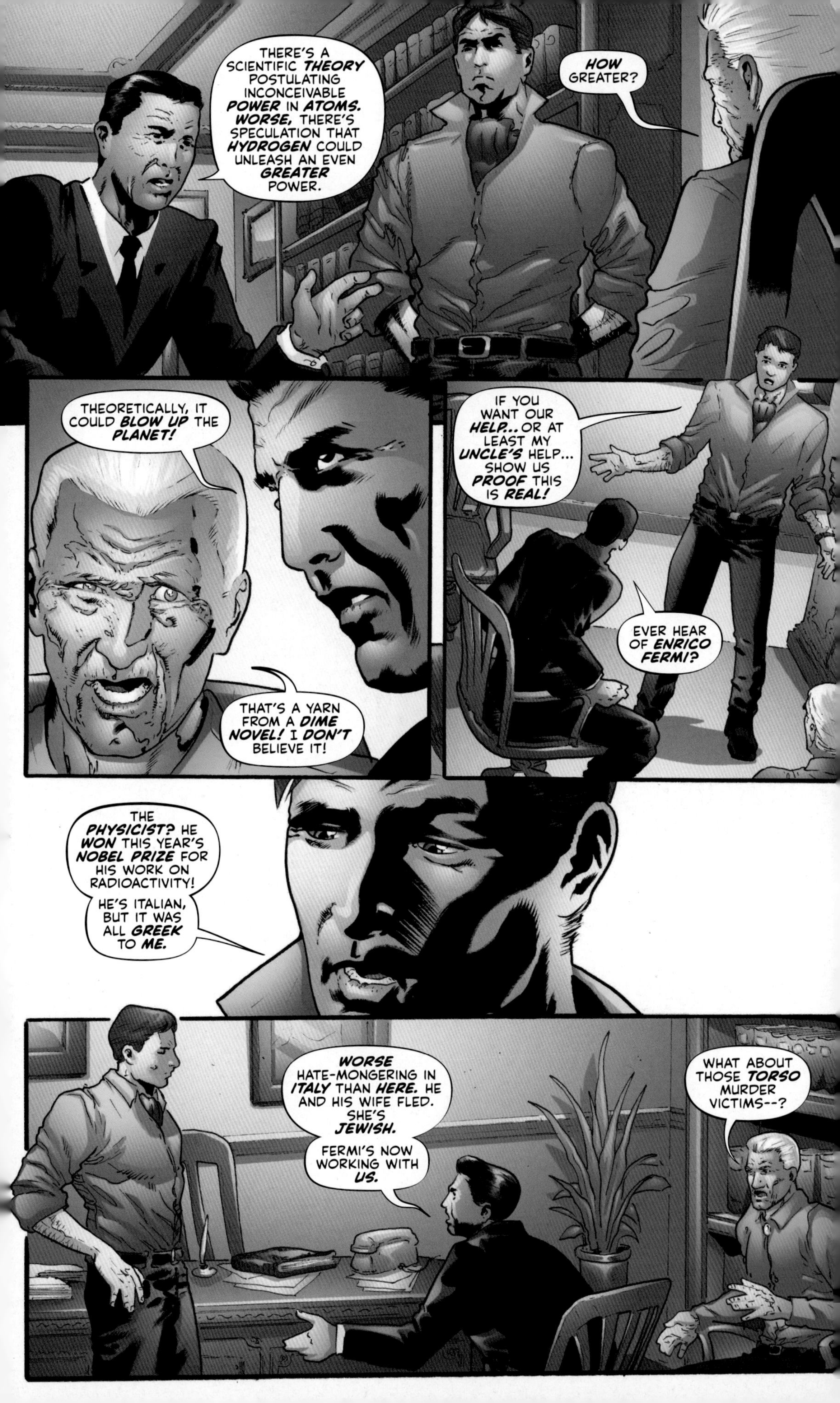

THERE'S A SCIENTIFIC THEORY POSTULATING INCONCEIVABLE POWER IN ATOMS. WORSE, THERE'S SPECULATION THAT HYDROGEN COULD UNLEASH AN EVEN GREATER POWER.
HOW GREATER?
THEORETICALLY, IT COULD BLOW UP THE PLANET!
THAT'S A YARN FROM A DIME NOVEL! I DON'T BELIEVE IT!
IF YOU WANT OUR HELP... OR AT LEAST MY UNCLE'S HELP... SHOW US PROOF THIS IS REAL!
EVER HEAR OF ENRICO FERMI?
THE PHYSICIST? HE WON THIS YEAR'S NOBEL PRIZE FOR HIS WORK ON RADIOACTIVITY!
HE'S ITALIAN, BUT IT WAS ALL GREEK TO ME.
WORSE HATE-MONGERING IN ITALY THAN HERE. HE AND HIS WIFE FLED. SHE'S JEWISH.
FERMI'S NOW WORKING WITH US.
WHAT ABOUT THOSE TORSO MURDER VICTIMS--?

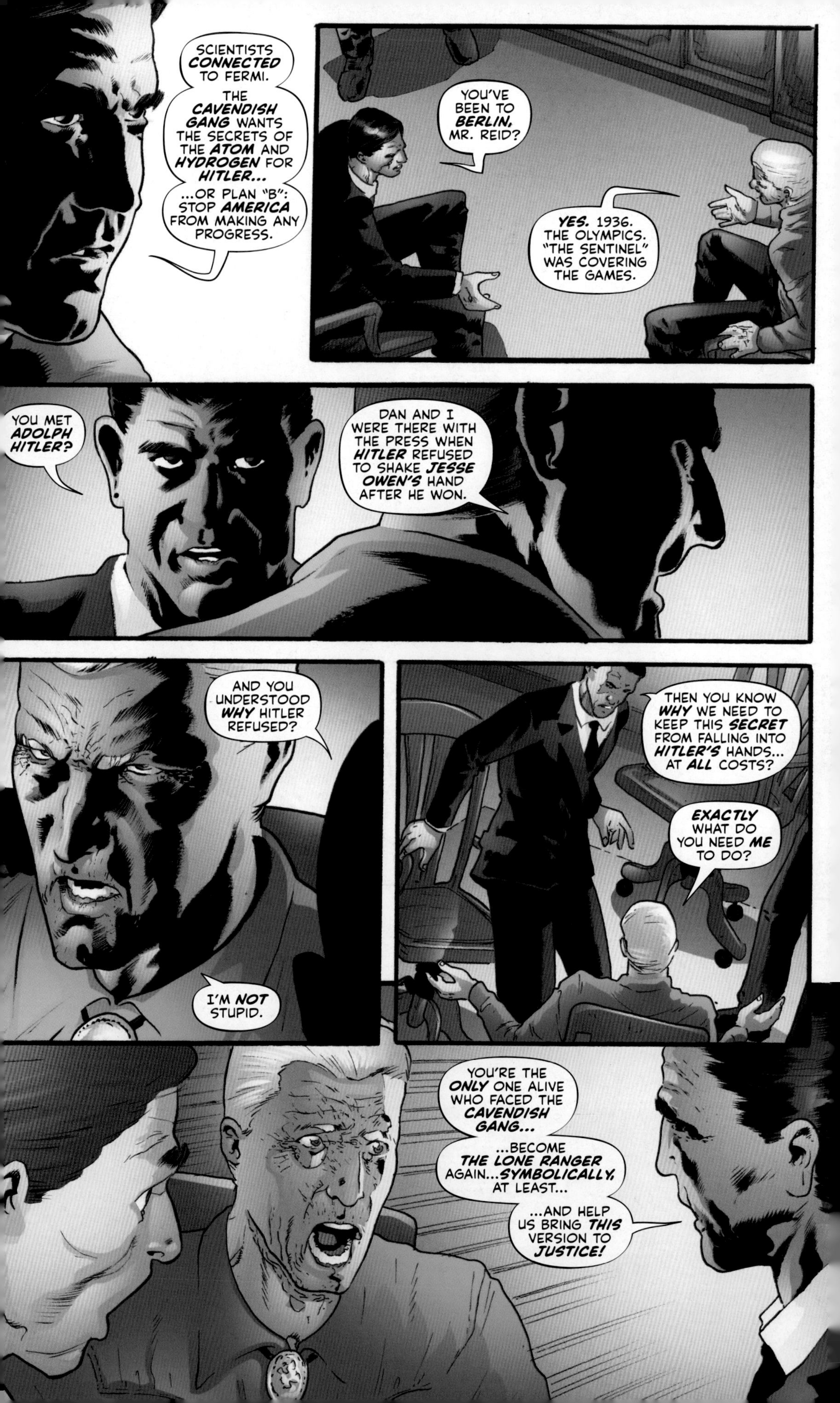
SCIENTISTS CONNECTED TO FERMI.
THE CAVENDISH GANG WANTS THE SECRETS OF THE ATOM AND HYDROGEN FOR HITLER...
...OR PLAN "B": STOP AMERICA FROM MAKING ANY PROGRESS.
YOU'VE BEEN TO BERLIN, MR. REID?
YES. 1936. THE OLYMPICS. "THE SENTINEL" WAS COVERING THE GAMES.
YOU MET ADOLPH HITLER?
DAN AND I WERE THERE WITH THE PRESS WHEN HITLER REFUSED TO SHAKE JESSE OWEN'S HAND AFTER HE WON.
AND YOU UNDERSTOOD WHY HITLER REFUSED?
I'M NOT STUPID.
THEN YOU KNOW WHY WE NEED TO KEEP THIS SECRET FROM FALLING INTO HITLER'S HANDS... AT ALL COSTS?
EXACTLY WHAT DO YOU NEED ME TO DO?
YOU'RE THE ONLY ONE ALIVE WHO FACED THE CAVENDISH GANG...
...BECOME THE LONE RANGER AGAIN...SYMBOLICALLY, AT LEAST...
...AND HELP US BRING THIS VERSION TO JUSTICE!

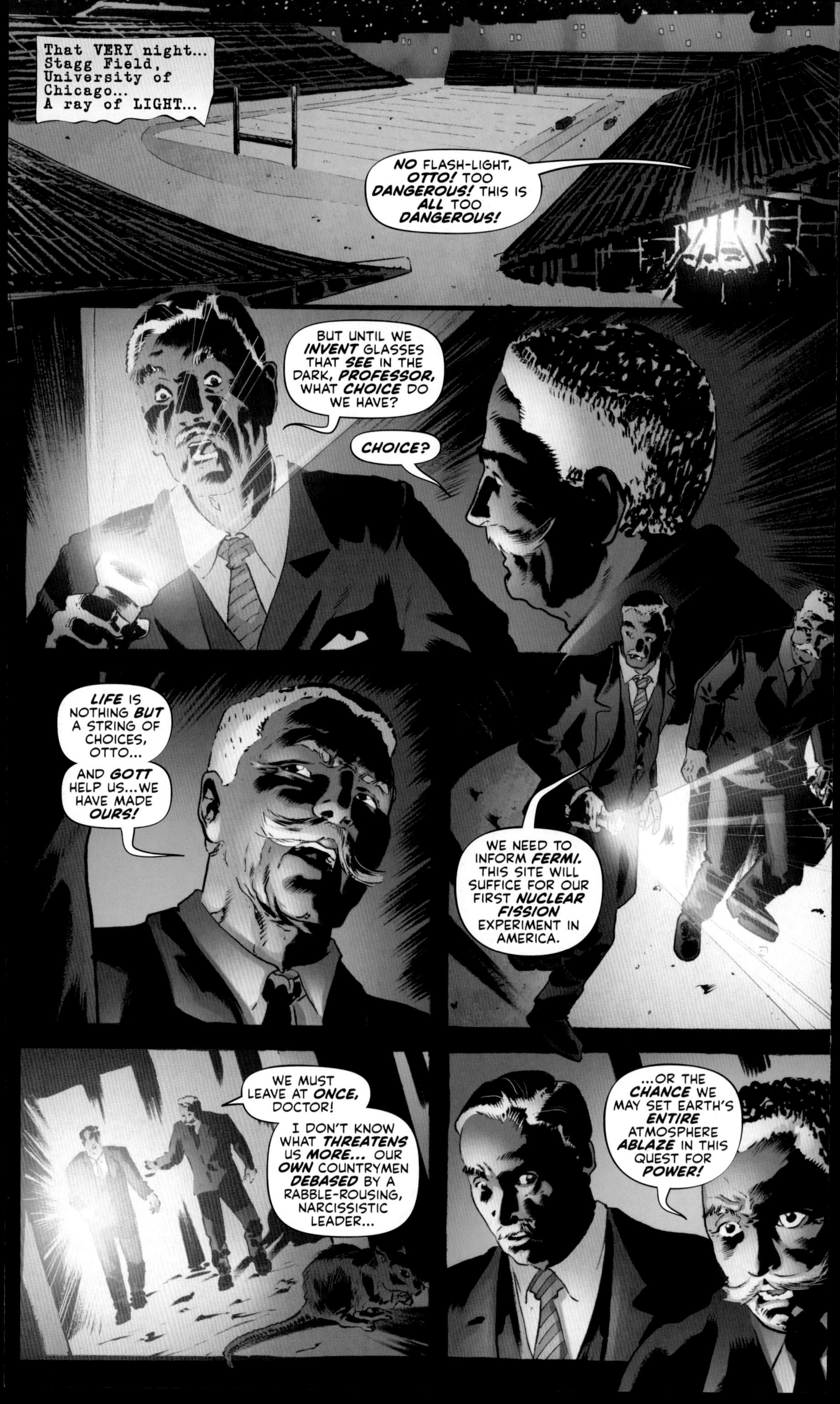
That VERY night... Stagg Field, University of Chicago... A ray of LIGHT...
NO FLASH-LIGHT, OTTO! TOO DANGEROUS! THIS IS ALL TOO DANGEROUS!
BUT UNTIL WE INVENT GLASSES THAT SEE IN THE DARK, PROFESSOR, WHAT CHOICE DO WE HAVE?
CHOICE?
LIFE IS NOTHING BUT A STRING OF CHOICES, OTTO...
AND GOTT HELP US...WE HAVE MADE OURS!
WE NEED TO INFORM FERMI. THIS SITE WILL SUFFICE FOR OUR FIRST NUCLEAR FISSION EXPERIMENT IN AMERICA.
WE MUST LEAVE AT ONCE, DOCTOR!
I DON'T KNOW WHAT THREATENS US MORE... OUR OWN COUNTRYMEN DEBASED BY A RABBLE-ROUSING, NARCISSISTIC LEADER...
...OR THE CHANCE WE MAY SET EARTH'S ENTIRE ATMOSPHERE ABLAZE IN THIS QUEST FOR POWER!

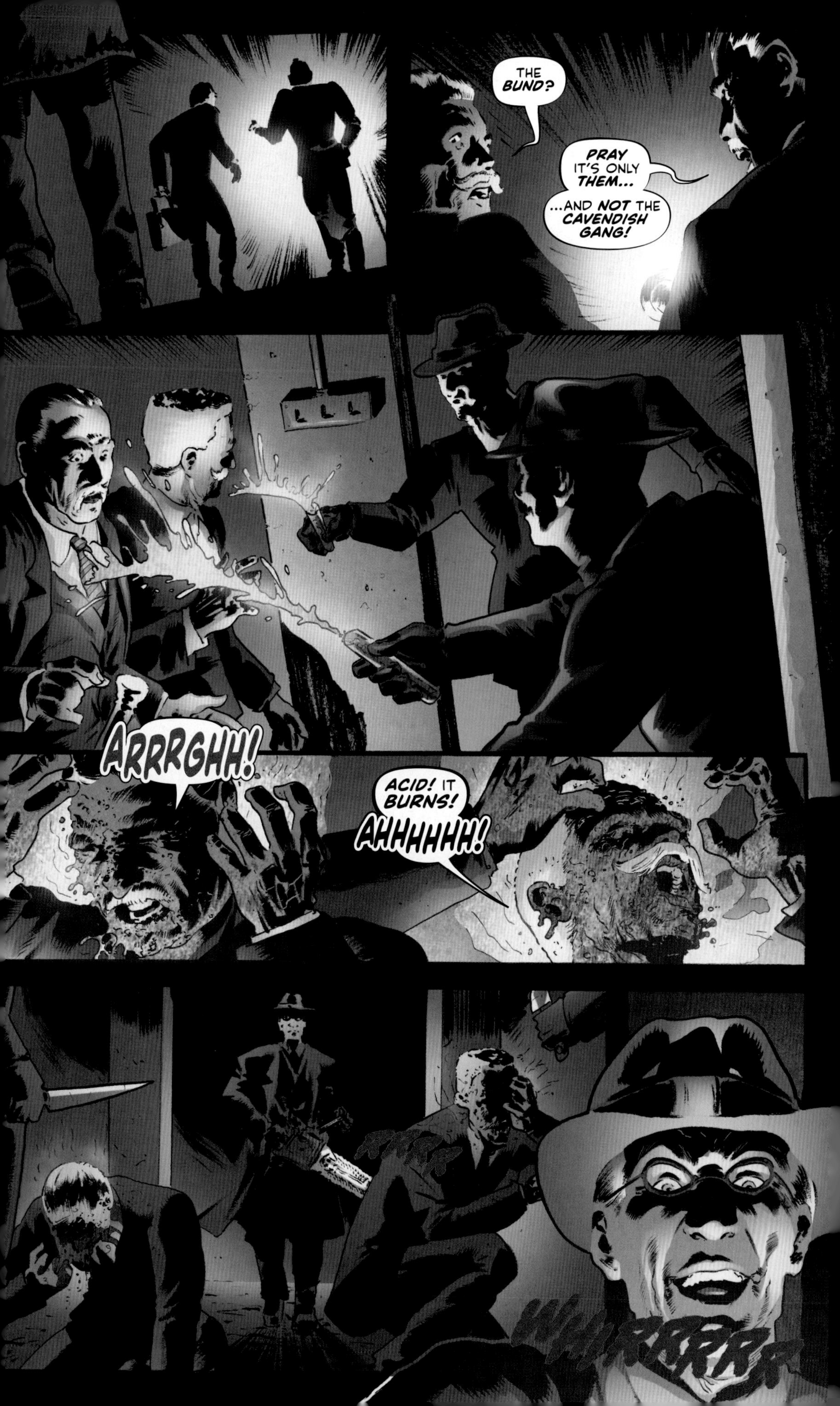

THE BUND?
PRAY IT'S ONLY THEM...
...AND NOT THE CAVENDISH GANG!
ARRRGHH!
ACID! IT BURNS! AHHHHHH!

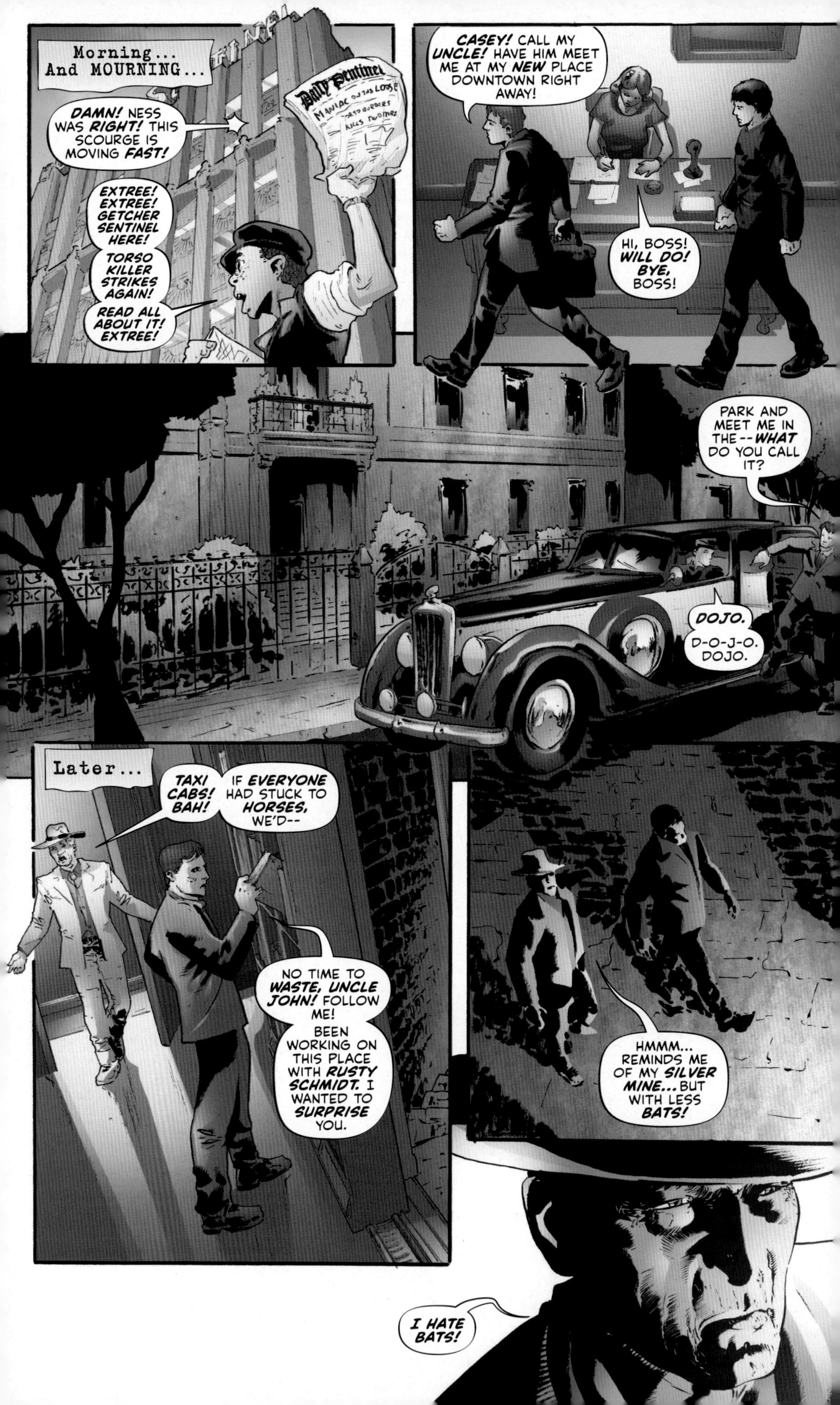

Morning... And MOURNING...
Daily Sentinel
MANIAC ON THE LOOSE
TORSO MURDERS KILLS TWO MORE
DAMN! NESS WAS RIGHT! THIS SCOURGE IS MOVING FAST!
EXTREE! EXTREE! GETCHER SENTINEL HERE!
TORSO KILLER STRIKES AGAIN!
READ ALL ABOUT IT! EXTREE!
CASEY! CALL MY UNCLE! HAVE HIM MEET ME AT MY NEW PLACE DOWNTOWN RIGHT AWAY!
HI, BOSS! WILL DO! BYE, BOSS!
PARK AND MEET ME IN THE --WHAT DO YOU CALL IT?
DOJO.
D-O-J-O. DOJO.
Later...
TAXI CABS! BAH!
IF EVERYONE HAD STUCK TO HORSES, WE'D--
NO TIME TO WASTE, UNCLE JOHN! FOLLOW ME!
BEEN WORKING ON THIS PLACE WITH RUSTY SCHMIDT. I WANTED TO SURPRISE YOU.
HMMM... REMINDS ME OF MY SILVER MINE... BUT WITH LESS BATS!
I HATE BATS!

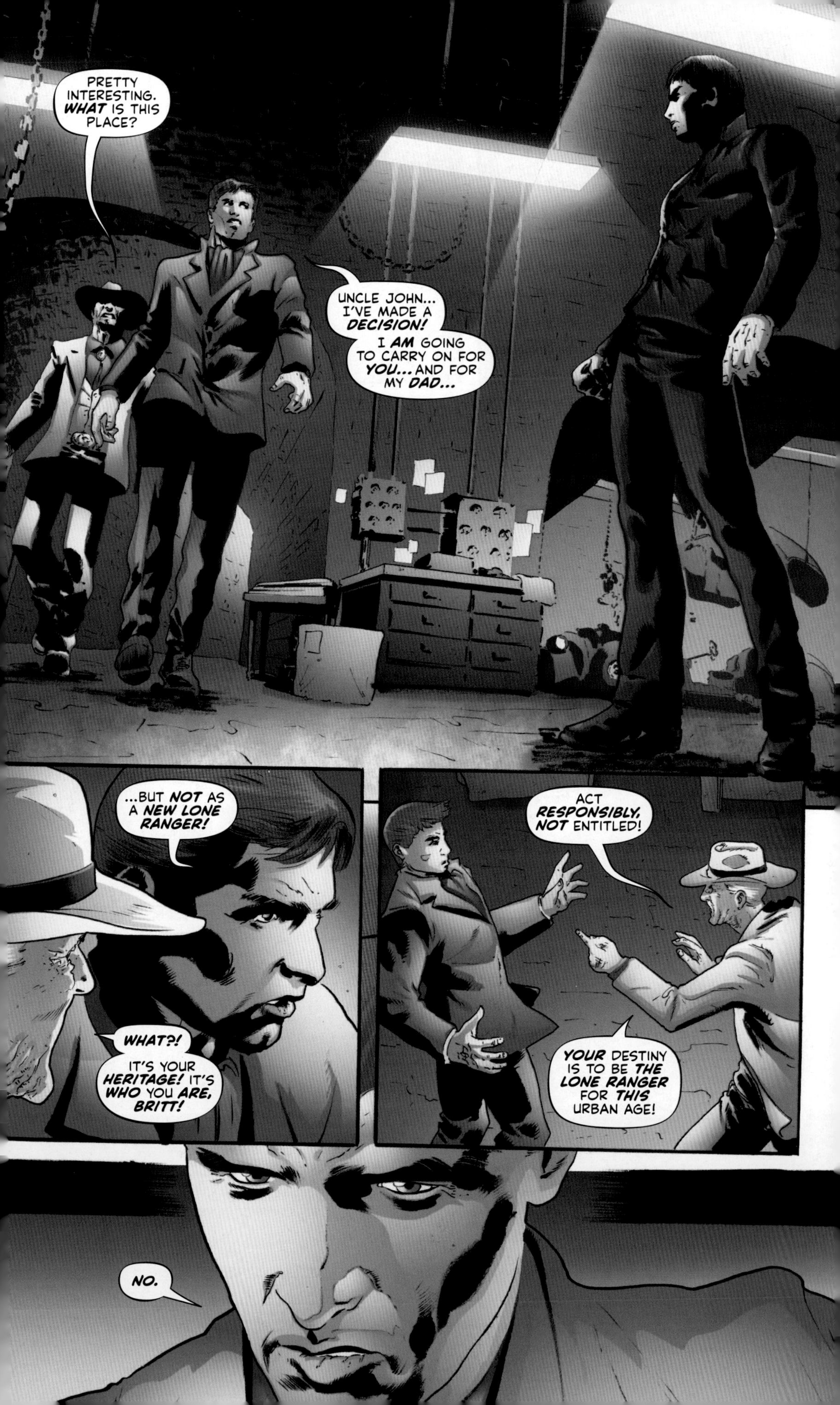

PRETTY INTERESTING. WHAT IS THIS PLACE?
UNCLE JOHN... I'VE MADE A DECISION!
I AM GOING TO CARRY ON FOR YOU... AND FOR MY DAD...
...BUT NOT AS A NEW LONE RANGER!
WHAT?!
IT'S YOUR HERITAGE! IT'S WHO YOU ARE, BRITT!
ACT RESPONSIBLY, NOT ENTITLED!
YOUR DESTINY IS TO BE THE LONE RANGER FOR THIS URBAN AGE!
NO.

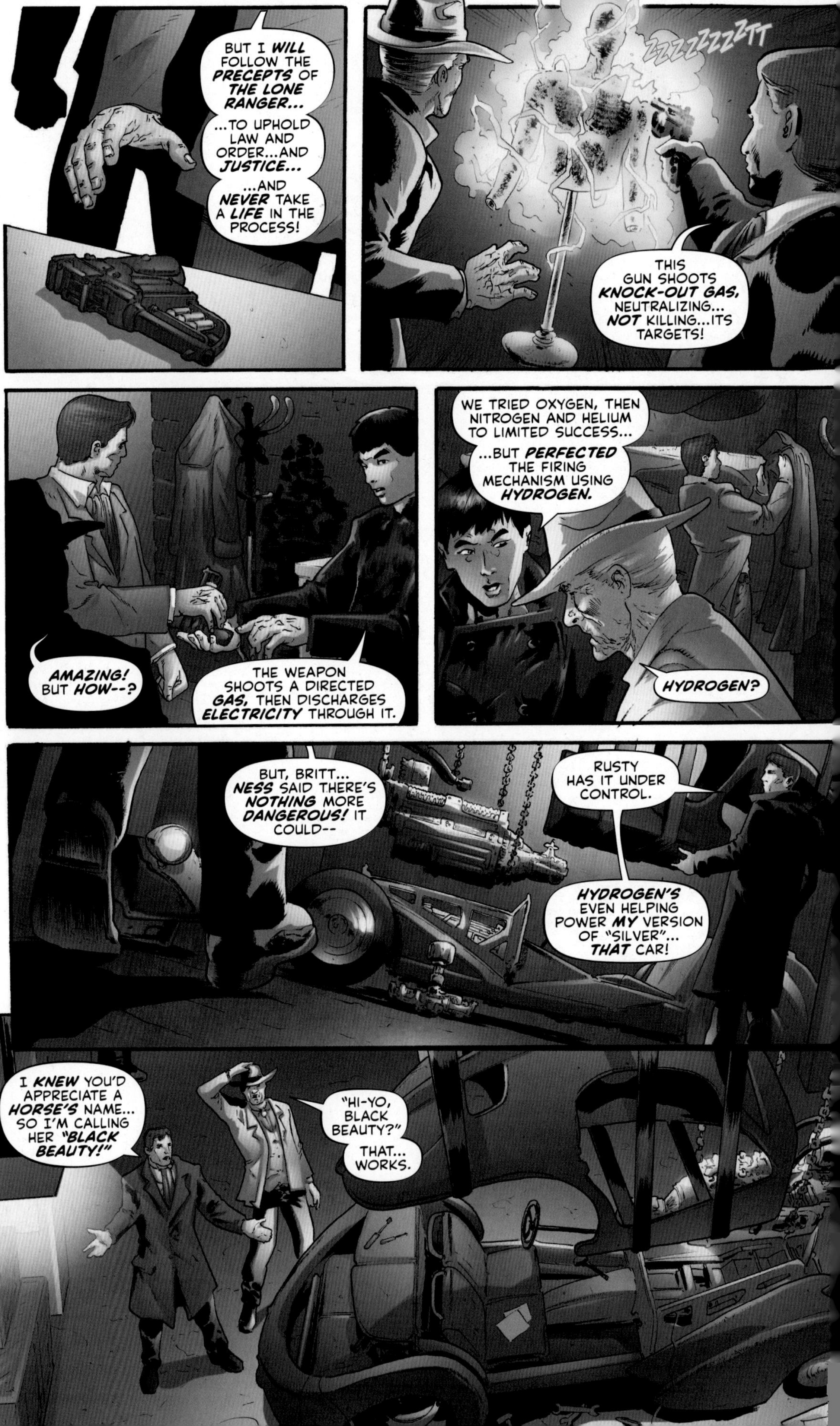

BUT I WILL FOLLOW THE PRECEPTS OF THE LONE RANGER...
...TO UPHOLD LAW AND ORDER...AND JUSTICE...
...AND NEVER TAKE A LIFE IN THE PROCESS!
ZZZZZZZZZTT
THIS GUN SHOOTS KNOCK-OUT GAS, NEUTRALIZING... NOT KILLING...ITS TARGETS!
AMAZING! BUT HOW--?
THE WEAPON SHOOTS A DIRECTED GAS, THEN DISCHARGES ELECTRICITY THROUGH IT.
WE TRIED OXYGEN, THEN NITROGEN AND HELIUM TO LIMITED SUCCESS...
...BUT PERFECTED THE FIRING MECHANISM USING HYDROGEN.
HYDROGEN?
BUT, BRITT... NESS SAID THERE'S NOTHING MORE DANGEROUS! IT COULD--
RUSTY HAS IT UNDER CONTROL.
HYDROGEN'S EVEN HELPING POWER MY VERSION OF "SILVER"... THAT CAR!
I KNEW YOU'D APPRECIATE A HORSE'S NAME... SO I'M CALLING HER "BLACK BEAUTY!"
"HI-YO, BLACK BEAUTY?"
THAT... WORKS.

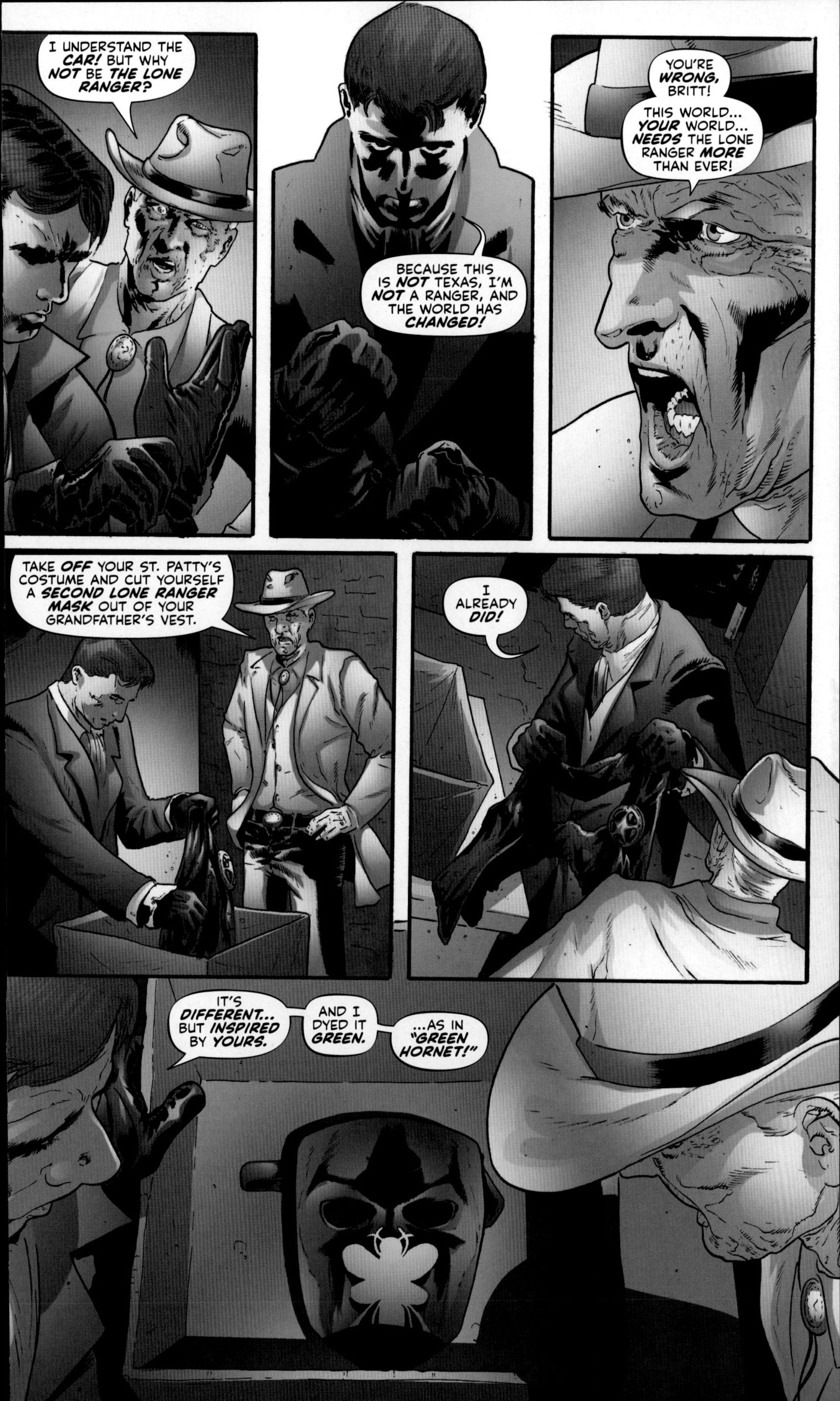
I UNDERSTAND THE CAR! BUT WHY NOT BE THE LONE RANGER?
BECAUSE THIS IS NOT TEXAS, I'M NOT A RANGER, AND THE WORLD HAS CHANGED!
YOU'RE WRONG, BRITT!
THIS WORLD... YOUR WORLD... NEEDS THE LONE RANGER MORE THAN EVER!
TAKE OFF YOUR ST. PATTY'S COSTUME AND CUT YOURSELF A SECOND LONE RANGER MASK OUT OF YOUR GRANDFATHER'S VEST.
I ALREADY DID!
IT'S DIFFERENT... BUT INSPIRED BY YOURS.
AND I DYED IT GREEN.
...AS IN "GREEN HORNET!"

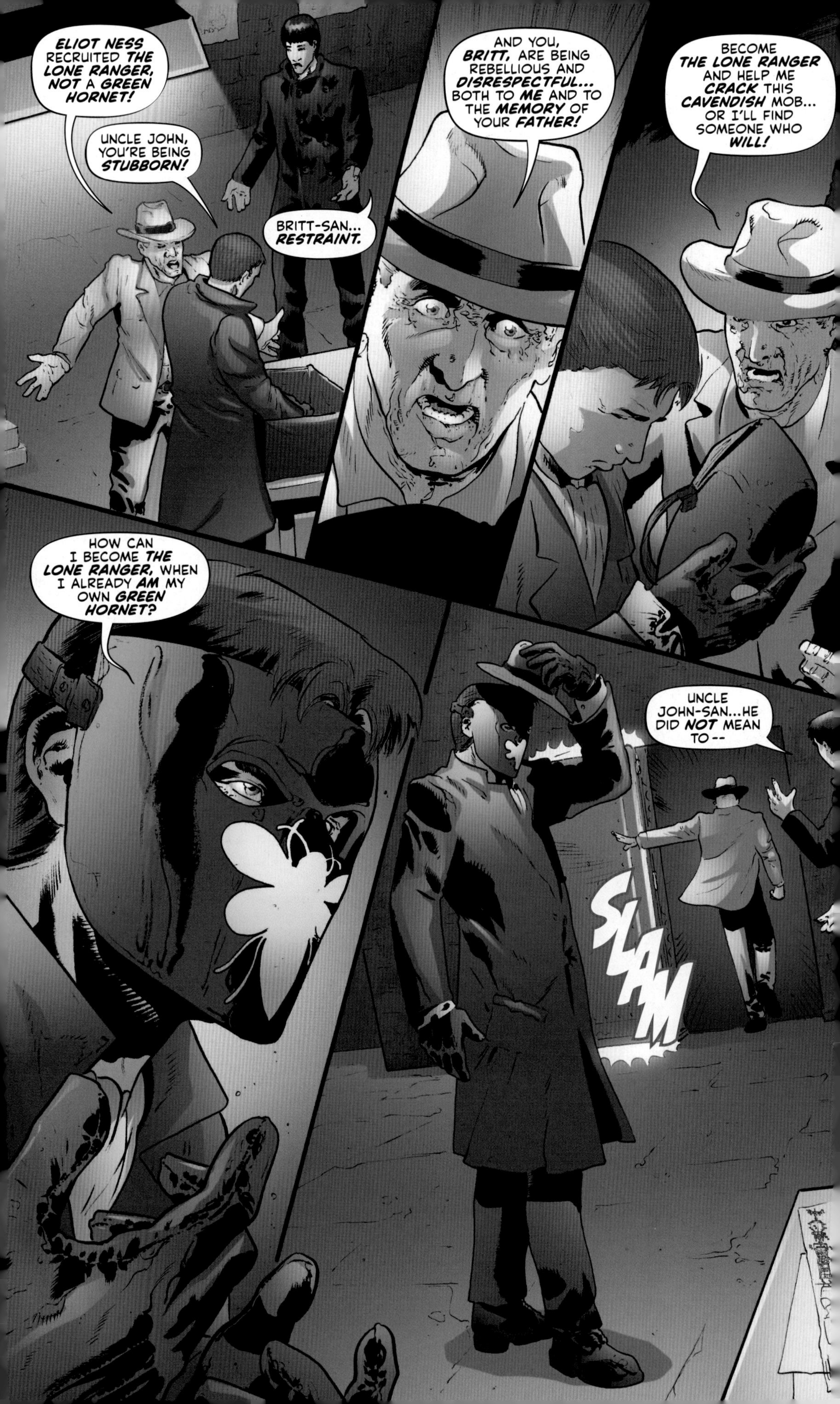

ELIOT NESS RECRUITED THE LONE RANGER, NOT A GREEN HORNET!
UNCLE JOHN, YOU'RE BEING STUBBORN!
BRITT-SAN... RESTRAINT.
AND YOU, BRITT, ARE BEING REBELLIOUS AND DISRESPECTFUL... BOTH TO ME AND TO THE MEMORY OF YOUR FATHER!
BECOME THE LONE RANGER AND HELP ME CRACK THIS CAVENDISH MOB... OR I'LL FIND SOMEONE WHO WILL!
HOW CAN I BECOME THE LONE RANGER, WHEN I ALREADY AM MY OWN GREEN HORNET?
UNCLE JOHN-SAN...HE DID NOT MEAN TO --
SLAM

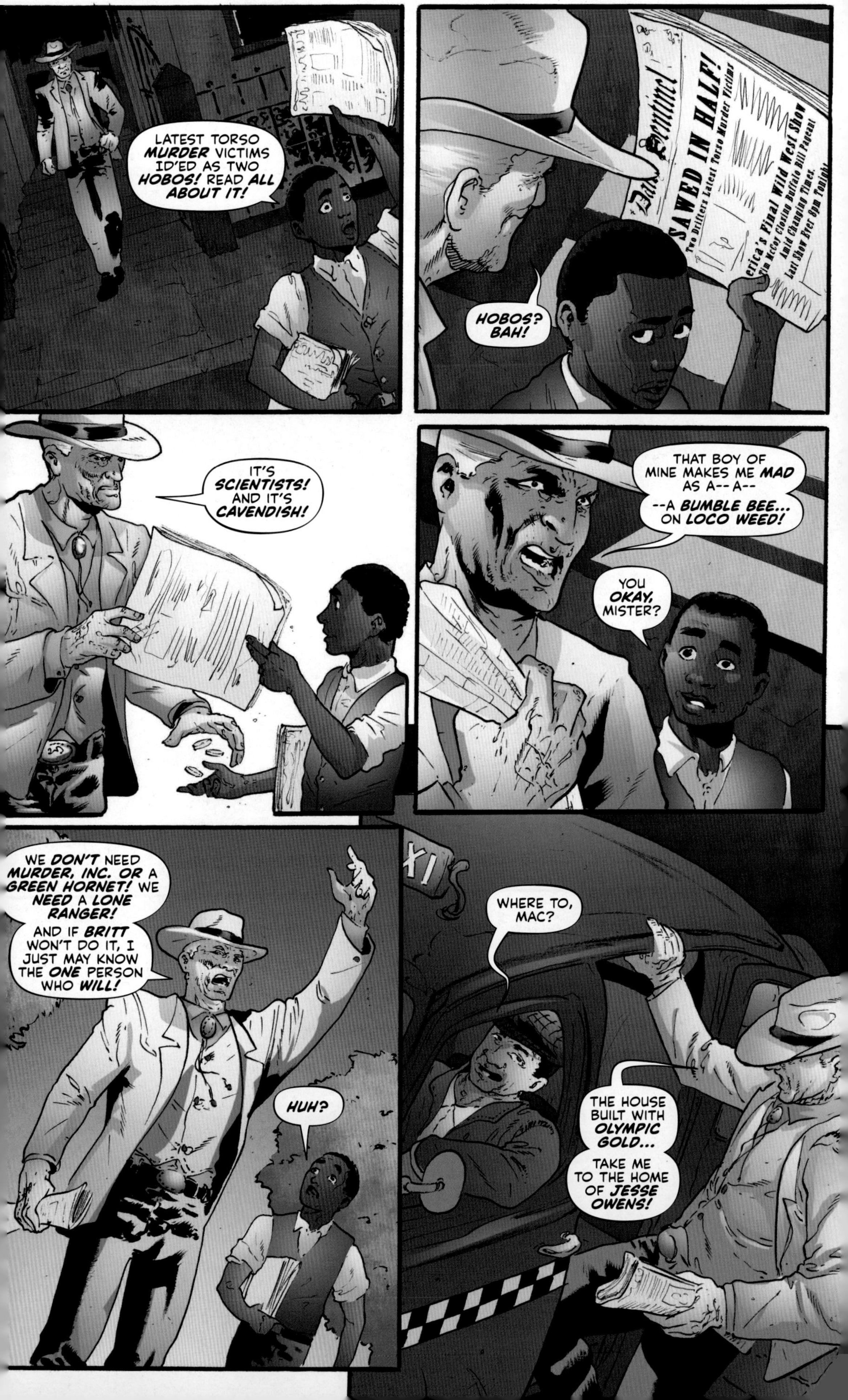

LATEST TORSO MURDER VICTIMS ID'ED AS TWO HOBOS! READ ALL ABOUT IT!
SAWED IN HALF!
Two Drifters Latest Torso Murder Victims
HOBOS? BAH!
IT'S SCIENTISTS! AND IT'S CAVENDISH!
THAT BOY OF MINE MAKES ME MAD AS A-- A--
--A BUMBLE BEE... ON LOCO WEED!
YOU OKAY, MISTER?
WE DON'T NEED MURDER, INC. OR A GREEN HORNET! WE NEED A LONE RANGER!
AND IF BRITT WON'T DO IT, I JUST MAY KNOW THE ONE PERSON WHO WILL!
HUH?
WHERE TO, MAC?
THE HOUSE BUILT WITH OLYMPIC GOLD...
TAKE ME TO THE HOME OF JESSE OWENS!

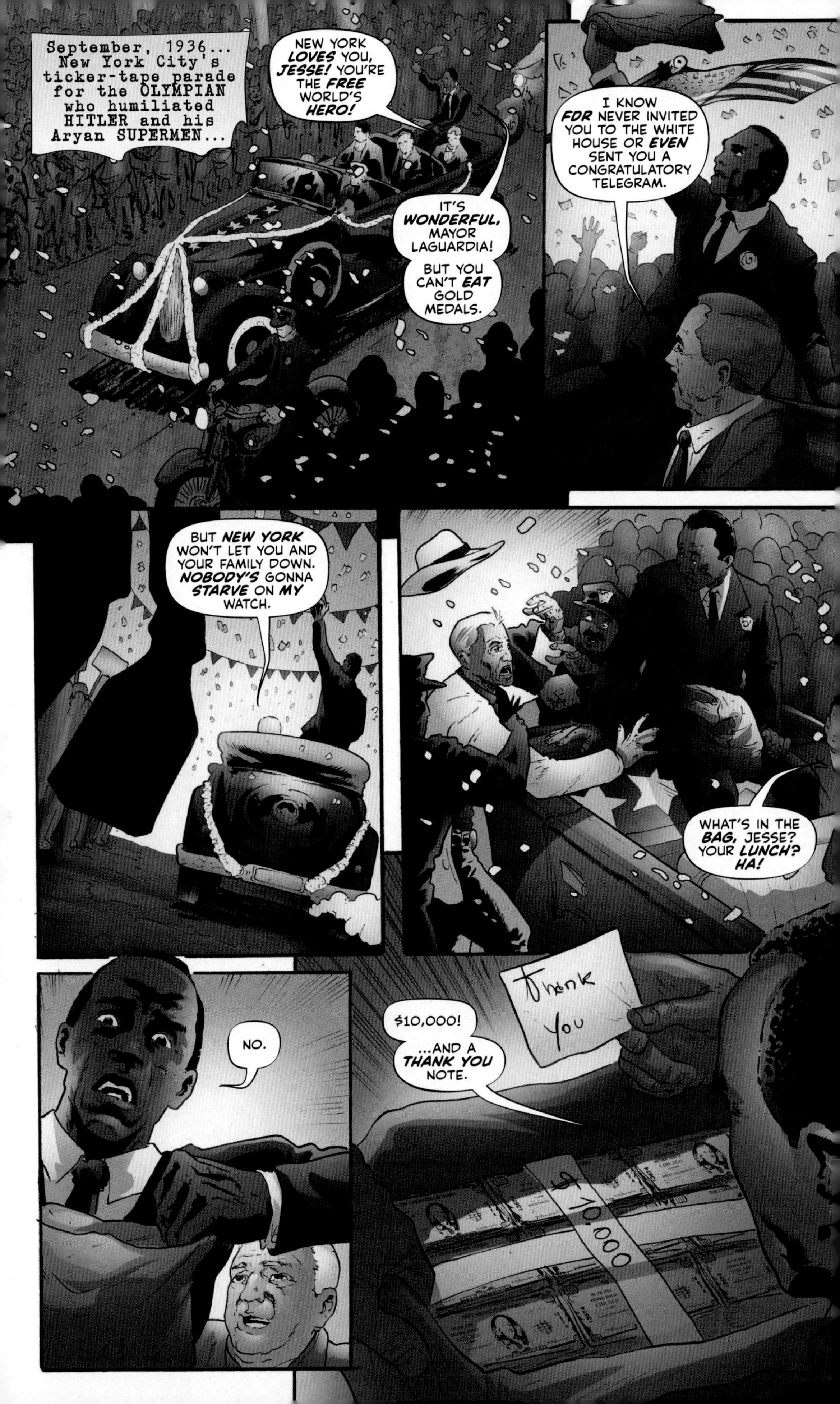
September, 1936... New York City's ticker-tape parade for the OLYMPIAN who humiliated HITLER and his Aryan SUPERMEN...
NEW YORK LOVES YOU, JESSE! YOU'RE THE FREE WORLD'S HERO!
IT'S WONDERFUL, MAYOR LAGUARDIA!
BUT YOU CAN'T EAT GOLD MEDALS.
I KNOW FDR NEVER INVITED YOU TO THE WHITE HOUSE OR EVEN SENT YOU A CONGRATULATORY TELEGRAM.
BUT NEW YORK WON'T LET YOU AND YOUR FAMILY DOWN. NOBODY'S GONNA STARVE ON MY WATCH.
WHAT'S IN THE BAG, JESSE? YOUR LUNCH? HA!
NO.
$10,000!
...AND A THANK YOU NOTE.
Thank You
$10,000

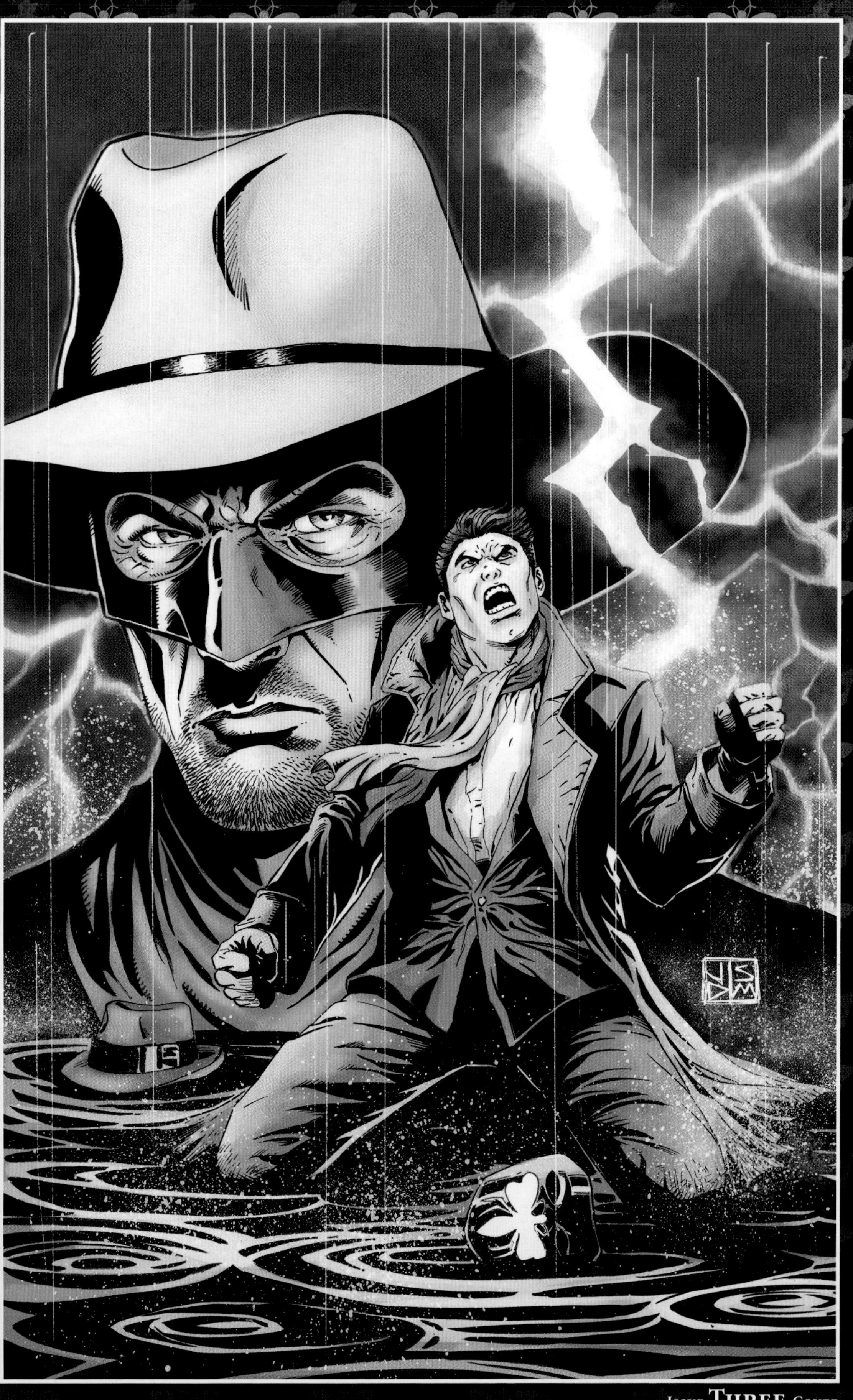

JS DM

Issue THREE Cover

Art by JAN DUURSEMA Colors by SIAN MANDRAKE

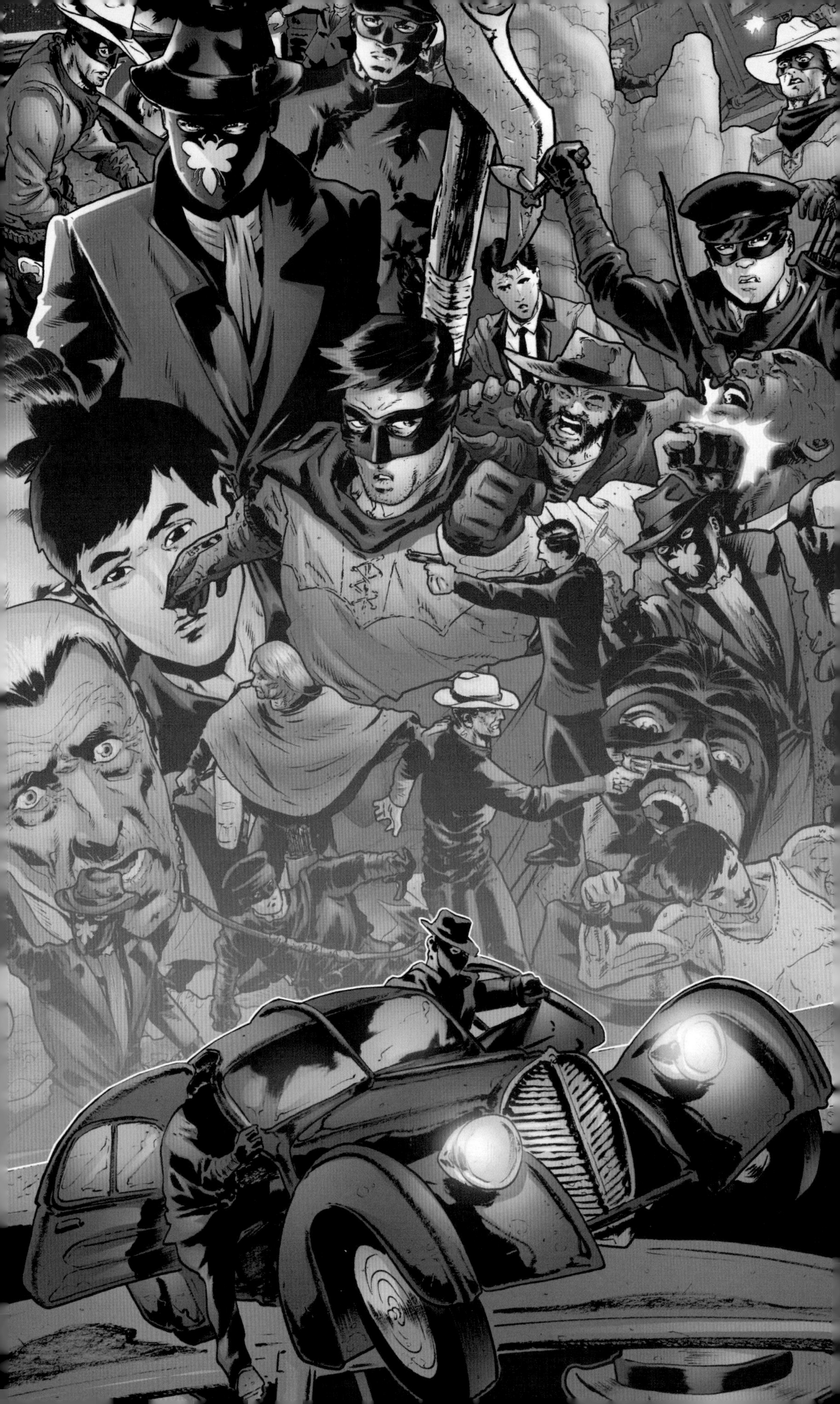

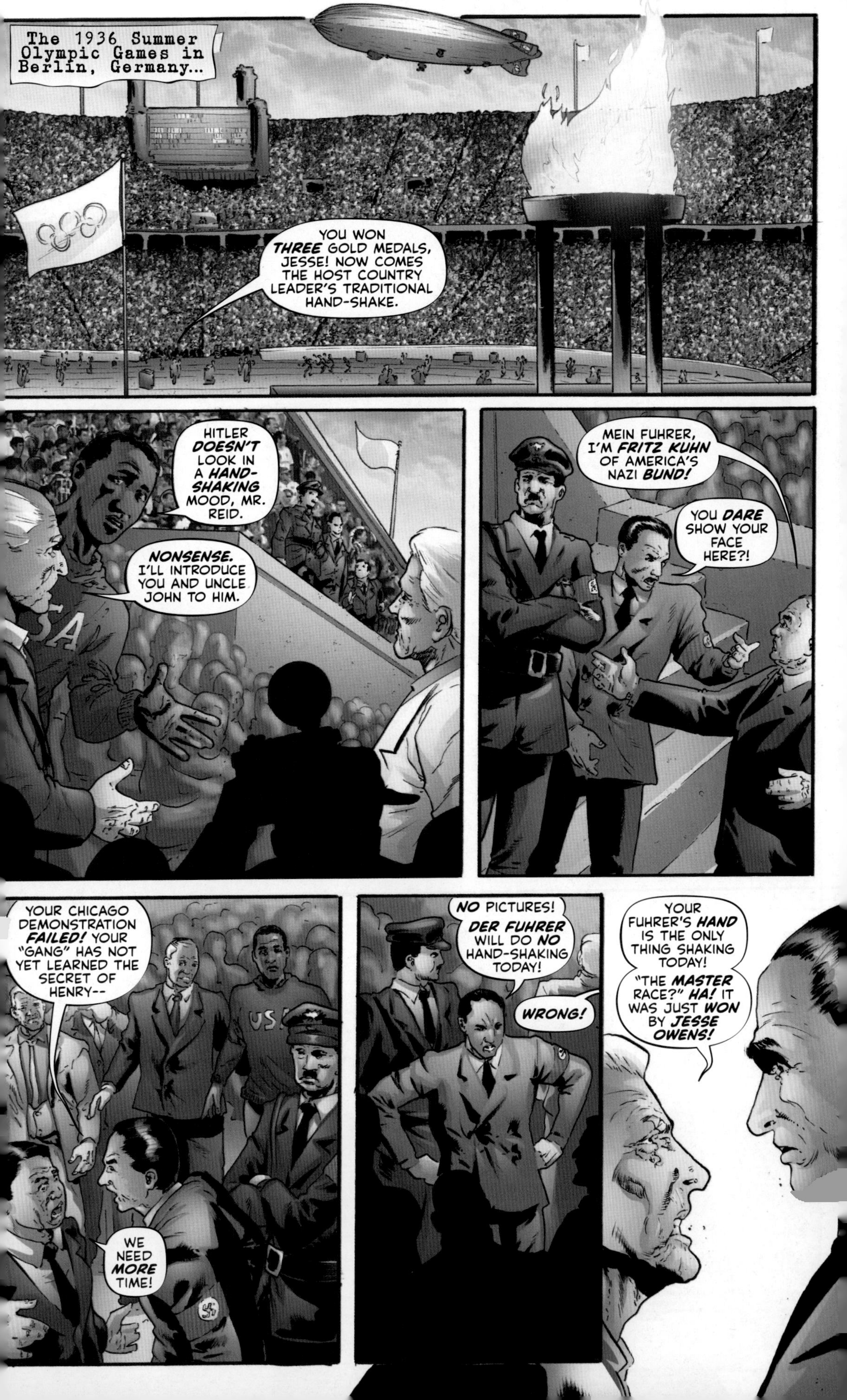
The 1936 Summer Olympic Games in Berlin, Germany...
YOU WON THREE GOLD MEDALS, JESSE! NOW COMES THE HOST COUNTRY LEADER'S TRADITIONAL HAND-SHAKE.
HITLER DOESN'T LOOK IN A HAND-SHAKING MOOD, MR. REID.
NONSENSE. I'LL INTRODUCE YOU AND UNCLE JOHN TO HIM.
MEIN FUHRER, I'M FRITZ KUHN OF AMERICA'S NAZI BUND!
YOU DARE SHOW YOUR FACE HERE?!
YOUR CHICAGO DEMONSTRATION FAILED! YOUR "GANG" HAS NOT YET LEARNED THE SECRET OF HENRY--
WE NEED MORE TIME!
NO PICTURES! DER FUHRER WILL DO NO HAND-SHAKING TODAY!
WRONG!
YOUR FUHRER'S HAND IS THE ONLY THING SHAKING TODAY!
"THE MASTER RACE?" HA! IT WAS JUST WON BY JESSE OWENS!

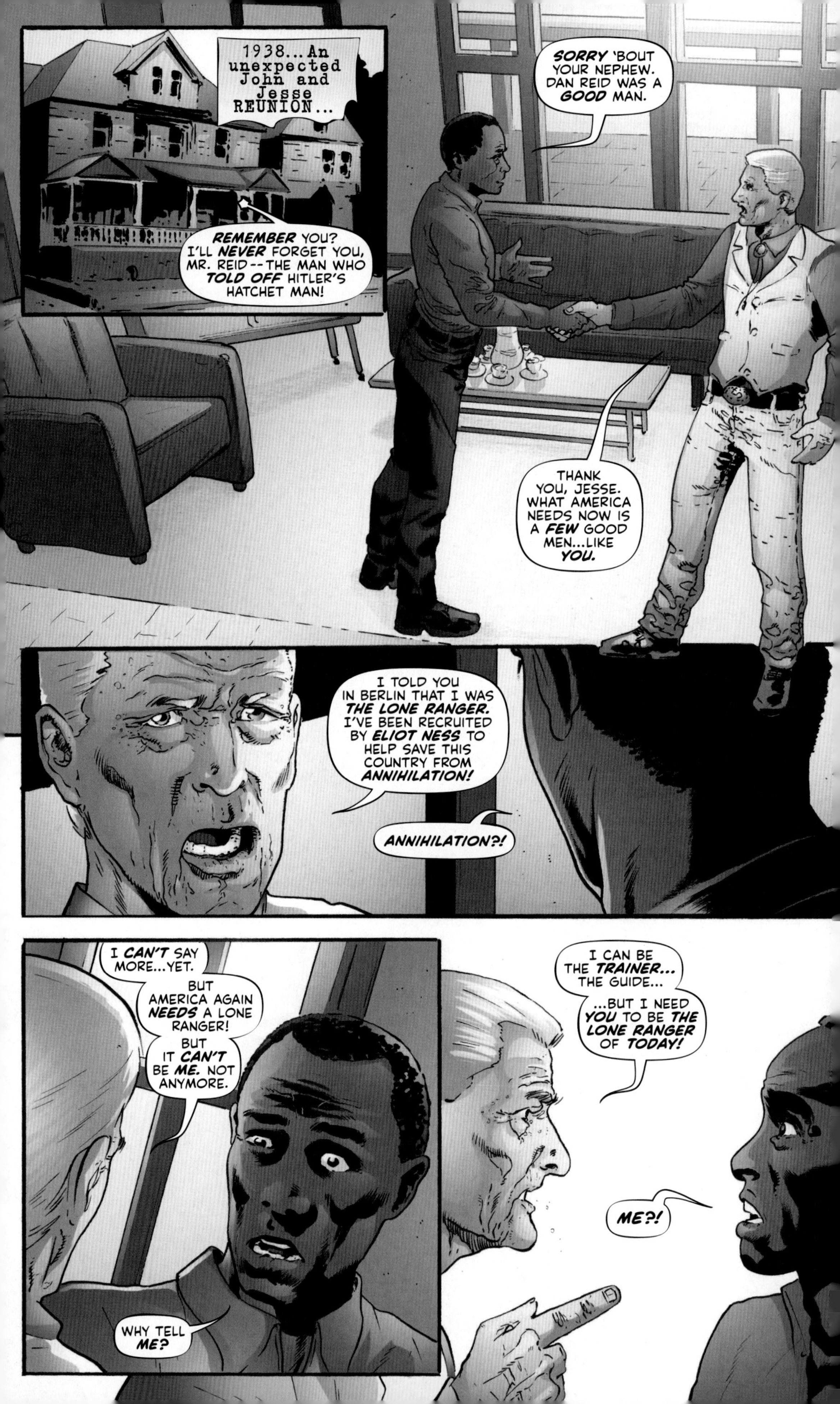

1938...An unexpected John and Jesse REUNION...
REMEMBER YOU? I'LL NEVER FORGET YOU, MR. REID--THE MAN WHO TOLD OFF HITLER'S HATCHET MAN!
SORRY 'BOUT YOUR NEPHEW. DAN REID WAS A GOOD MAN.
THANK YOU, JESSE. WHAT AMERICA NEEDS NOW IS A FEW GOOD MEN...LIKE YOU.
I TOLD YOU IN BERLIN THAT I WAS THE LONE RANGER. I'VE BEEN RECRUITED BY ELIOT NESS TO HELP SAVE THIS COUNTRY FROM ANNIHILATION!
ANNIHILATION?!
I CAN'T SAY MORE...YET.
BUT AMERICA AGAIN NEEDS A LONE RANGER!
BUT IT CAN'T BE ME. NOT ANYMORE.
WHY TELL ME?
I CAN BE THE TRAINER... THE GUIDE...
...BUT I NEED YOU TO BE THE LONE RANGER OF TODAY!
ME?!

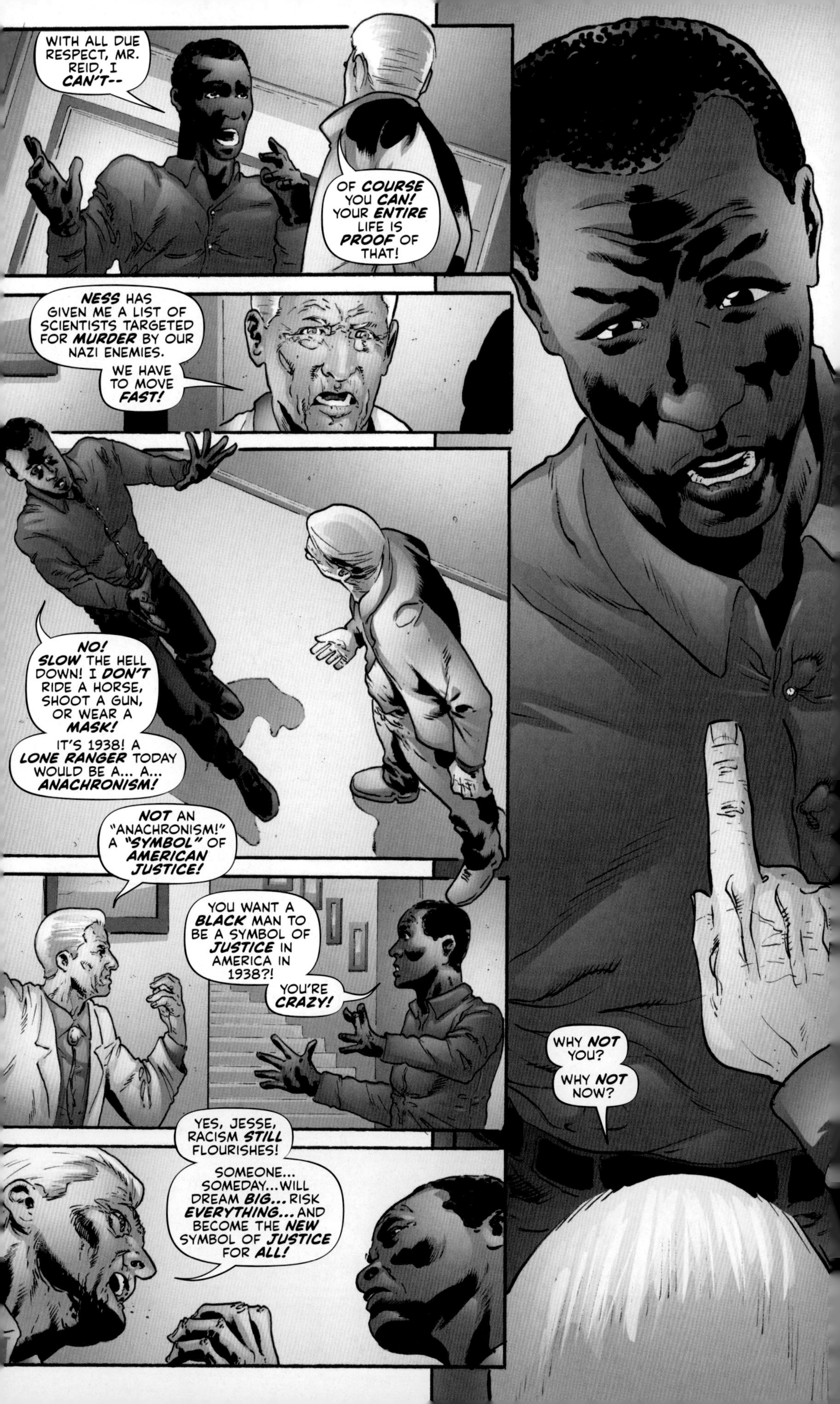

WITH ALL DUE RESPECT, MR. REID, I CAN'T--
OF COURSE YOU CAN! YOUR ENTIRE LIFE IS PROOF OF THAT!
NESS HAS GIVEN ME A LIST OF SCIENTISTS TARGETED FOR MURDER BY OUR NAZI ENEMIES.
WE HAVE TO MOVE FAST!
NO! SLOW THE HELL DOWN! I DON'T RIDE A HORSE, SHOOT A GUN, OR WEAR A MASK!
IT'S 1938! A LONE RANGER TODAY WOULD BE A... A... ANACHRONISM!
NOT AN "ANACHRONISM!" A "SYMBOL" OF AMERICAN JUSTICE!
YOU WANT A BLACK MAN TO BE A SYMBOL OF JUSTICE IN AMERICA IN 1938?!
YOU'RE CRAZY!
YES, JESSE, RACISM STILL FLOURISHES!
SOMEONE... SOMEDAY...WILL DREAM BIG... RISK EVERYTHING... AND BECOME THE NEW SYMBOL OF JUSTICE FOR ALL!
WHY NOT YOU?
WHY NOT NOW?

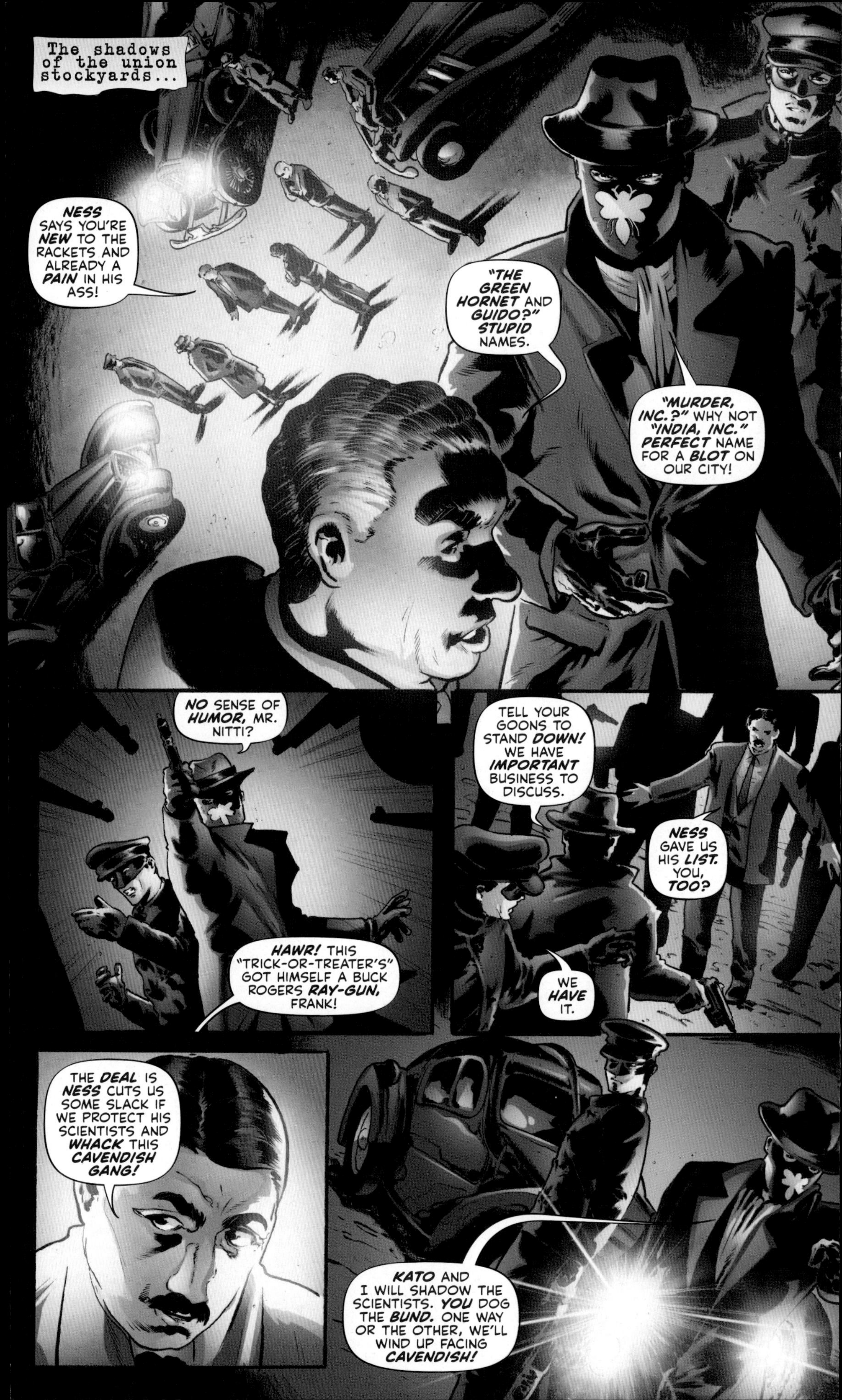
The shadows of the union stockyards...
NESS SAYS YOU'RE NEW TO THE RACKETS AND ALREADY A PAIN IN HIS ASS!
"THE GREEN HORNET AND GUIDO?" STUPID NAMES.
"MURDER, INC.?" WHY NOT "INDIA, INC." PERFECT NAME FOR A BLOT ON OUR CITY!
NO SENSE OF HUMOR, MR. NITTI?
HAWR! THIS "TRICK-OR-TREATER'S" GOT HIMSELF A BUCK ROGERS RAY-GUN, FRANK!
TELL YOUR GOONS TO STAND DOWN! WE HAVE IMPORTANT BUSINESS TO DISCUSS.
NESS GAVE US HIS LIST. YOU, TOO?
WE HAVE IT.
THE DEAL IS NESS CUTS US SOME SLACK IF WE PROTECT HIS SCIENTISTS AND WHACK THIS CAVENDISH GANG!
KATO AND I WILL SHADOW THE SCIENTISTS. YOU DOG THE BUND. ONE WAY OR THE OTHER, WE'LL WIND UP FACING CAVENDISH!

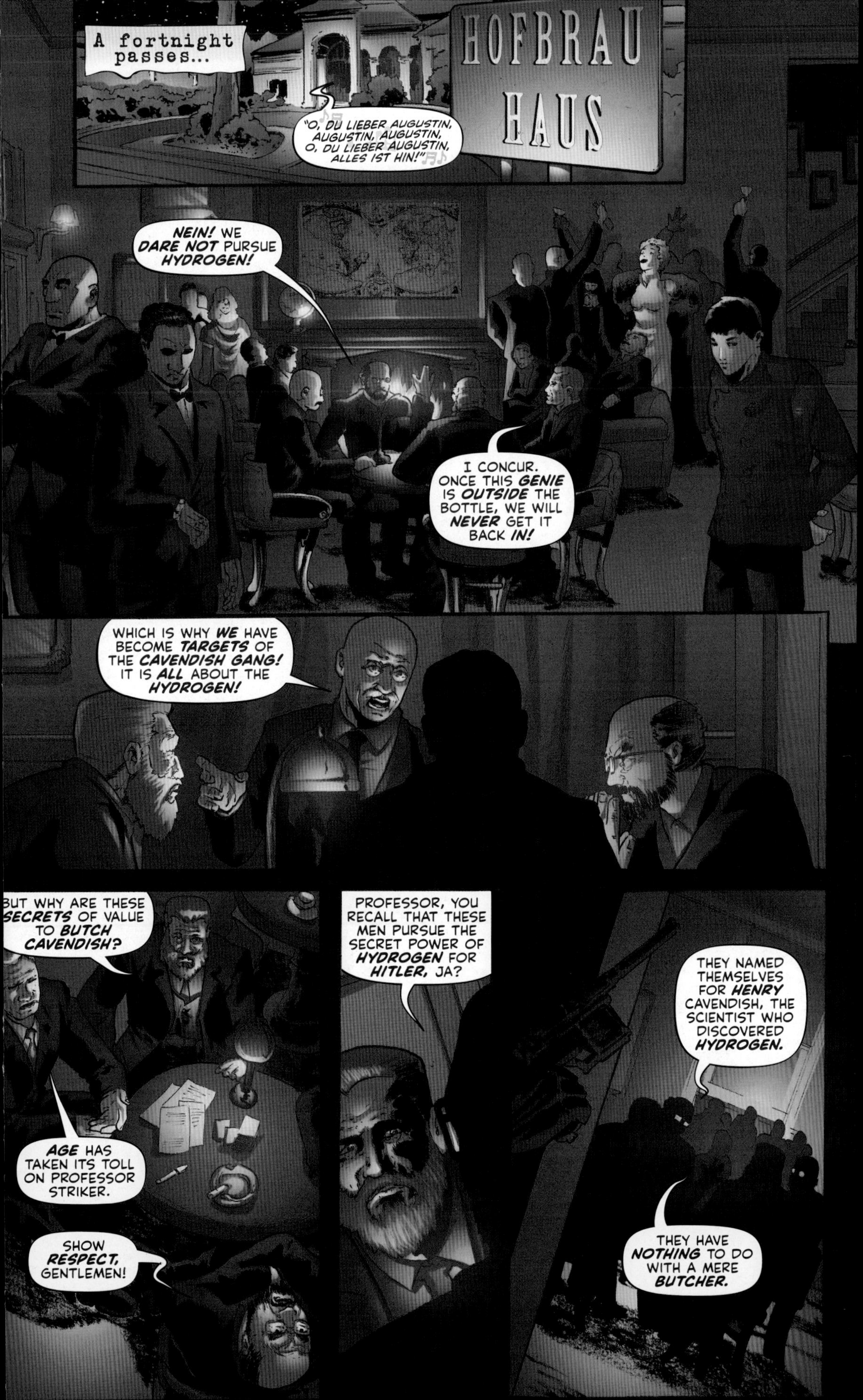
A fortnight passes...
HOFBRAU HAUS
"O, DU LIEBER AUGUSTIN, AUGUSTIN, AUGUSTIN, O, DU LIEBER AUGUSTIN, ALLES IST HIN!"
NEIN! WE DARE NOT PURSUE HYDROGEN!
I CONCUR. ONCE THIS GENIE IS OUTSIDE THE BOTTLE, WE WILL NEVER GET IT BACK IN!
WHICH IS WHY WE HAVE BECOME TARGETS OF THE CAVENDISH GANG! IT IS ALL ABOUT THE HYDROGEN!
BUT WHY ARE THESE SECRETS OF VALUE TO BUTCH CAVENDISH?
AGE HAS TAKEN ITS TOLL ON PROFESSOR STRIKER.
SHOW RESPECT, GENTLEMEN!
PROFESSOR, YOU RECALL THAT THESE MEN PURSUE THE SECRET POWER OF HYDROGEN FOR HITLER, JA?
THEY NAMED THEMSELVES FOR HENRY CAVENDISH, THE SCIENTIST WHO DISCOVERED HYDROGEN.
THEY HAVE NOTHING TO DO WITH A MERE BUTCHER.

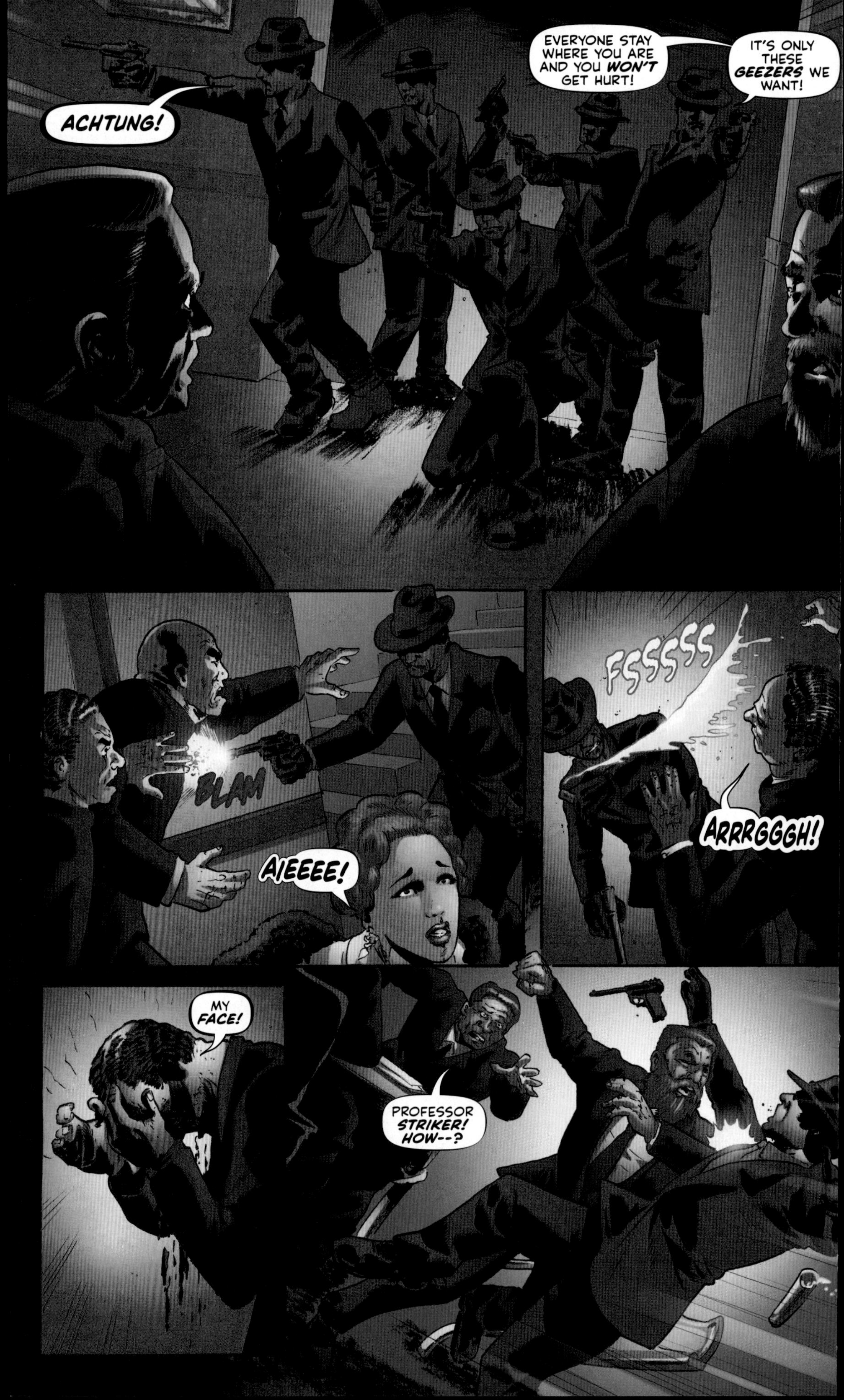
ACHTUNG!
EVERYONE STAY WHERE YOU ARE AND YOU WON'T GET HURT!
IT'S ONLY THESE GEEZERS WE WANT!
BLAM
AIEEEE!
FSSSSS
ARRRGGGH!
MY FACE!
PROFESSOR STRIKER! HOW--?

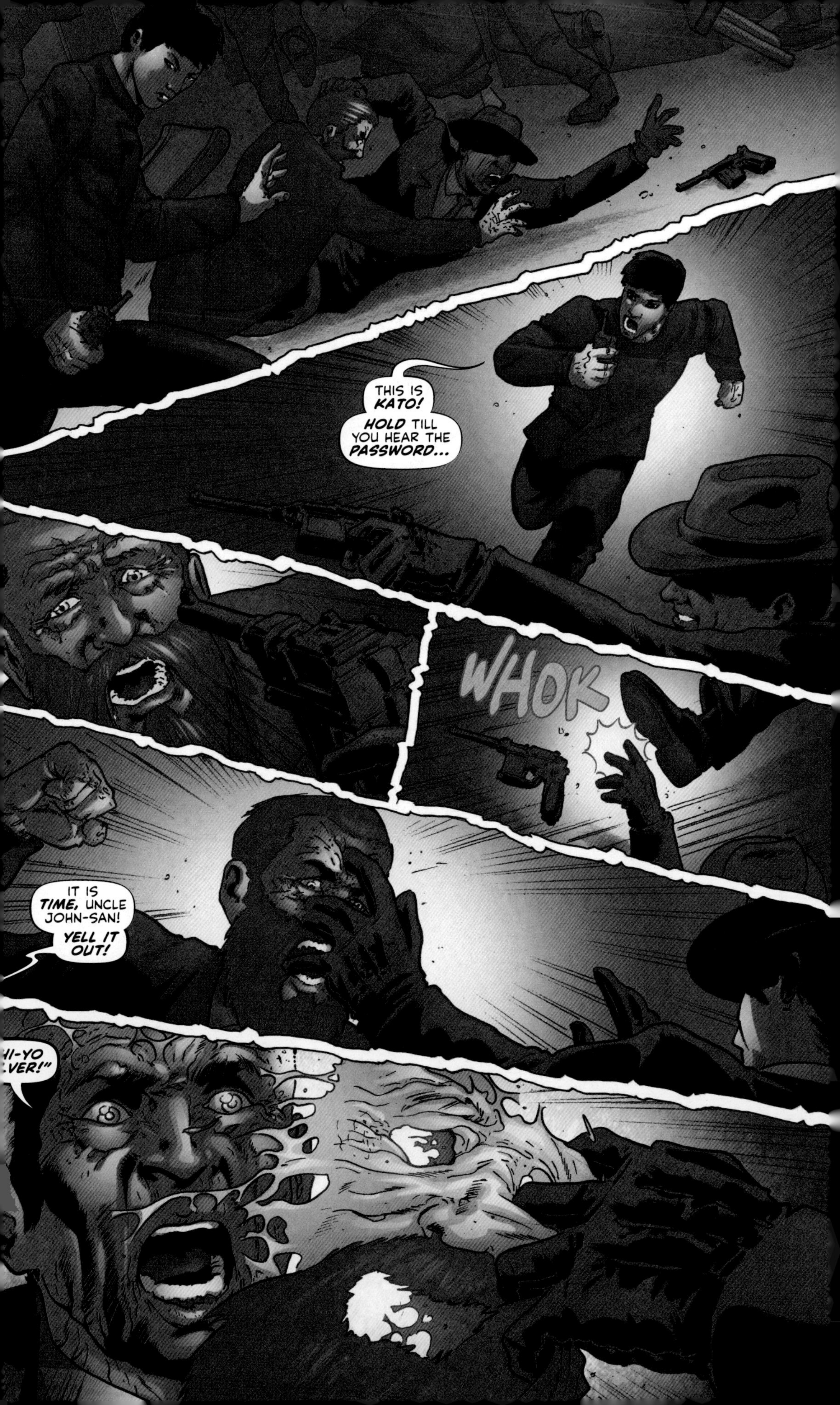

THIS IS KATO! HOLD TILL YOU HEAR THE PASSWORD...
WHOK
IT IS TIME, UNCLE JOHN-SAN! YELL IT OUT!
"HI-YO
VER!"

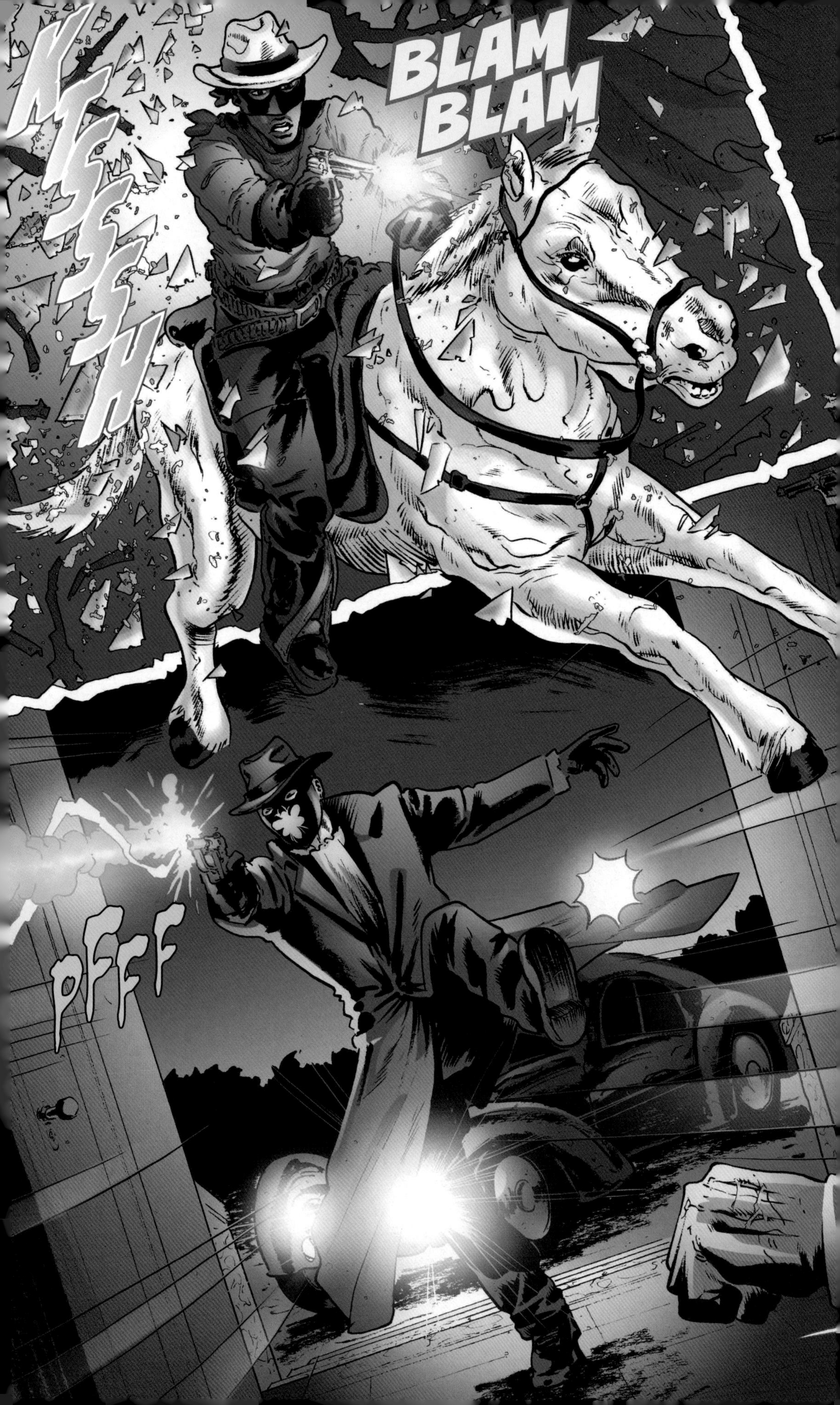
KTSSSH
BLAM
BLAM
PFFF

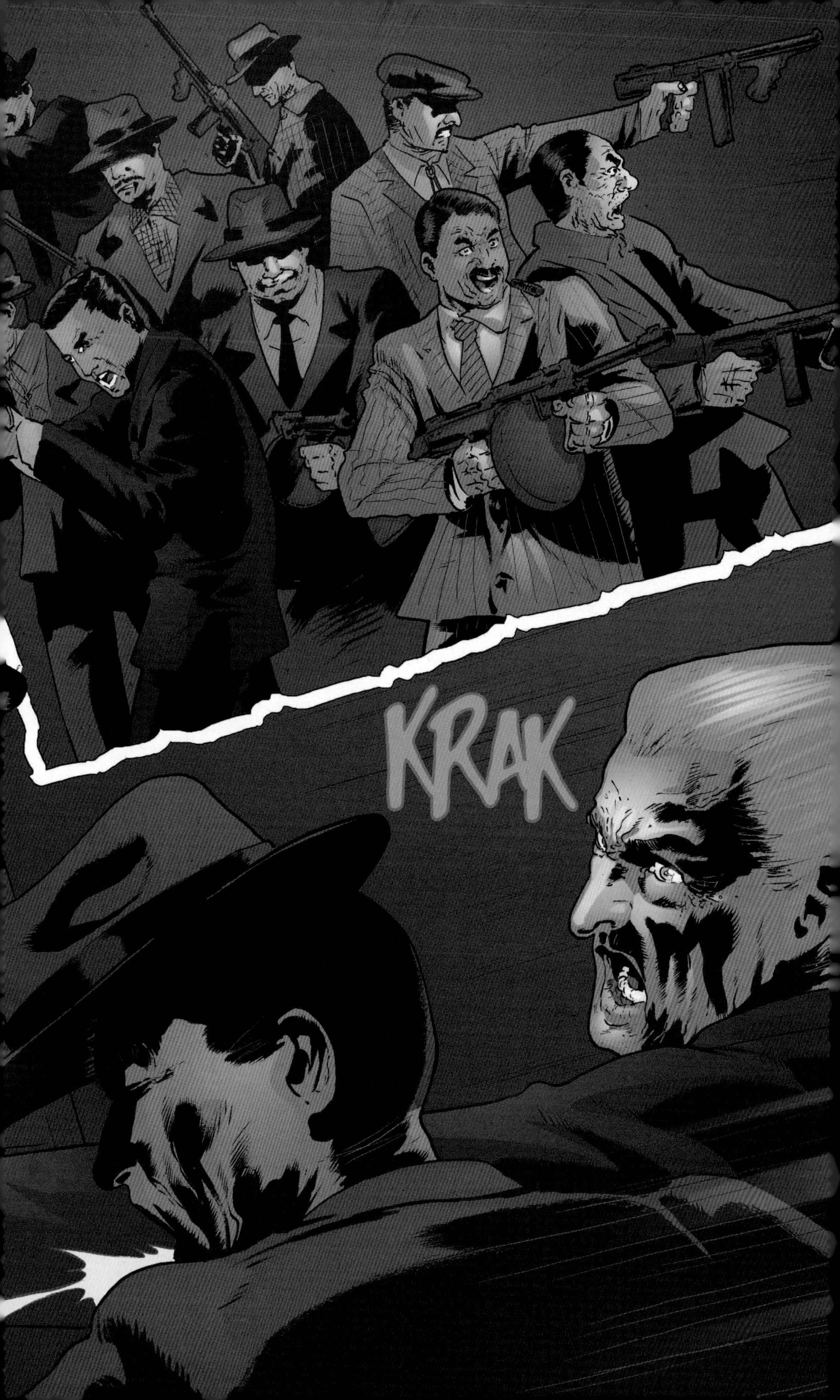
KRAK

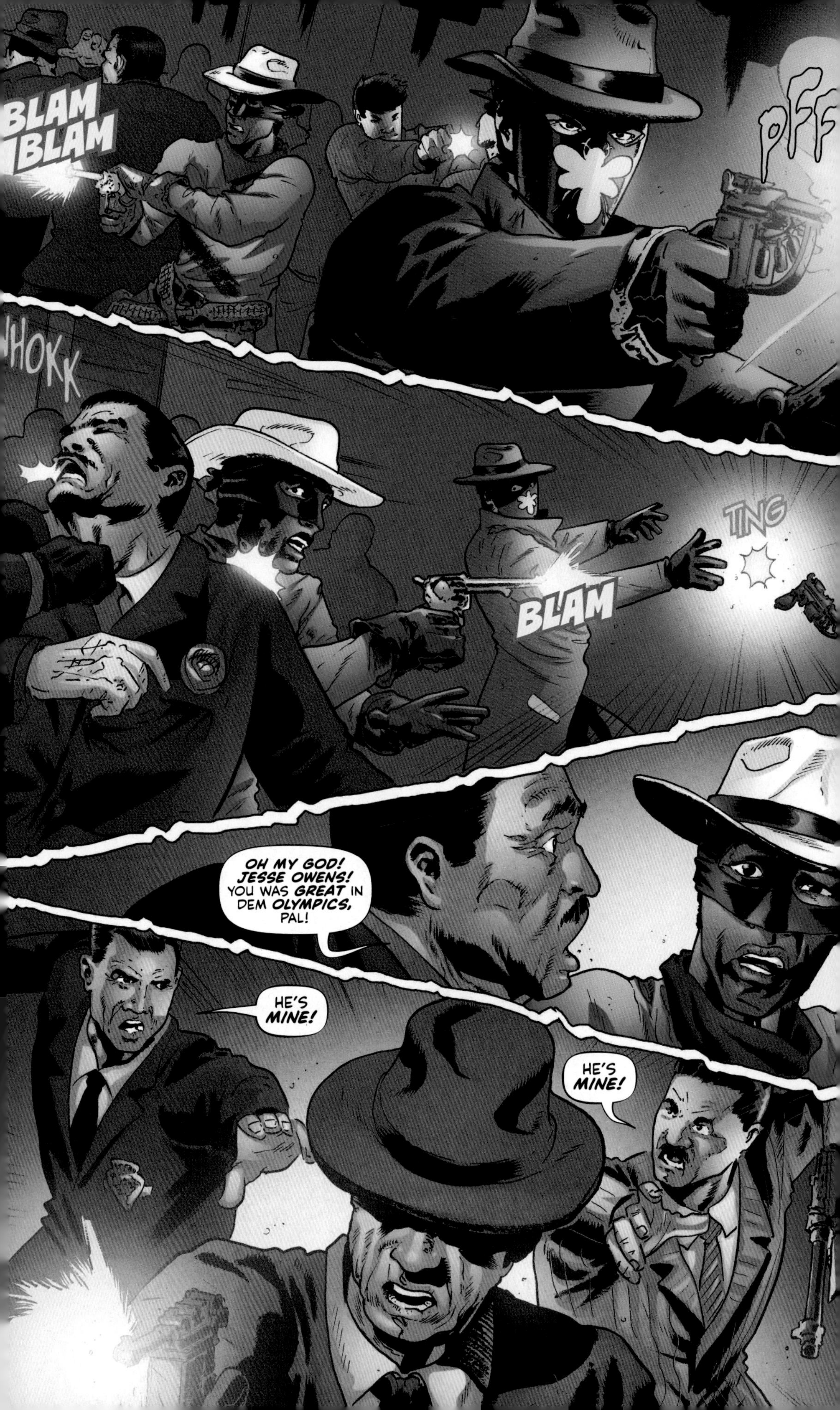

BLAM BLAM
pFF
WHOKK
TING
BLAM
OH MY GOD! JESSE OWENS! YOU WAS GREAT IN DEM OLYMPICS, PAL!
HE'S MINE!
HE'S MINE!

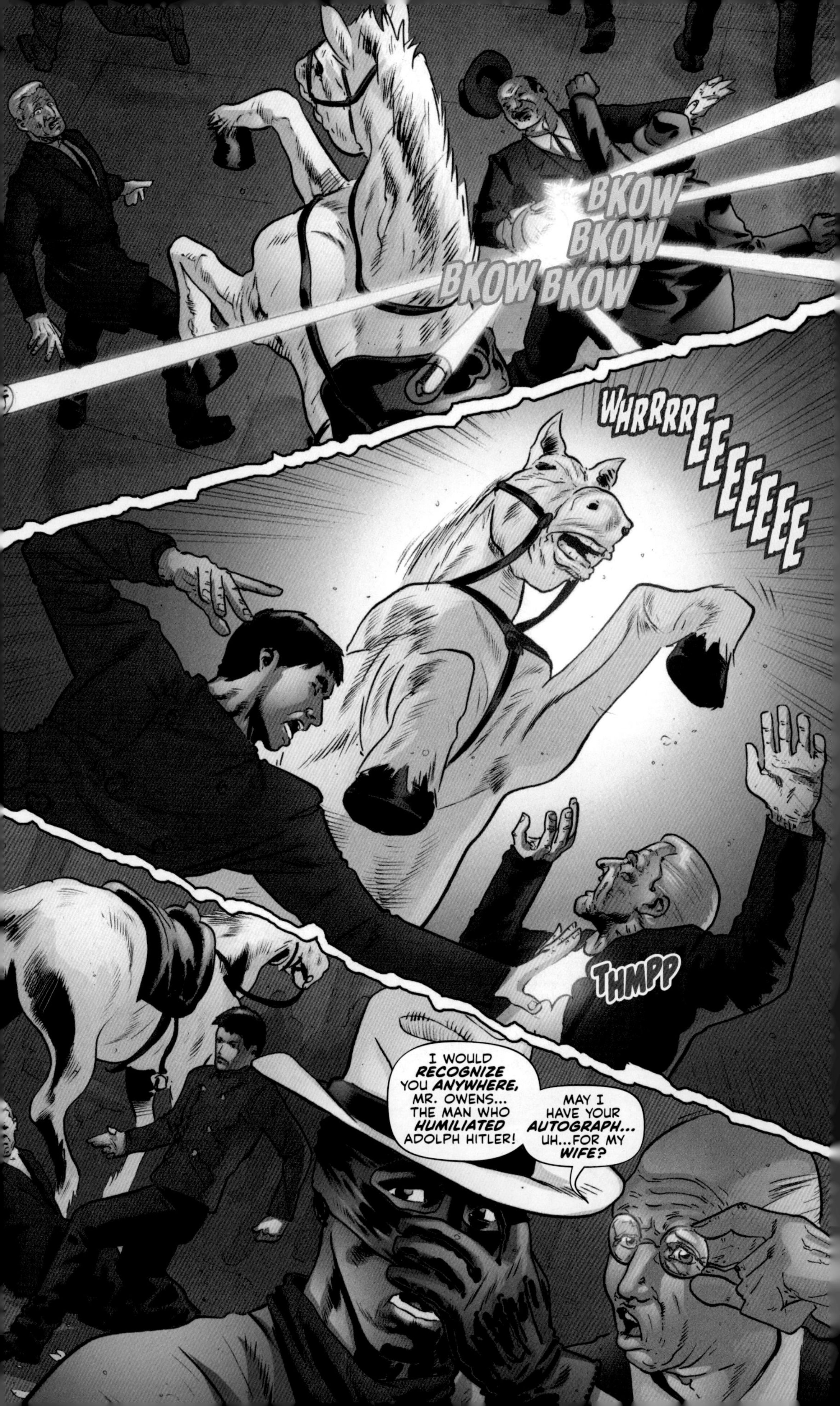
BKOW
BKOW
BKOW BKOW
WHRRRREEEEEEE
THMPP
I WOULD RECOGNIZE YOU ANYWHERE, MR. OWENS... THE MAN WHO HUMILIATED ADOLPH HITLER!
MAY I HAVE YOUR AUTOGRAPH... UH...FOR MY WIFE?

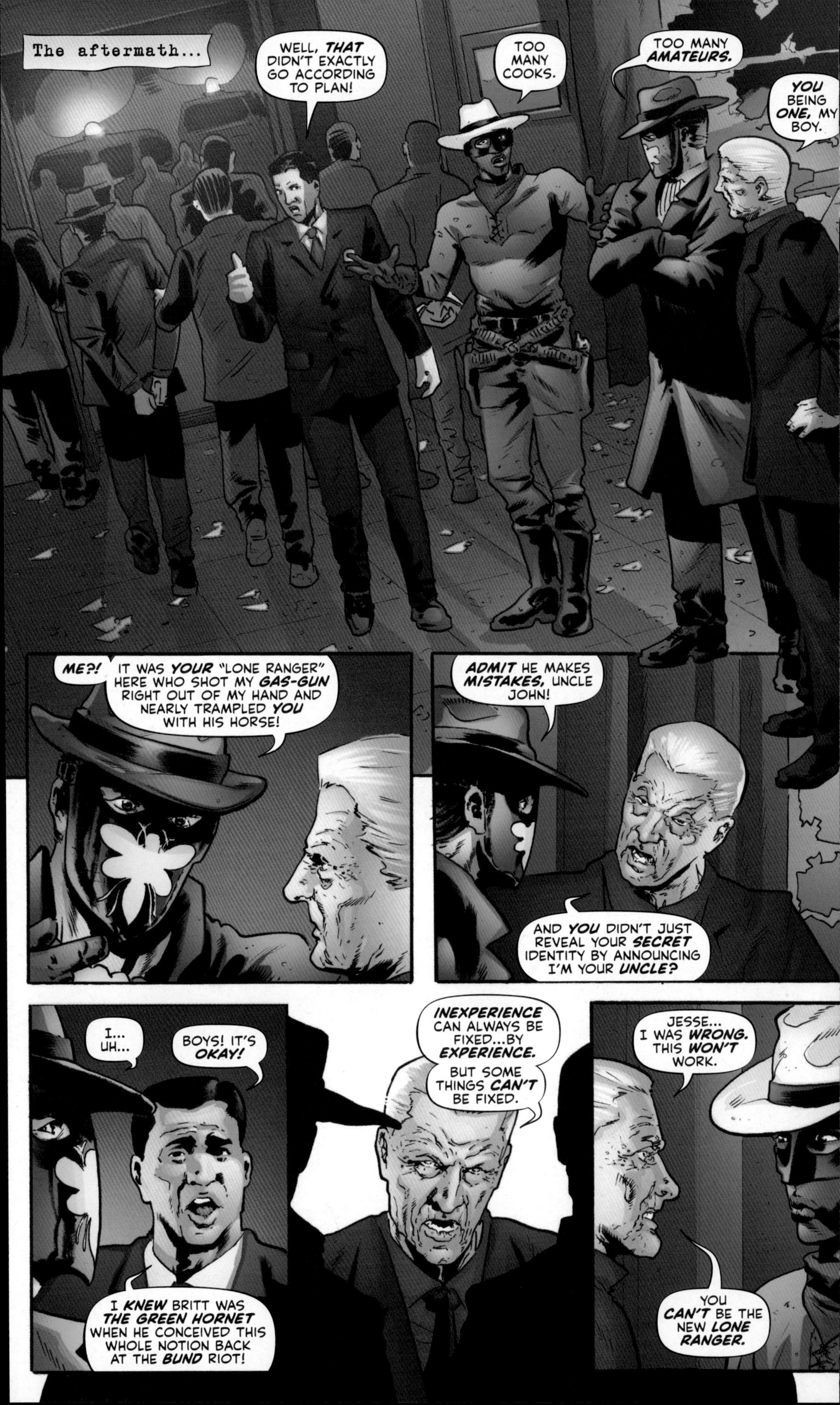

The aftermath...
WELL, THAT DIDN'T EXACTLY GO ACCORDING TO PLAN!
TOO MANY COOKS.
TOO MANY AMATEURS.
YOU BEING ONE, MY BOY.
ME?!
IT WAS YOUR "LONE RANGER" HERE WHO SHOT MY GAS-GUN RIGHT OUT OF MY HAND AND NEARLY TRAMPLED YOU WITH HIS HORSE!
ADMIT HE MAKES MISTAKES, UNCLE JOHN!
AND YOU DIDN'T JUST REVEAL YOUR SECRET IDENTITY BY ANNOUNCING I'M YOUR UNCLE?
I... UH...
BOYS! IT'S OKAY!
I KNEW BRITT WAS THE GREEN HORNET WHEN HE CONCEIVED THIS WHOLE NOTION BACK AT THE BUND RIOT!
INEXPERIENCE CAN ALWAYS BE FIXED...BY EXPERIENCE.
BUT SOME THINGS CAN'T BE FIXED.
JESSE... I WAS WRONG. THIS WON'T WORK.
YOU CAN'T BE THE NEW LONE RANGER.

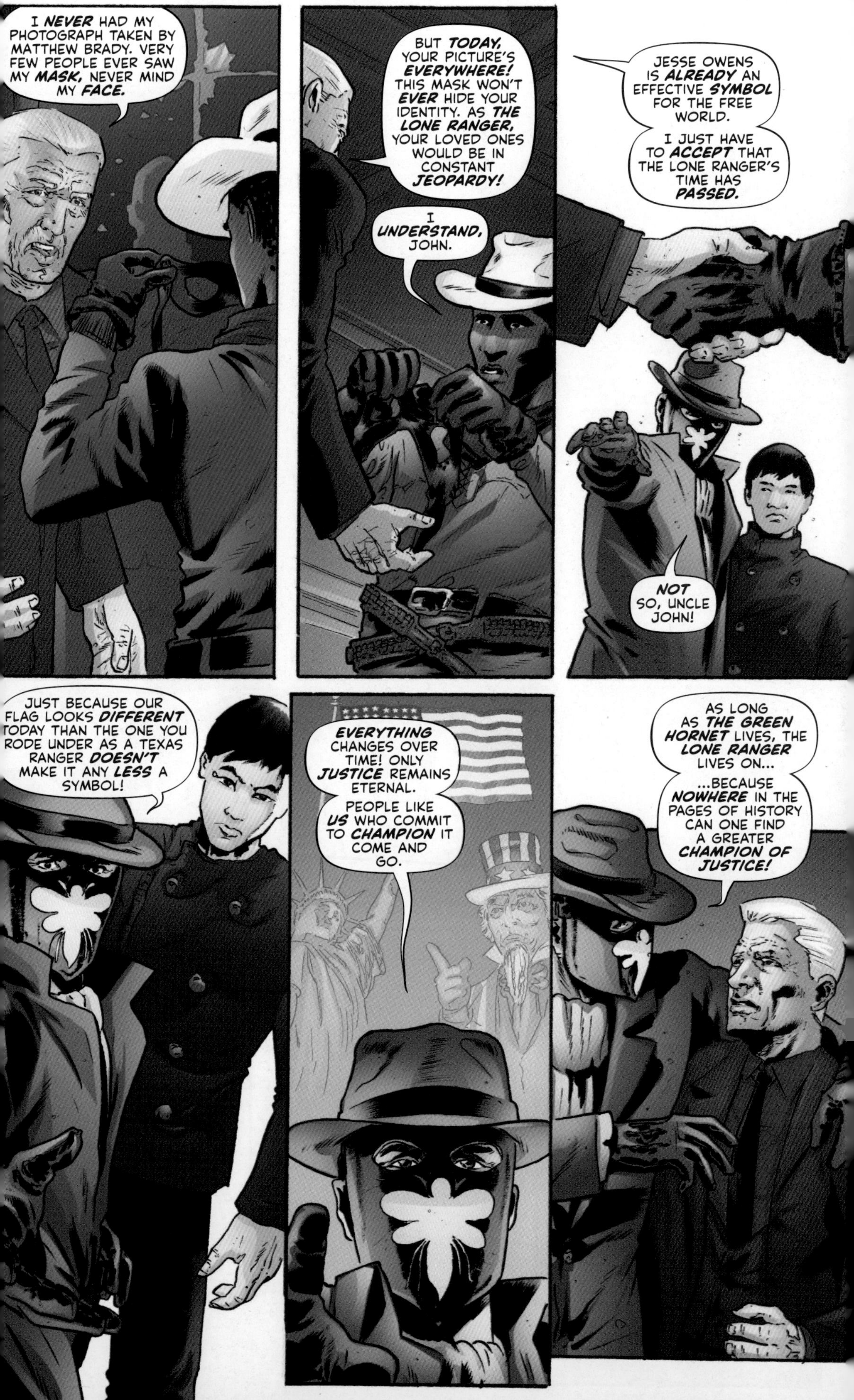

I NEVER HAD MY PHOTOGRAPH TAKEN BY MATTHEW BRADY. VERY FEW PEOPLE EVER SAW MY MASK, NEVER MIND MY FACE.
BUT TODAY, YOUR PICTURE'S EVERYWHERE! THIS MASK WON'T EVER HIDE YOUR IDENTITY. AS THE LONE RANGER, YOUR LOVED ONES WOULD BE IN CONSTANT JEOPARDY!
I UNDERSTAND, JOHN.
JESSE OWENS IS ALREADY AN EFFECTIVE SYMBOL FOR THE FREE WORLD.
I JUST HAVE TO ACCEPT THAT THE LONE RANGER'S TIME HAS PASSED.
NOT SO, UNCLE JOHN!
JUST BECAUSE OUR FLAG LOOKS DIFFERENT TODAY THAN THE ONE YOU RODE UNDER AS A TEXAS RANGER DOESN'T MAKE IT ANY LESS A SYMBOL!
EVERYTHING CHANGES OVER TIME! ONLY JUSTICE REMAINS ETERNAL.
PEOPLE LIKE US WHO COMMIT TO CHAMPION IT COME AND GO.
AS LONG AS THE GREEN HORNET LIVES, THE LONE RANGER LIVES ON...
...BECAUSE NOWHERE IN THE PAGES OF HISTORY CAN ONE FIND A GREATER CHAMPION OF JUSTICE!

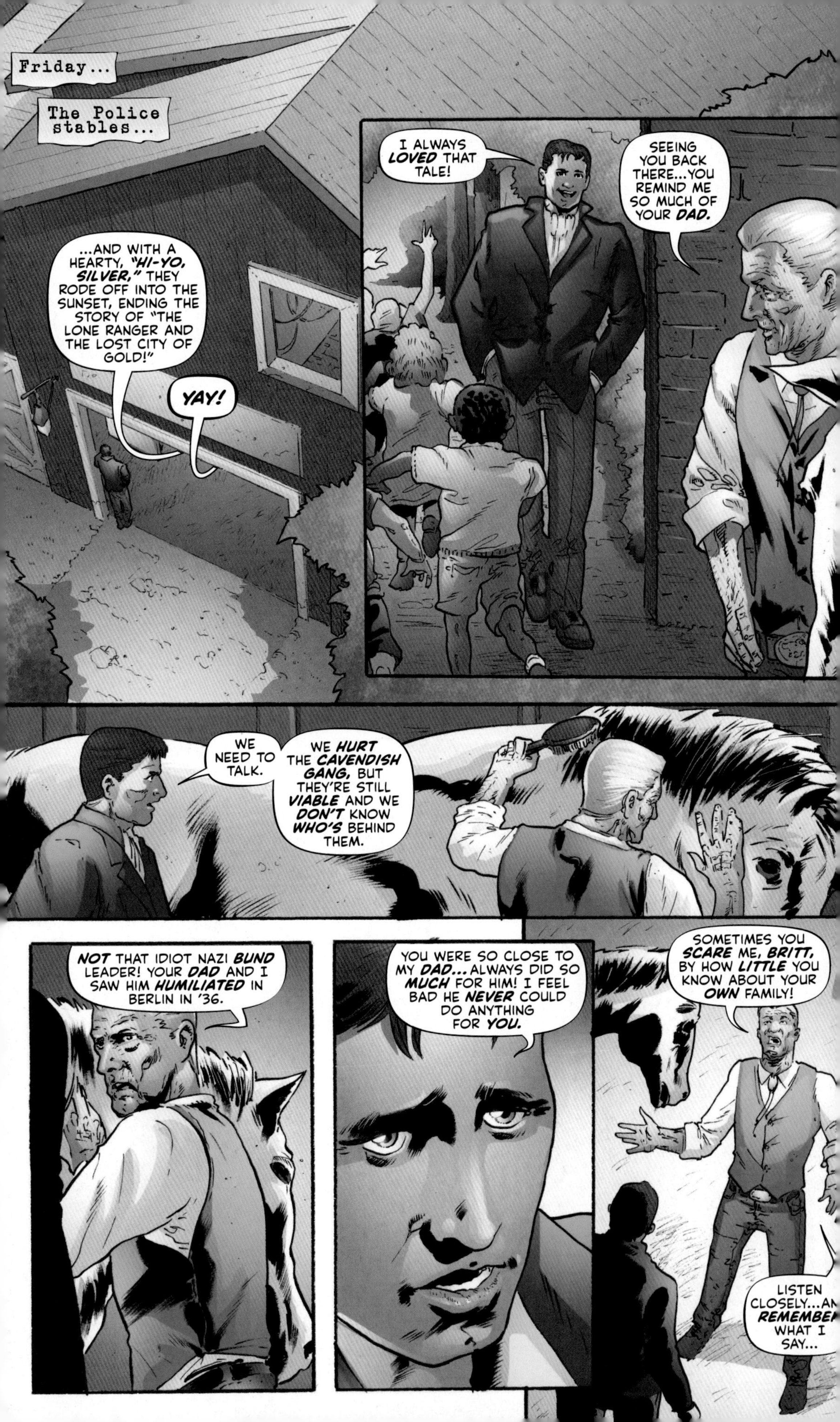
Friday...
The Police stables...
...AND WITH A HEARTY, "HI-YO, SILVER," THEY RODE OFF INTO THE SUNSET, ENDING THE STORY OF "THE LONE RANGER AND THE LOST CITY OF GOLD!"
YAY!
I ALWAYS LOVED THAT TALE!
SEEING YOU BACK THERE...YOU REMIND ME SO MUCH OF YOUR DAD.
WE NEED TO TALK.
WE HURT THE CAVENDISH GANG, BUT THEY'RE STILL VIABLE AND WE DON'T KNOW WHO'S BEHIND THEM.
NOT THAT IDIOT NAZI BUND LEADER! YOUR DAD AND I SAW HIM HUMILIATED IN BERLIN IN '36.
YOU WERE SO CLOSE TO MY DAD... ALWAYS DID SO MUCH FOR HIM! I FEEL BAD HE NEVER COULD DO ANYTHING FOR YOU.
SOMETIMES YOU SCARE ME, BRITT, BY HOW LITTLE YOU KNOW ABOUT YOUR OWN FAMILY!
LISTEN CLOSELY...AN
WHAT I SAY...

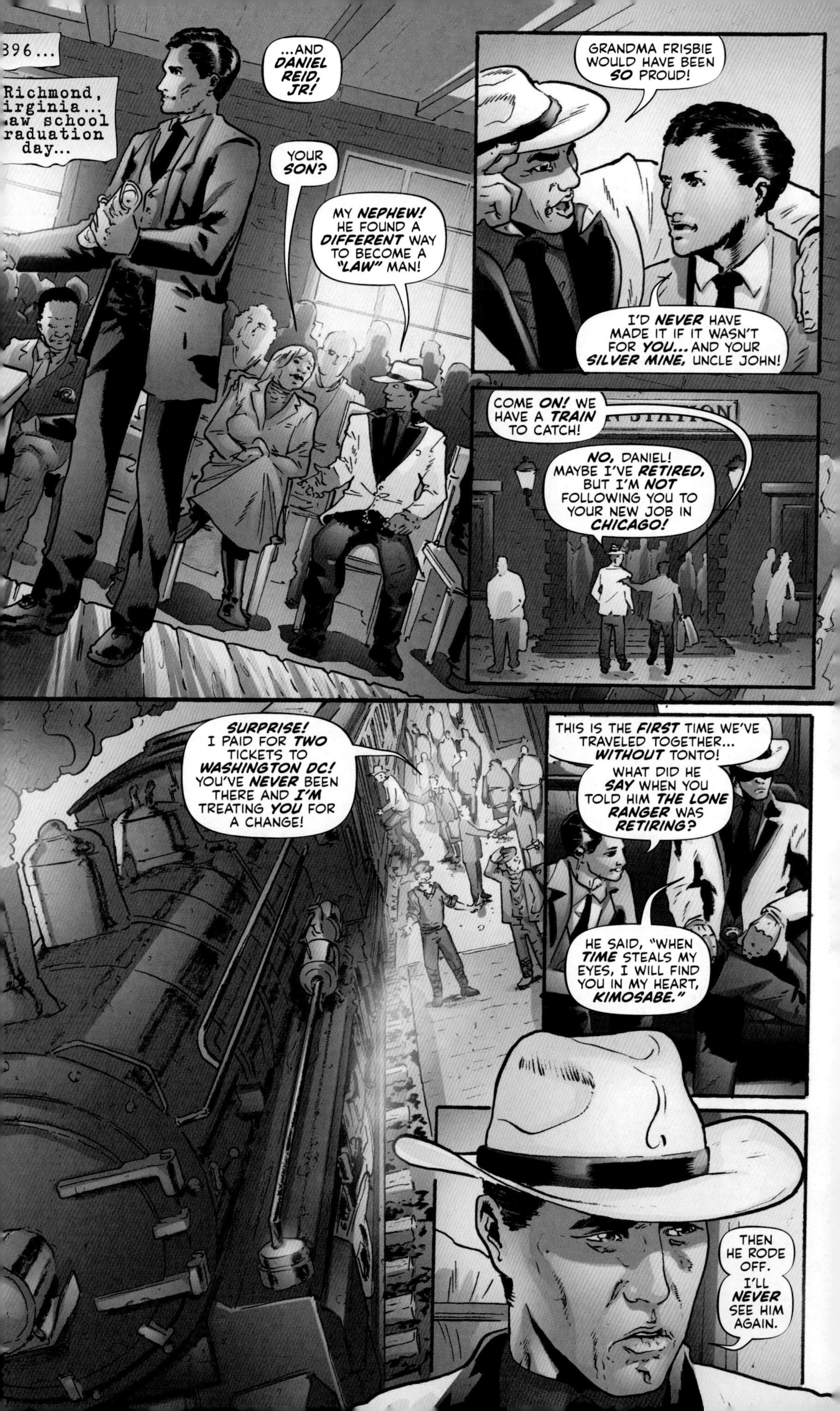

396...
Richmond, irginia... aw school raduation day...
...AND DANIEL REID, JR!
YOUR SON?
MY NEPHEW! HE FOUND A DIFFERENT WAY TO BECOME A "LAW" MAN!
GRANDMA FRISBIE WOULD HAVE BEEN SO PROUD!
I'D NEVER HAVE MADE IT IF IT WASN'T FOR YOU... AND YOUR SILVER MINE, UNCLE JOHN!
COME ON! WE HAVE A TRAIN TO CATCH!
NO, DANIEL! MAYBE I'VE RETIRED, BUT I'M NOT FOLLOWING YOU TO YOUR NEW JOB IN CHICAGO!
SURPRISE! I PAID FOR TWO TICKETS TO WASHINGTON DC! YOU'VE NEVER BEEN THERE AND I'M TREATING YOU FOR A CHANGE!
THIS IS THE FIRST TIME WE'VE TRAVELED TOGETHER... WITHOUT TONTO!
WHAT DID HE SAY WHEN YOU TOLD HIM THE LONE RANGER WAS RETIRING?
HE SAID, "WHEN TIME STEALS MY EYES, I WILL FIND YOU IN MY HEART, KIMOSABE."
THEN HE RODE OFF. I'LL NEVER SEE HIM AGAIN.

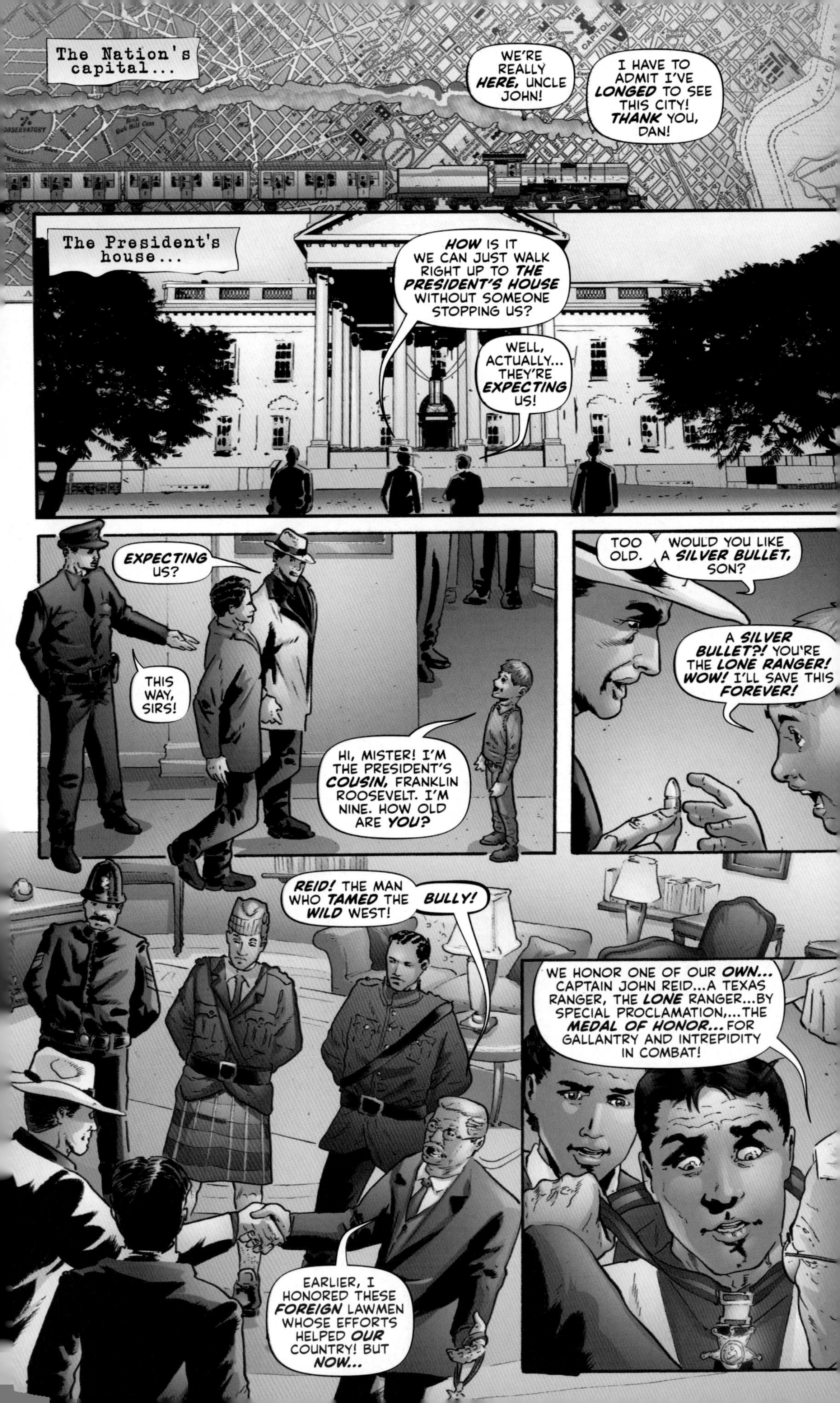
The Nation's capital...
WE'RE REALLY HERE, UNCLE JOHN!
I HAVE TO ADMIT I'VE LONGED TO SEE THIS CITY! THANK YOU, DAN!
The President's house...
HOW IS IT WE CAN JUST WALK RIGHT UP TO THE PRESIDENT'S HOUSE WITHOUT SOMEONE STOPPING US?
WELL, ACTUALLY... THEY'RE EXPECTING US!
EXPECTING US?
THIS WAY, SIRS!
HI, MISTER! I'M THE PRESIDENT'S COUSIN, FRANKLIN ROOSEVELT. I'M NINE. HOW OLD ARE YOU?
TOO OLD.
WOULD YOU LIKE A SILVER BULLET, SON?
A SILVER BULLET?! YOU'RE THE LONE RANGER! WOW! I'LL SAVE THIS FOREVER!
REID! THE MAN WHO TAMED THE WILD WEST!
BULLY!
EARLIER, I HONORED THESE FOREIGN LAWMEN WHOSE EFFORTS HELPED OUR COUNTRY! BUT NOW...
WE HONOR ONE OF OUR OWN... CAPTAIN JOHN REID...A TEXAS RANGER, THE LONE RANGER...BY SPECIAL PROCLAMATION,...THE MEDAL OF HONOR... FOR GALLANTRY AND INTREPIDITY IN COMBAT!

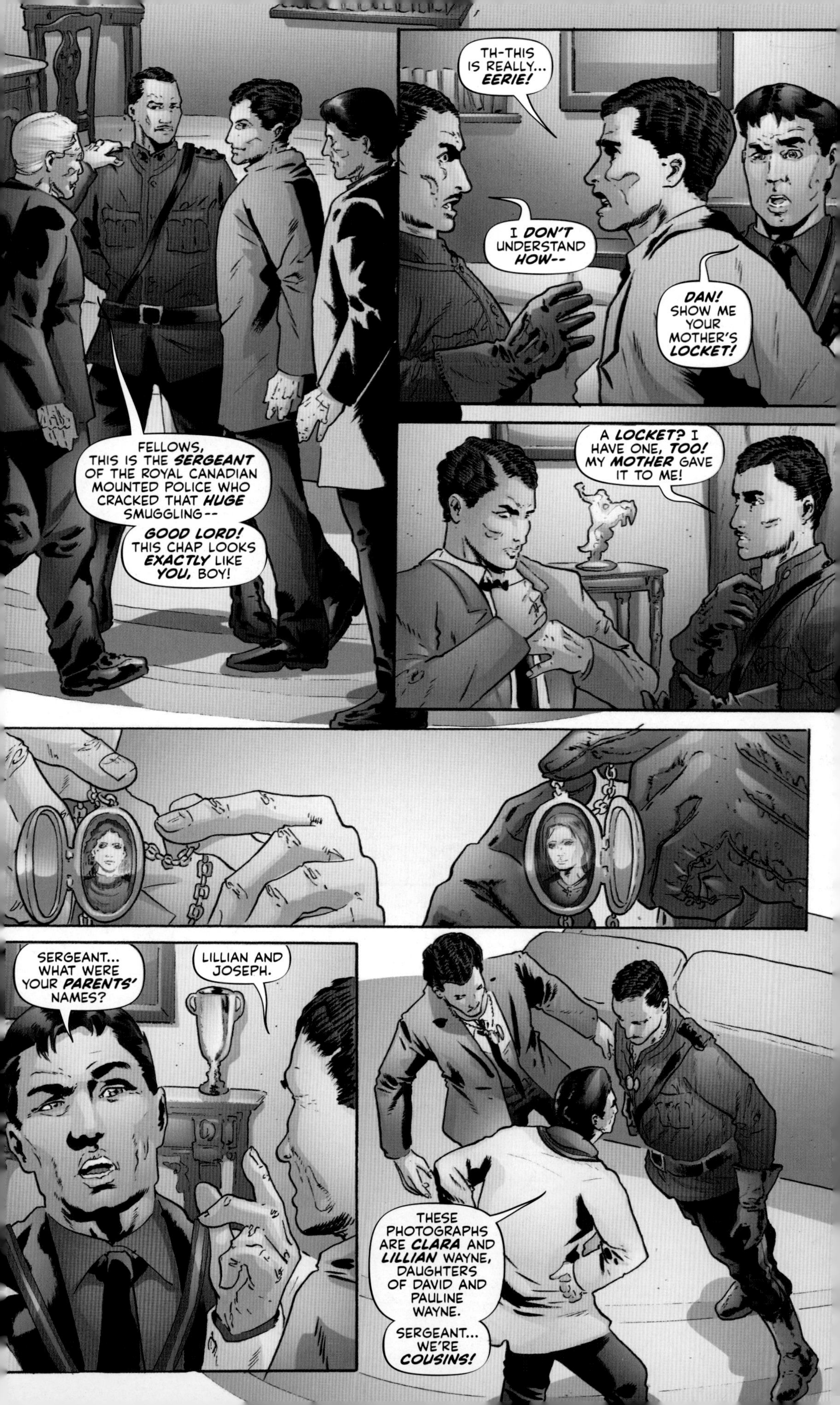
FELLOWS, THIS IS THE SERGEANT OF THE ROYAL CANADIAN MOUNTED POLICE WHO CRACKED THAT HUGE SMUGGLING--
GOOD LORD! THIS CHAP LOOKS EXACTLY LIKE YOU, BOY!
TH-THIS IS REALLY... EERIE!
I DON'T UNDERSTAND HOW--
DAN! SHOW ME YOUR MOTHER'S LOCKET!
A LOCKET? I HAVE ONE, TOO! MY MOTHER GAVE IT TO ME!
SERGEANT... WHAT WERE YOUR PARENTS' NAMES?
LILLIAN AND JOSEPH.
THESE PHOTOGRAPHS ARE CLARA AND LILLIAN WAYNE, DAUGHTERS OF DAVID AND PAULINE WAYNE.
SERGEANT... WE'RE COUSINS!

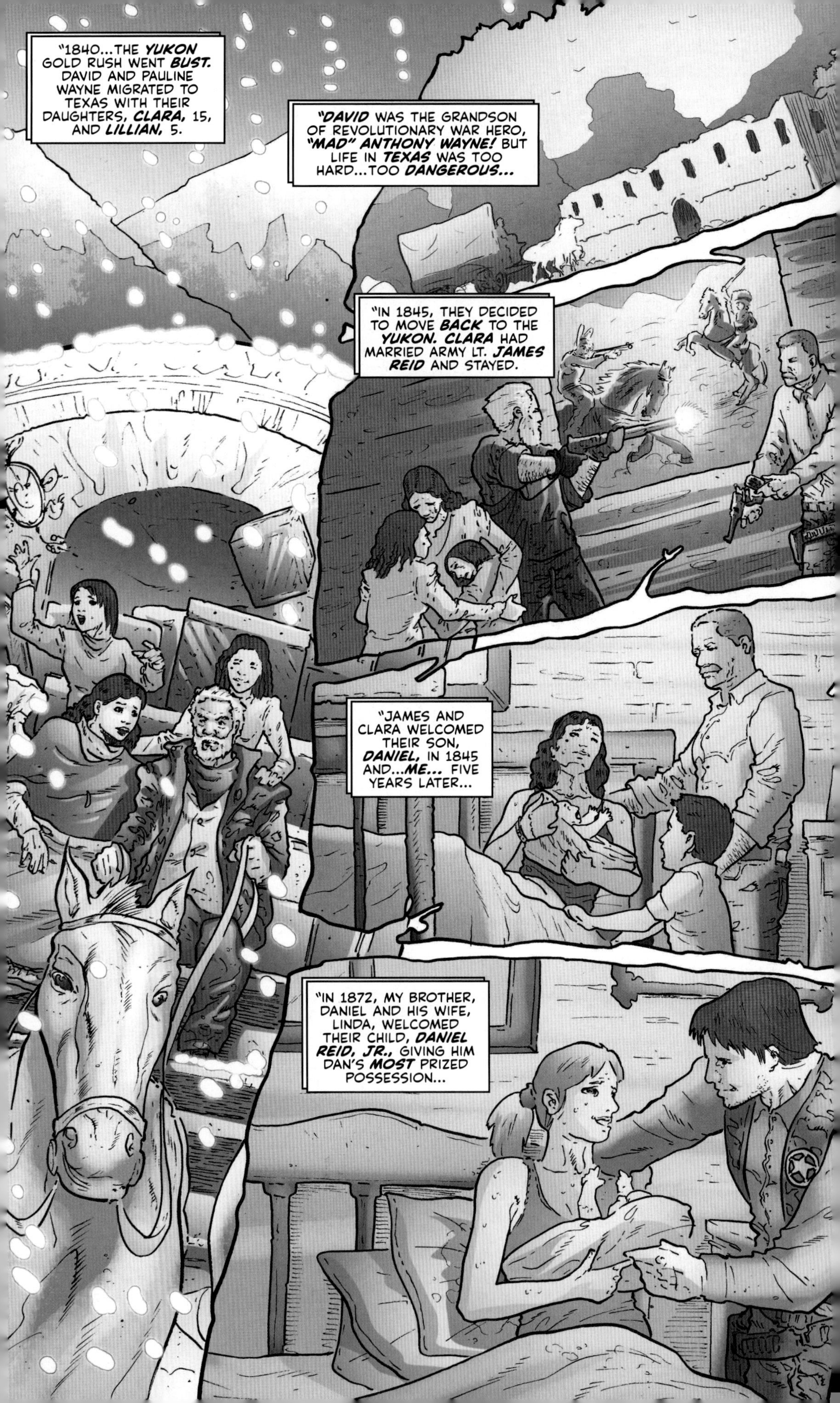
"1840...THE YUKON GOLD RUSH WENT BUST. DAVID AND PAULINE WAYNE MIGRATED TO TEXAS WITH THEIR DAUGHTERS, CLARA, 15, AND LILLIAN, 5.
"DAVID WAS THE GRANDSON OF REVOLUTIONARY WAR HERO, "MAD" ANTHONY WAYNE! BUT LIFE IN TEXAS WAS TOO HARD...TOO DANGEROUS...
"IN 1845, THEY DECIDED TO MOVE BACK TO THE YUKON. CLARA HAD MARRIED ARMY LT. JAMES REID AND STAYED.
"JAMES AND CLARA WELCOMED THEIR SON, DANIEL, IN 1845 AND...ME... FIVE YEARS LATER...
"IN 1872, MY BROTHER, DANIEL AND HIS WIFE, LINDA, WELCOMED THEIR CHILD, DANIEL REID, JR., GIVING HIM DAN'S MOST PRIZED POSSESSION...

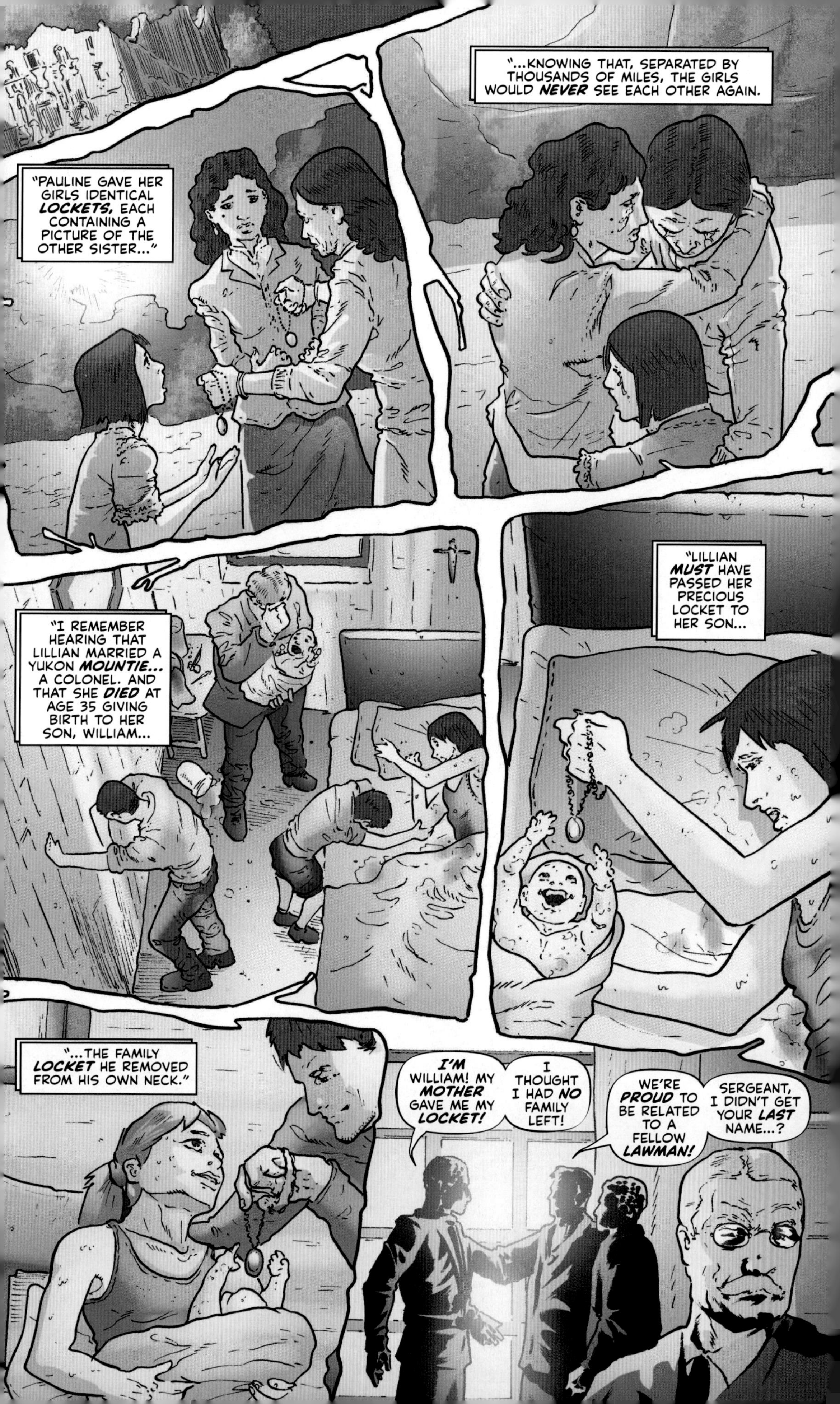
"PAULINE GAVE HER GIRLS IDENTICAL LOCKETS, EACH CONTAINING A PICTURE OF THE OTHER SISTER..."
"...KNOWING THAT, SEPARATED BY THOUSANDS OF MILES, THE GIRLS WOULD NEVER SEE EACH OTHER AGAIN.
"I REMEMBER HEARING THAT LILLIAN MARRIED A YUKON MOUNTIE... A COLONEL. AND THAT SHE DIED AT AGE 35 GIVING BIRTH TO HER SON, WILLIAM...
"LILLIAN MUST HAVE PASSED HER PRECIOUS LOCKET TO HER SON...
"...THE FAMILY LOCKET HE REMOVED FROM HIS OWN NECK."
I'M WILLIAM! MY MOTHER GAVE ME MY LOCKET!
I THOUGHT I HAD NO FAMILY LEFT!
WE'RE PROUD TO BE RELATED TO A FELLOW LAWMAN!
SERGEANT, I DIDN'T GET YOUR LAST NAME...?

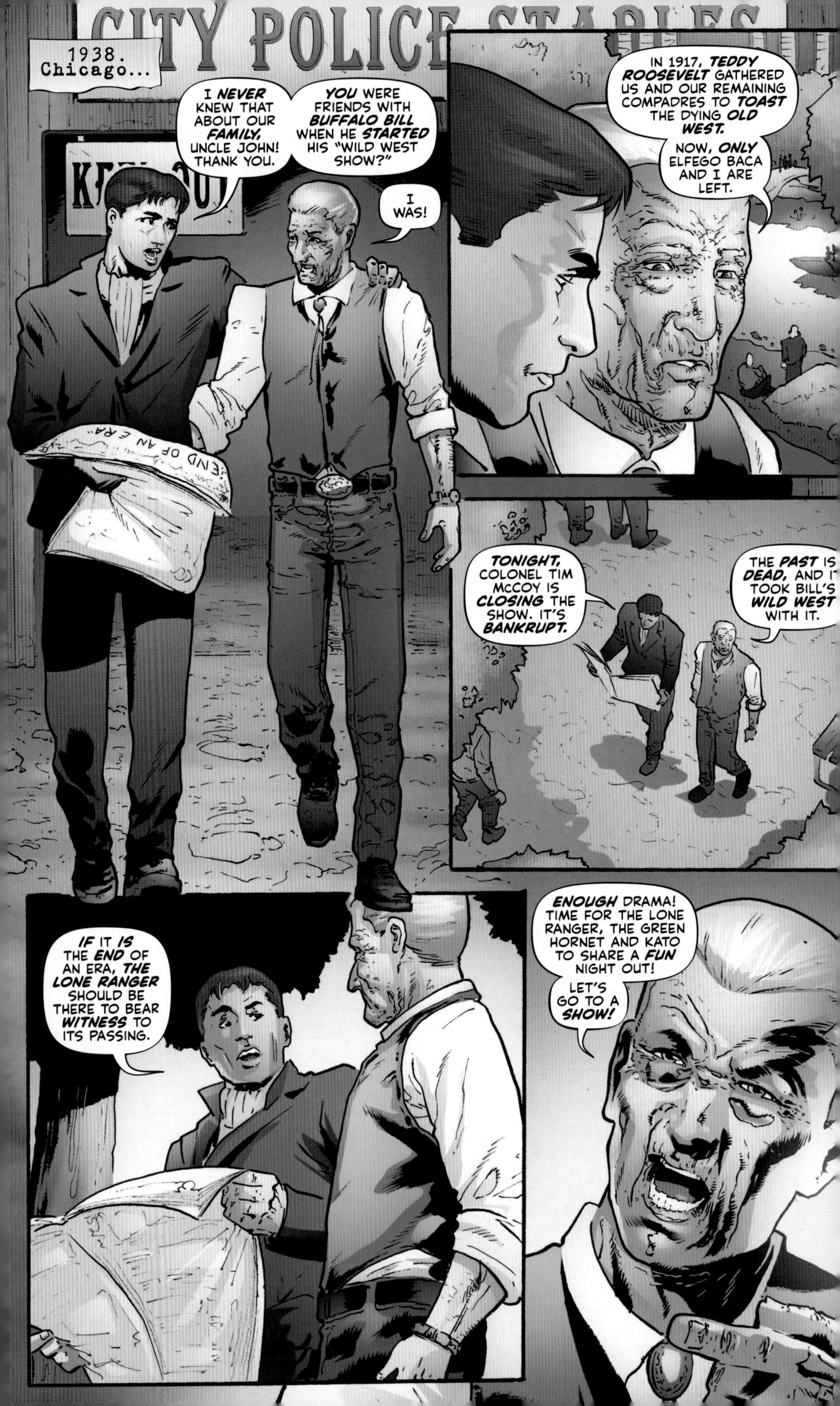

CITY POLICE STABLES
1938. Chicago...
I NEVER KNEW THAT ABOUT OUR FAMILY, UNCLE JOHN! THANK YOU.
YOU WERE FRIENDS WITH BUFFALO BILL WHEN HE STARTED HIS "WILD WEST SHOW?"
I WAS!
END OF AN ERA
IN 1917, TEDDY ROOSEVELT GATHERED US AND OUR REMAINING COMPADRES TO TOAST THE DYING OLD WEST.
NOW, ONLY ELFEGO BACA AND I ARE LEFT.
TONIGHT, COLONEL TIM McCOY IS CLOSING THE SHOW. IT'S BANKRUPT.
THE PAST IS DEAD, AND IT TOOK BILL'S WILD WEST WITH IT.
IF IT IS THE END OF AN ERA, THE LONE RANGER SHOULD BE THERE TO BEAR WITNESS TO ITS PASSING.
ENOUGH DRAMA! TIME FOR THE LONE RANGER, THE GREEN HORNET AND KATO TO SHARE A FUN NIGHT OUT!
LET'S GO TO A SHOW!

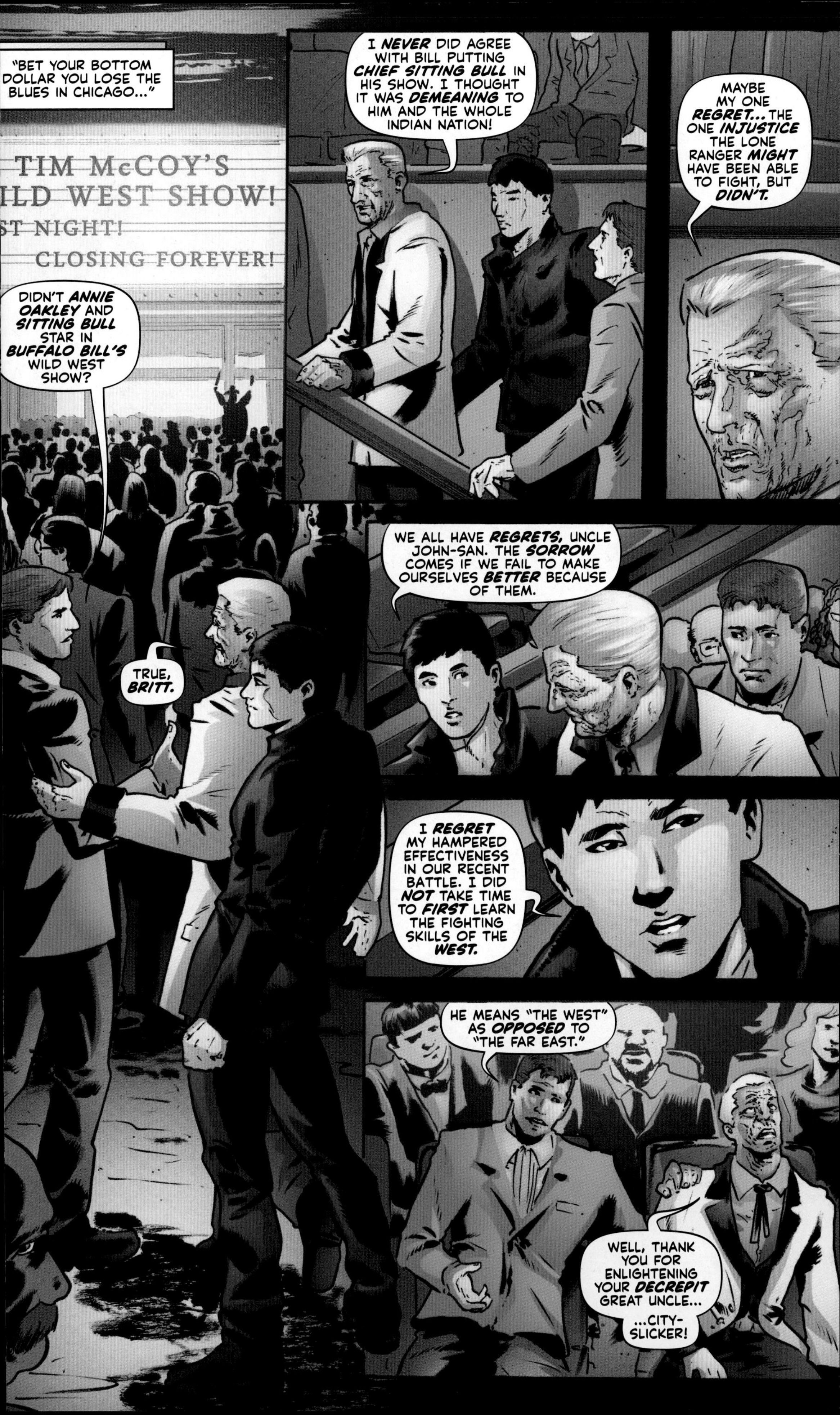
"BET YOUR BOTTOM DOLLAR YOU LOSE THE BLUES IN CHICAGO..."
TIM McCOY'S
ILD WEST SHOW!
ST NIGHT!
CLOSING FOREVER!
DIDN'T ANNIE OAKLEY AND SITTING BULL STAR IN BUFFALO BILL'S WILD WEST SHOW?
TRUE, BRITT.
I NEVER DID AGREE WITH BILL PUTTING CHIEF SITTING BULL IN HIS SHOW. I THOUGHT IT WAS DEMEANING TO HIM AND THE WHOLE INDIAN NATION!
MAYBE MY ONE REGRET... THE ONE INJUSTICE THE LONE RANGER MIGHT HAVE BEEN ABLE TO FIGHT, BUT DIDN'T.
WE ALL HAVE REGRETS, UNCLE JOHN-SAN. THE SORROW COMES IF WE FAIL TO MAKE OURSELVES BETTER BECAUSE OF THEM.
I REGRET MY HAMPERED EFFECTIVENESS IN OUR RECENT BATTLE. I DID NOT TAKE TIME TO FIRST LEARN THE FIGHTING SKILLS OF THE WEST.
HE MEANS "THE WEST" AS OPPOSED TO "THE FAR EAST."
WELL, THANK YOU FOR ENLIGHTENING YOUR DECREPIT GREAT UNCLE...
...CITY-SLICKER!

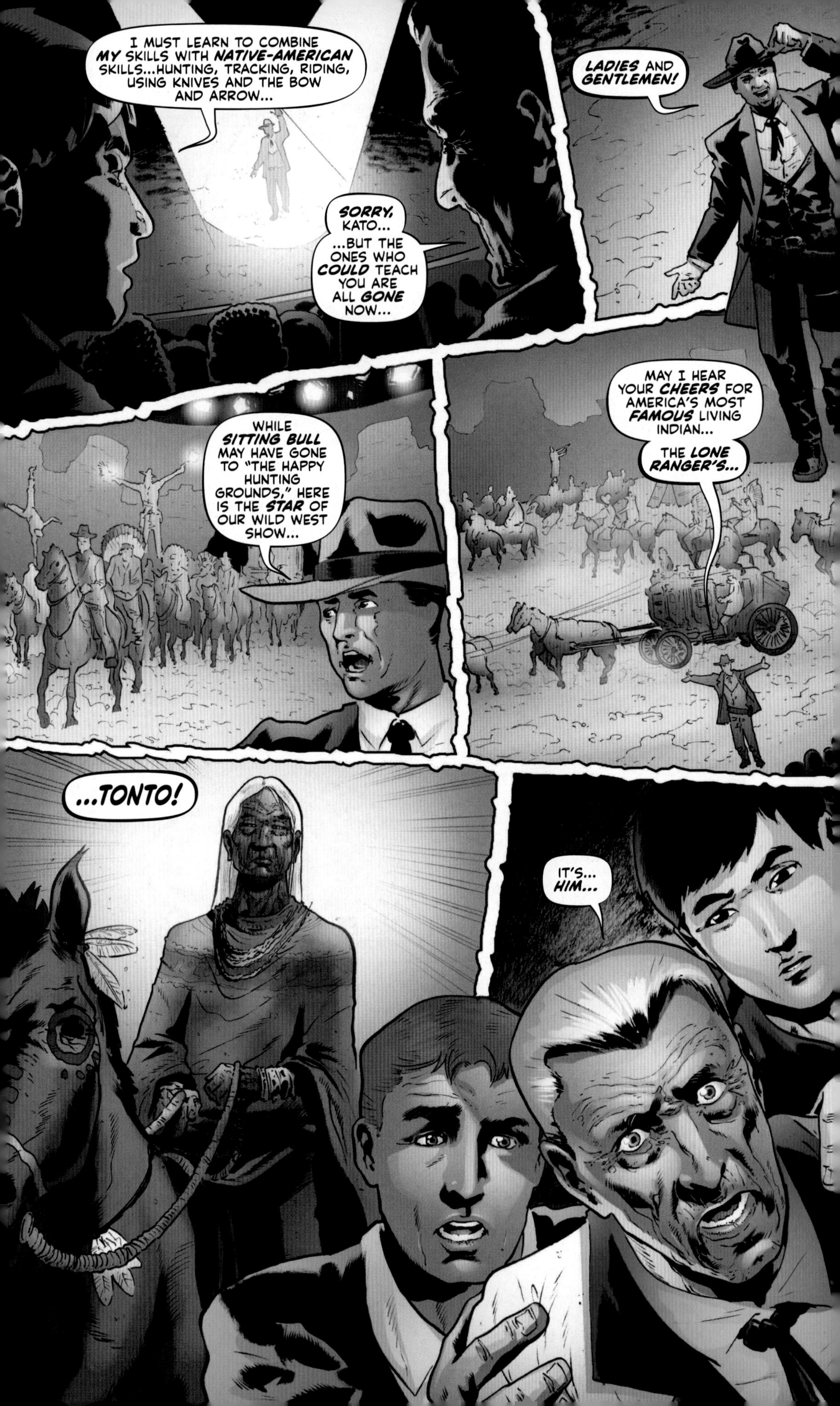
I MUST LEARN TO COMBINE MY SKILLS WITH NATIVE-AMERICAN SKILLS...HUNTING, TRACKING, RIDING, USING KNIVES AND THE BOW AND ARROW...
SORRY, KATO...
...BUT THE ONES WHO COULD TEACH YOU ARE ALL GONE NOW...
LADIES AND GENTLEMEN!
WHILE SITTING BULL MAY HAVE GONE TO "THE HAPPY HUNTING GROUNDS," HERE IS THE STAR OF OUR WILD WEST SHOW...
MAY I HEAR YOUR CHEERS FOR AMERICA'S MOST FAMOUS LIVING INDIAN...
THE LONE RANGER'S...
...TONTO!
IT'S... HIM...

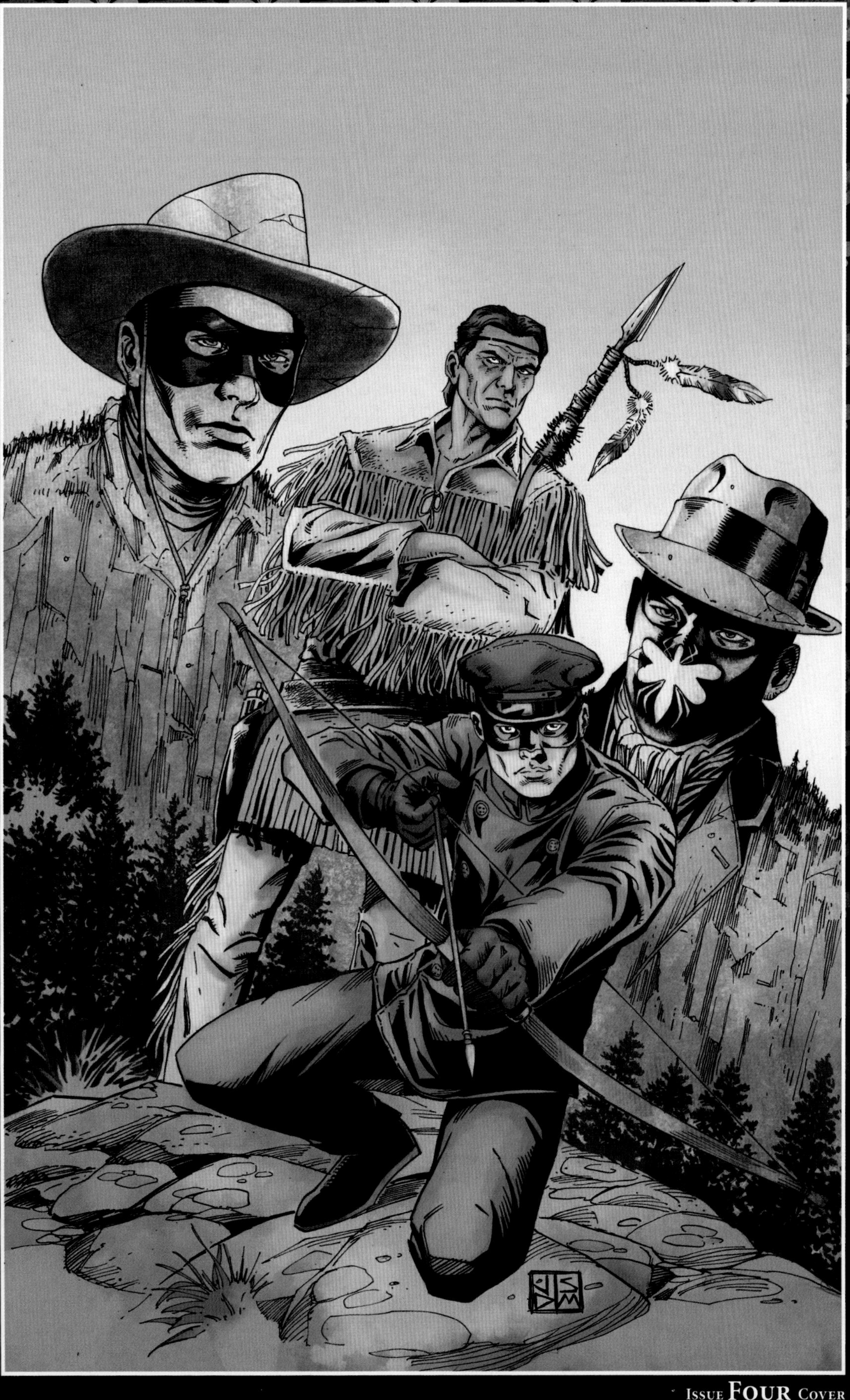

Issue **Four** Cover

Art by **Jan Duursema** Colors by **Sian Mandrake**

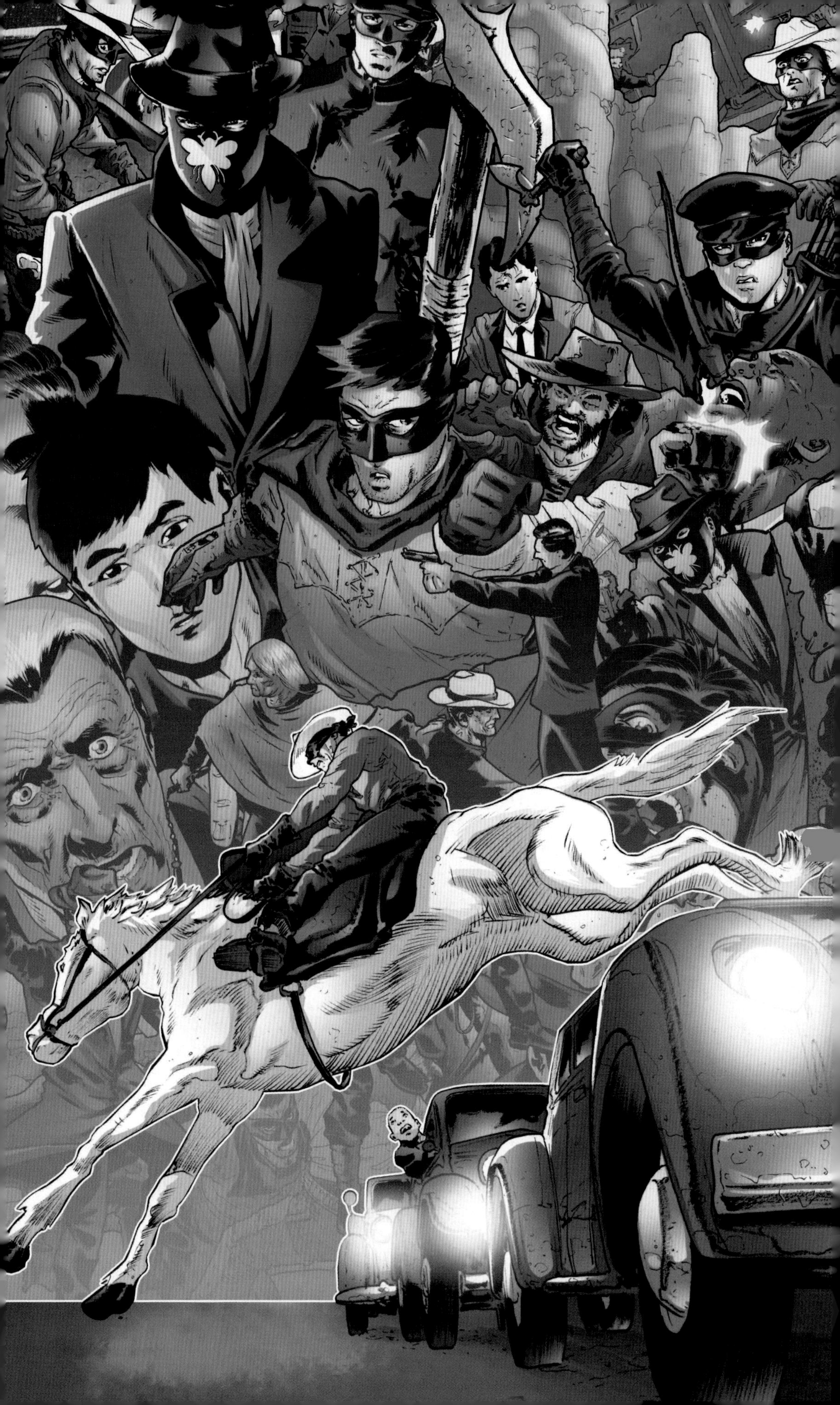

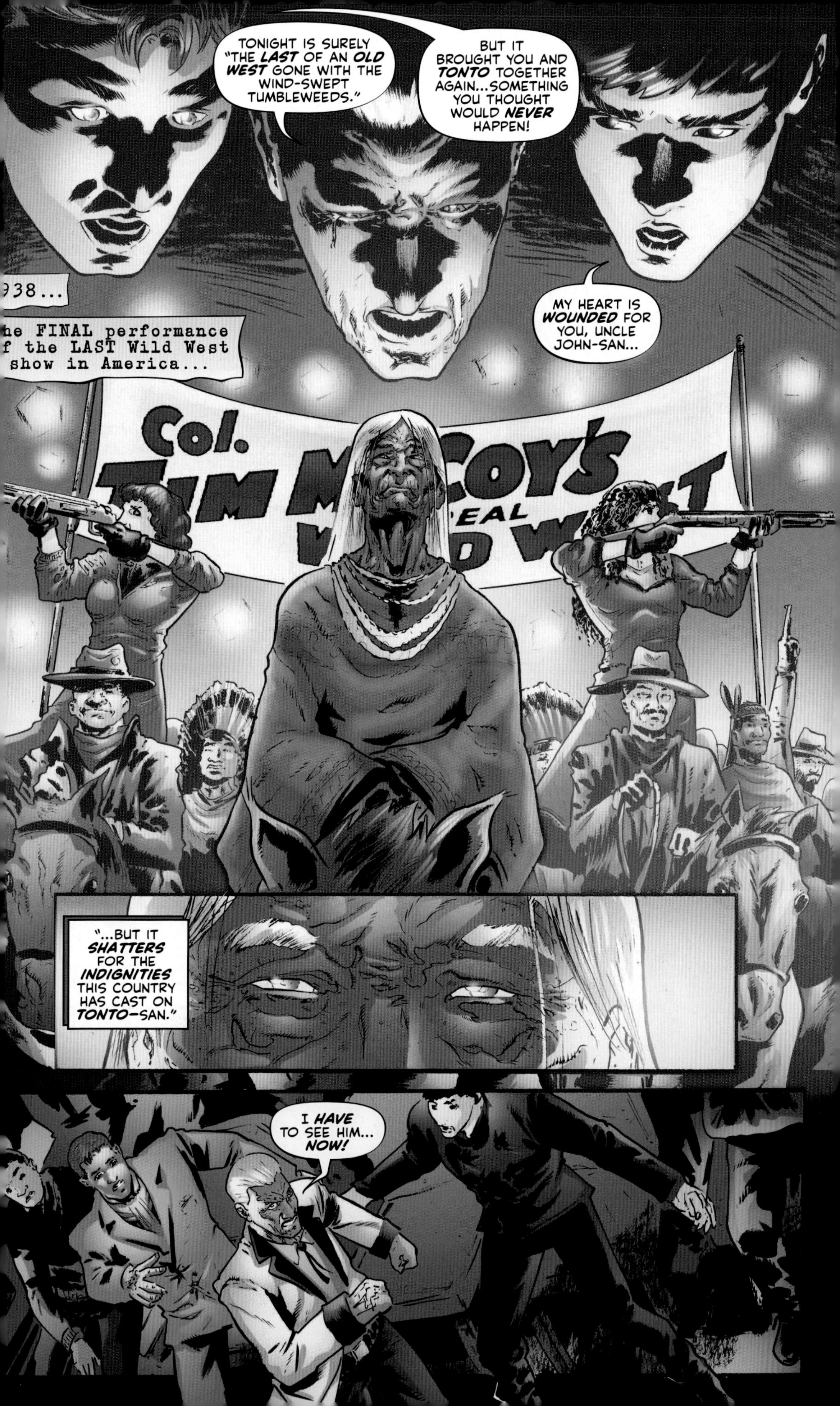
TONIGHT IS SURELY "THE LAST OF AN OLD WEST GONE WITH THE WIND-SWEPT TUMBLEWEEDS."
BUT IT BROUGHT YOU AND TONTO TOGETHER AGAIN...SOMETHING YOU THOUGHT WOULD NEVER HAPPEN!
938...
he FINAL performance f the LAST Wild West show in America...
MY HEART IS WOUNDED FOR YOU, UNCLE JOHN-SAN...
Col. TIM McCOY'S
"...BUT IT SHATTERS FOR THE INDIGNITIES THIS COUNTRY HAS CAST ON TONTO-SAN."
I HAVE TO SEE HIM... NOW!

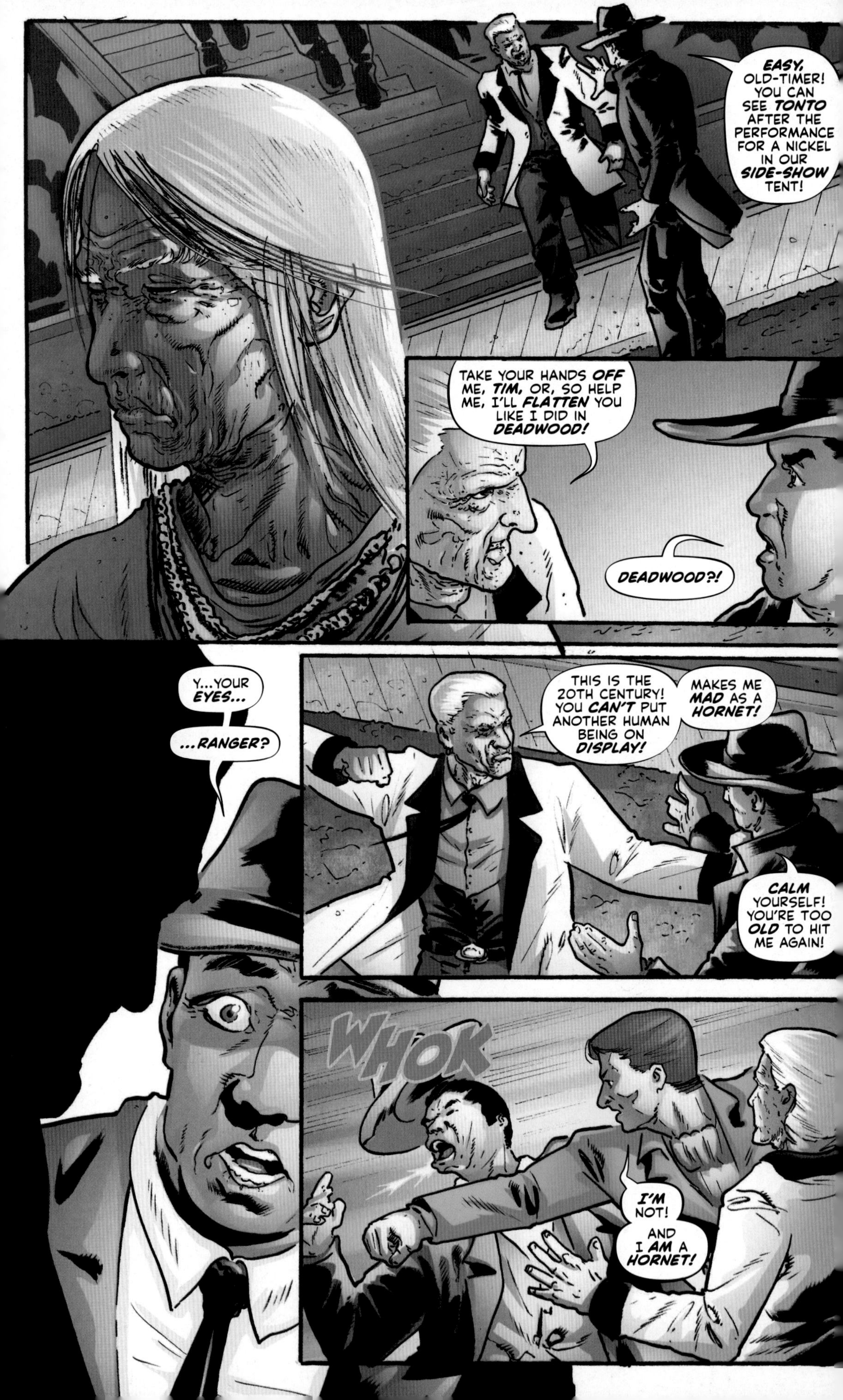

EASY, OLD-TIMER! YOU CAN SEE TONTO AFTER THE PERFORMANCE FOR A NICKEL IN OUR SIDE-SHOW TENT!
TAKE YOUR HANDS OFF ME, TIM, OR, SO HELP ME, I'LL FLATTEN YOU LIKE I DID IN DEADWOOD!
DEADWOOD?!
Y...YOUR EYES...
...RANGER?
THIS IS THE 20TH CENTURY! YOU CAN'T PUT ANOTHER HUMAN BEING ON DISPLAY!
MAKES ME MAD AS A HORNET!
CALM YOURSELF! YOU'RE TOO OLD TO HIT ME AGAIN!
WHOK
I'M NOT!
AND I AM A HORNET!

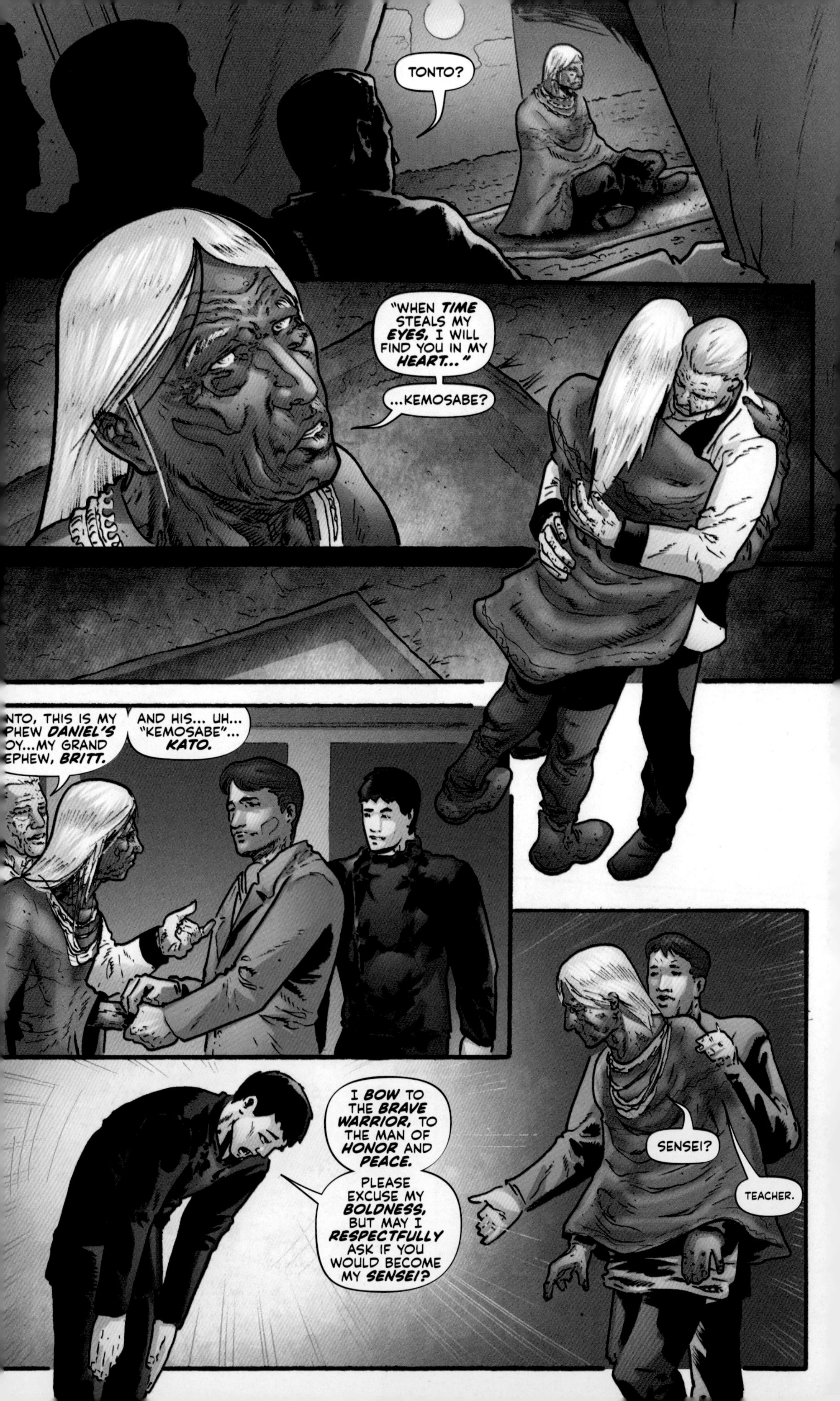

TONTO?
"WHEN TIME STEALS MY EYES, I WILL FIND YOU IN MY HEART..."
...KEMOSABE?
NTO, THIS IS MY PHEW DANIEL'S OY...MY GRAND EPHEW, BRITT.
AND HIS... UH... "KEMOSABE"... KATO.
I BOW TO THE BRAVE WARRIOR, TO THE MAN OF HONOR AND PEACE.
PLEASE EXCUSE MY BOLDNESS, BUT MAY I RESPECTFULLY ASK IF YOU WOULD BECOME MY SENSEI?
SENSEI?
TEACHER.

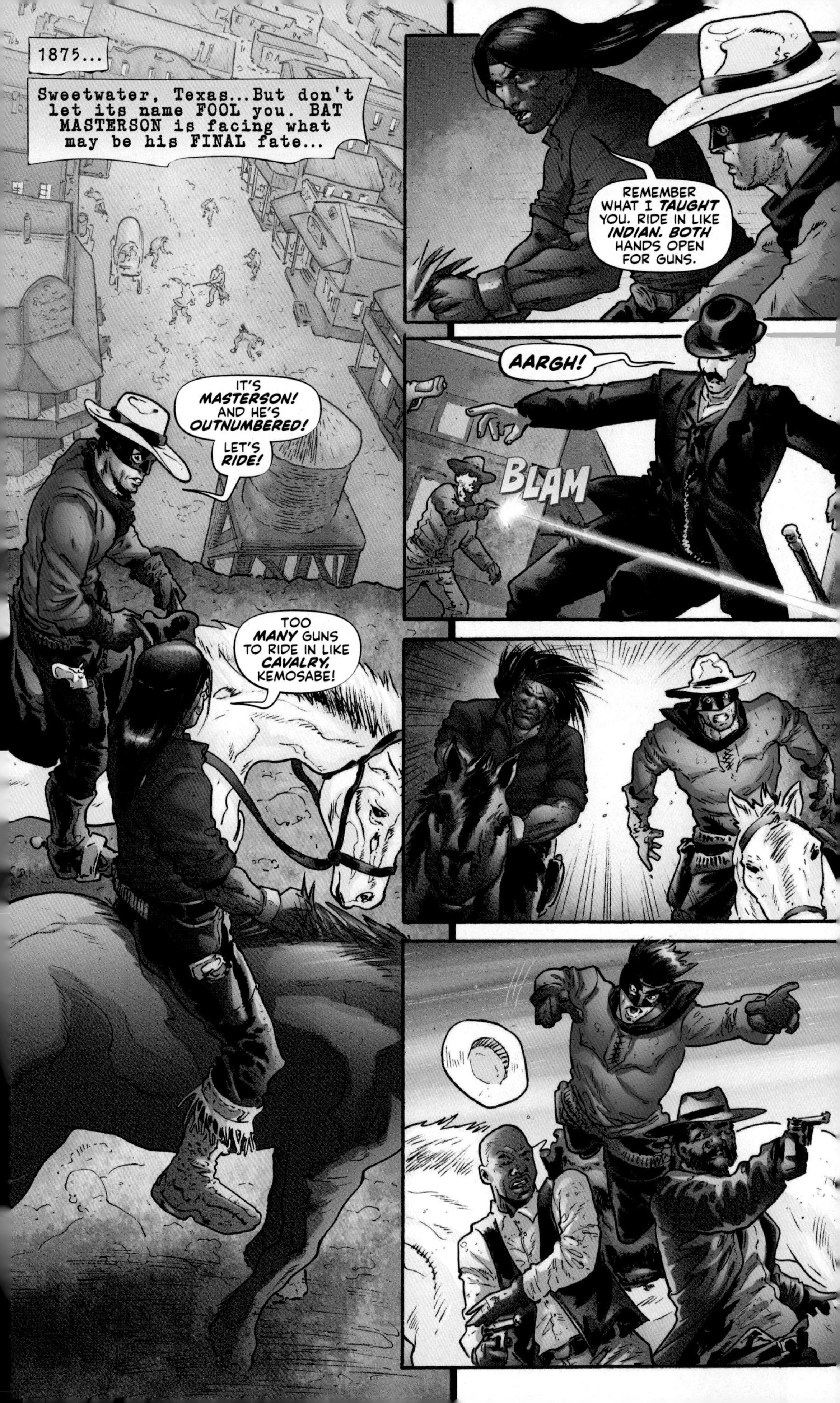
1875...
Sweetwater, Texas...But don't let its name FOOL you. BAT MASTERSON is facing what may be his FINAL fate...
IT'S MASTERSON! AND HE'S OUTNUMBERED!
LET'S RIDE!
TOO MANY GUNS TO RIDE IN LIKE CAVALRY, KEMOSABE!
REMEMBER WHAT I TAUGHT YOU. RIDE IN LIKE INDIAN. BOTH HANDS OPEN FOR GUNS.
AARGH!
BLAM

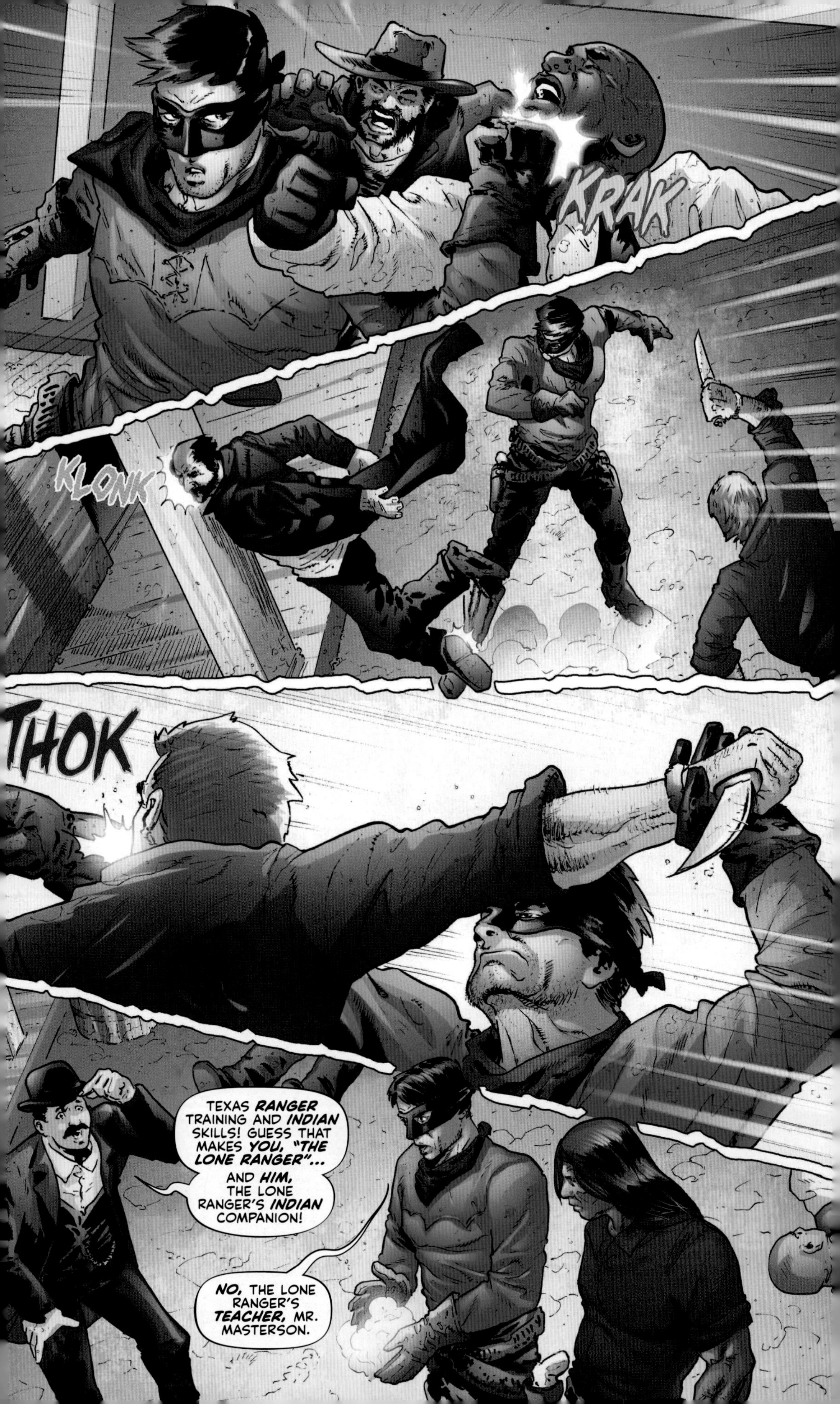
KRAK
KLONK
THOK
TEXAS *RANGER* TRAINING AND *INDIAN* SKILLS! GUESS THAT MAKES *YOU,* *"THE LONE RANGER"...*
AND *HIM,* THE LONE RANGER'S *INDIAN* COMPANION!
NO, THE LONE RANGER'S *TEACHER,* MR. MASTERSON.

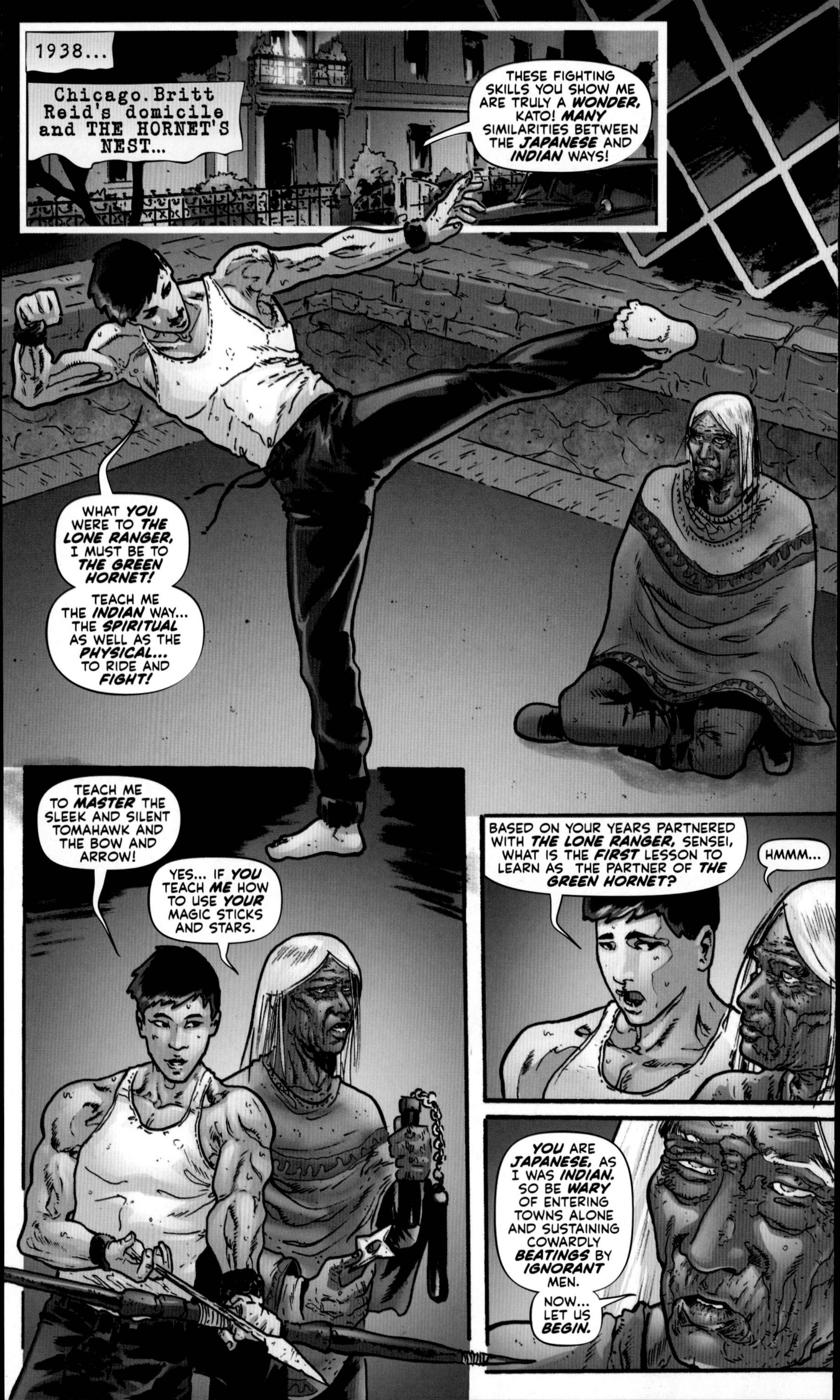

1938...
Chicago. Britt Reid's domicile and THE HORNET'S NEST...
THESE FIGHTING SKILLS YOU SHOW ME ARE TRULY A WONDER, KATO! MANY SIMILARITIES BETWEEN THE JAPANESE AND INDIAN WAYS!
WHAT YOU WERE TO THE LONE RANGER, I MUST BE TO THE GREEN HORNET!
TEACH ME THE INDIAN WAY... THE SPIRITUAL AS WELL AS THE PHYSICAL... TO RIDE AND FIGHT!
TEACH ME TO MASTER THE SLEEK AND SILENT TOMAHAWK AND THE BOW AND ARROW!
YES... IF YOU TEACH ME HOW TO USE YOUR MAGIC STICKS AND STARS.
BASED ON YOUR YEARS PARTNERED WITH THE LONE RANGER, SENSEI, WHAT IS THE FIRST LESSON TO LEARN AS THE PARTNER OF THE GREEN HORNET?
HMMM...
YOU ARE JAPANESE, AS I WAS INDIAN. SO BE WARY OF ENTERING TOWNS ALONE AND SUSTAINING COWARDLY BEATINGS BY IGNORANT MEN.
NOW... LET US BEGIN.

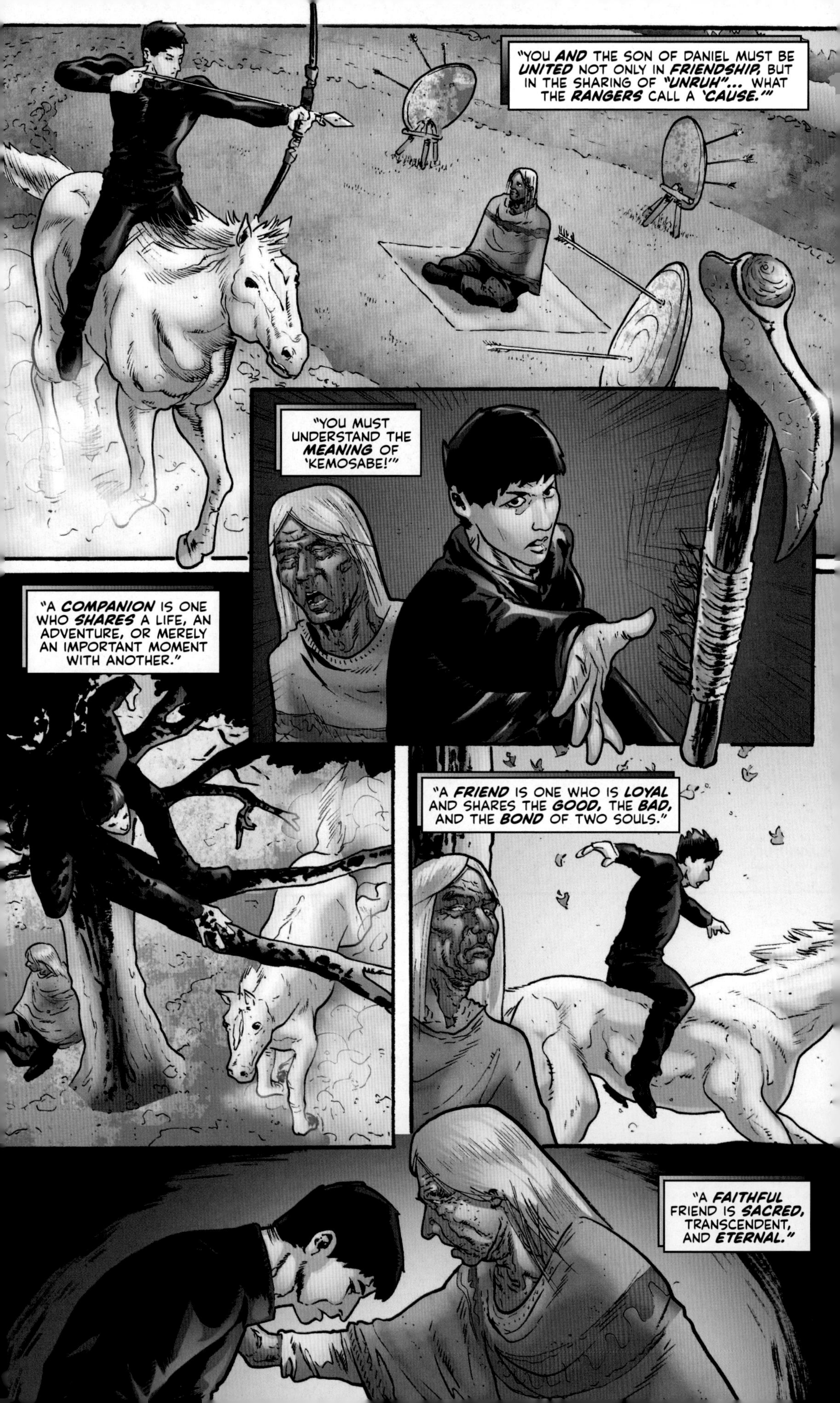
"YOU AND THE SON OF DANIEL MUST BE UNITED NOT ONLY IN FRIENDSHIP, BUT IN THE SHARING OF "UNRUH"... WHAT THE RANGERS CALL A 'CAUSE.'"
"YOU MUST UNDERSTAND THE MEANING OF 'KEMOSABE!'"
"A COMPANION IS ONE WHO SHARES A LIFE, AN ADVENTURE, OR MERELY AN IMPORTANT MOMENT WITH ANOTHER."
"A FRIEND IS ONE WHO IS LOYAL AND SHARES THE GOOD, THE BAD, AND THE BOND OF TWO SOULS."
"A FAITHFUL FRIEND IS SACRED, TRANSCENDENT, AND ETERNAL."

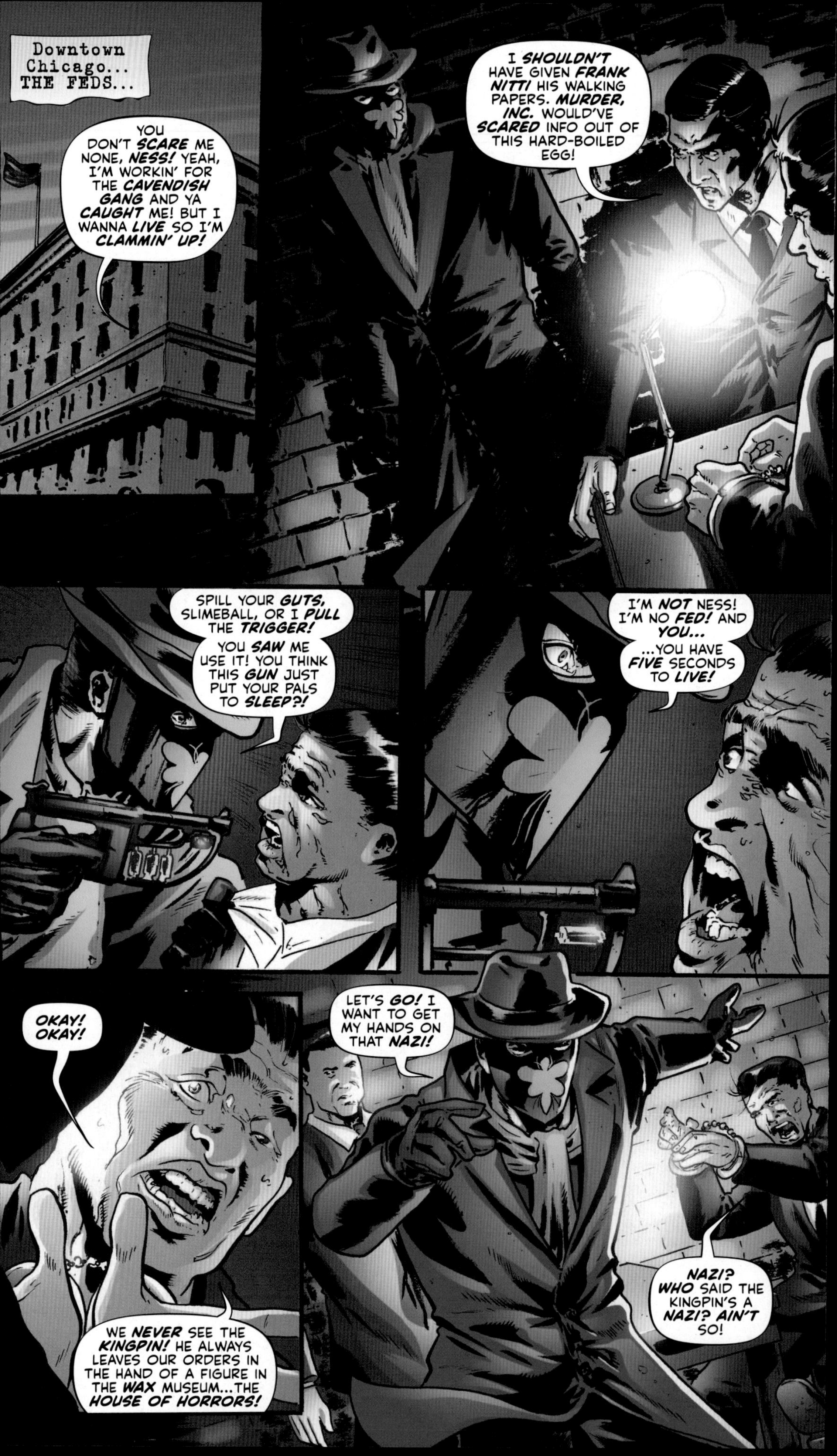

Downtown Chicago... THE FEDS...
YOU DON'T SCARE ME NONE, NESS! YEAH, I'M WORKIN' FOR THE CAVENDISH GANG AND YA CAUGHT ME! BUT I WANNA LIVE SO I'M CLAMMIN' UP!
I SHOULDN'T HAVE GIVEN FRANK NITTI HIS WALKING PAPERS. MURDER, INC. WOULD'VE SCARED INFO OUT OF THIS HARD-BOILED EGG!
SPILL YOUR GUTS, SLIMEBALL, OR I PULL THE TRIGGER!
YOU SAW ME USE IT! YOU THINK THIS GUN JUST PUT YOUR PALS TO SLEEP?!
I'M NOT NESS! I'M NO FED! AND YOU...
...YOU HAVE FIVE SECONDS TO LIVE!
OKAY! OKAY!
WE NEVER SEE THE KINGPIN! HE ALWAYS LEAVES OUR ORDERS IN THE HAND OF A FIGURE IN THE WAX MUSEUM...THE HOUSE OF HORRORS!
LET'S GO! I WANT TO GET MY HANDS ON THAT NAZI!
NAZI? WHO SAID THE KINGPIN'S A NAZI? AIN'T SO!

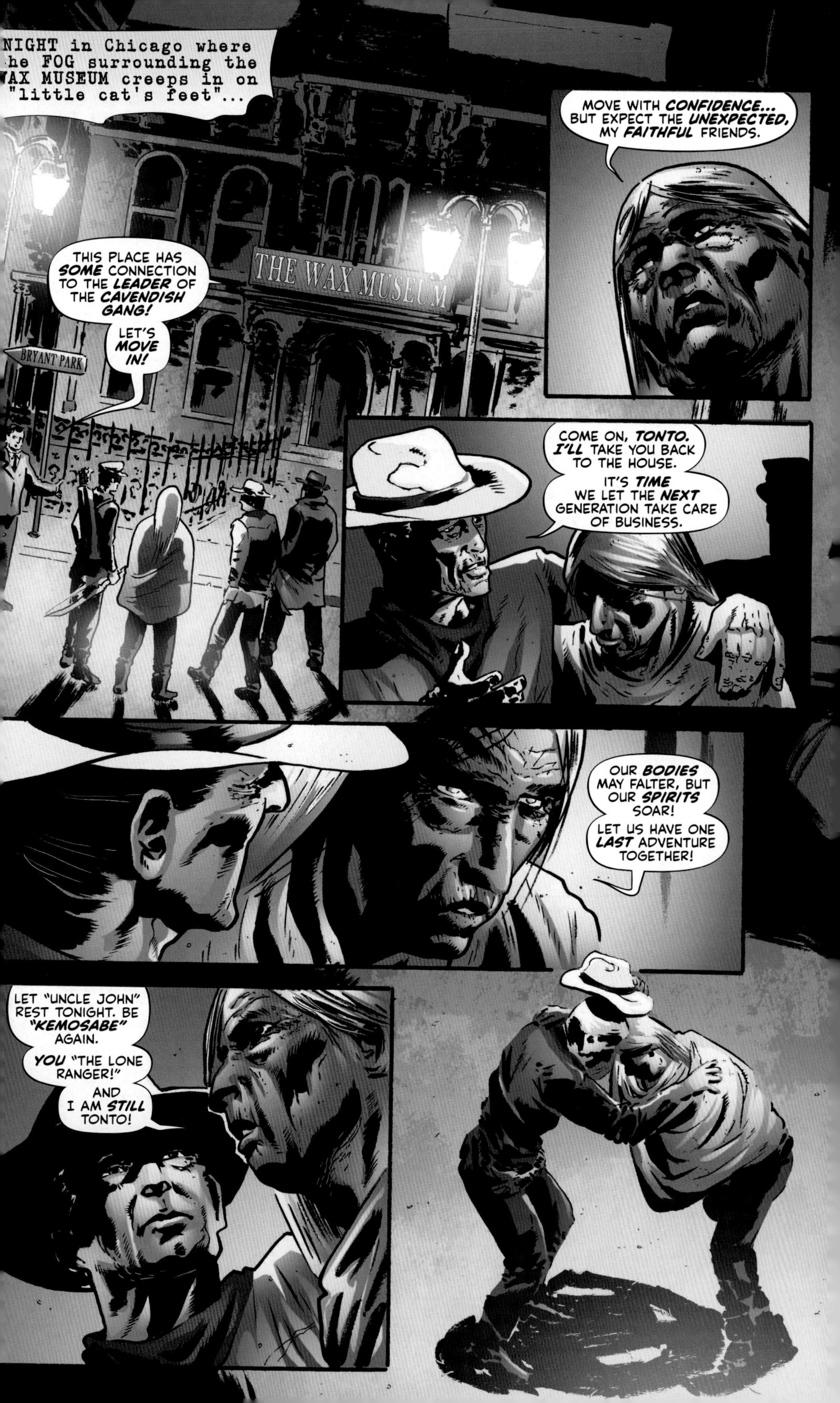
NIGHT in Chicago where the FOG surrounding the WAX MUSEUM creeps in on "little cat's feet"...
THE WAX MUSEUM
BRYANT PARK
THIS PLACE HAS SOME CONNECTION TO THE LEADER OF THE CAVENDISH GANG!
LET'S MOVE IN!
MOVE WITH CONFIDENCE... BUT EXPECT THE UNEXPECTED, MY FAITHFUL FRIENDS.
COME ON, TONTO. I'LL TAKE YOU BACK TO THE HOUSE.
IT'S TIME WE LET THE NEXT GENERATION TAKE CARE OF BUSINESS.
OUR BODIES MAY FALTER, BUT OUR SPIRITS SOAR!
LET US HAVE ONE LAST ADVENTURE TOGETHER!
LET "UNCLE JOHN" REST TONIGHT. BE "KEMOSABE" AGAIN.
YOU "THE LONE RANGER!"
AND I AM STILL TONTO!

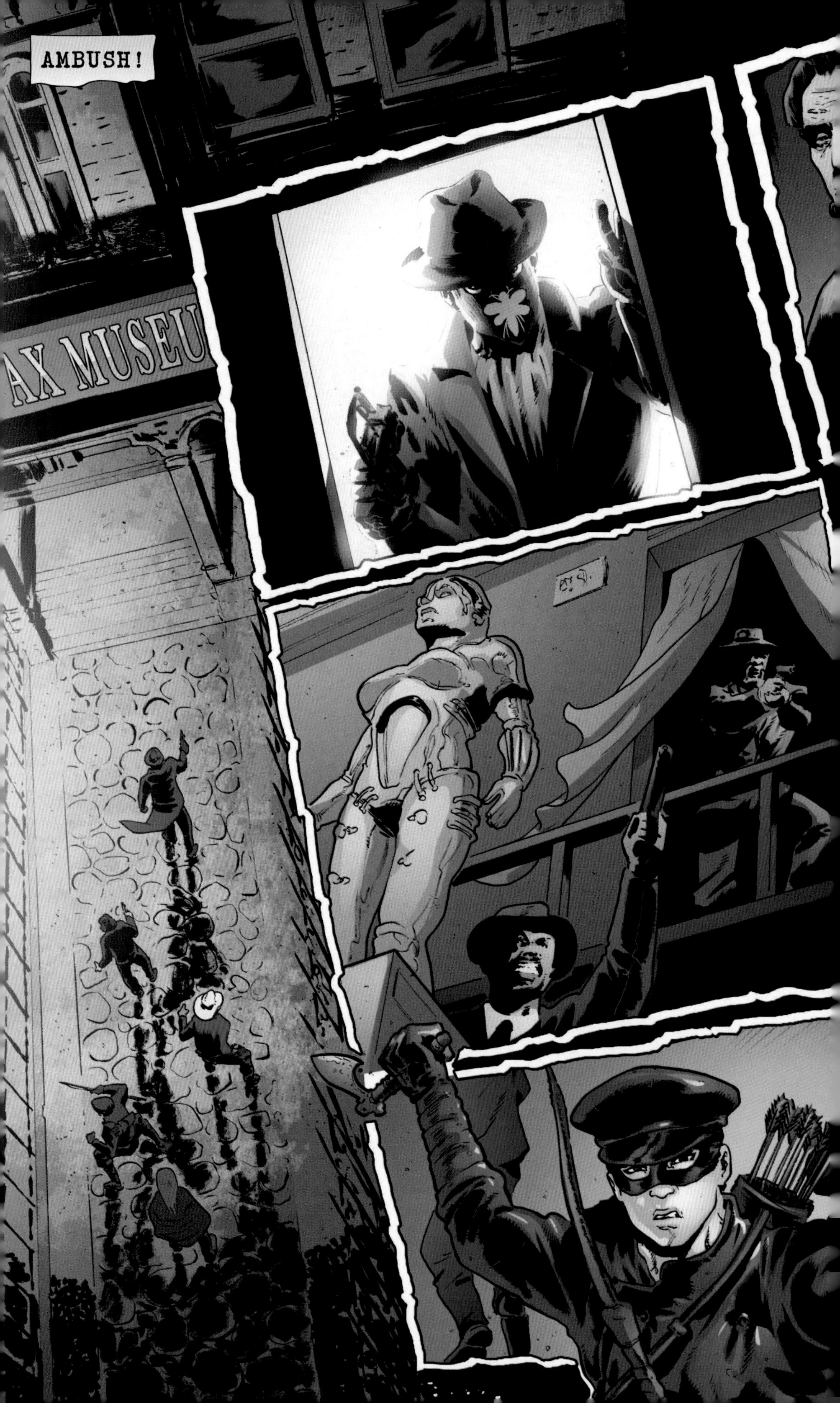
AMBUSH!
AX MUSEU

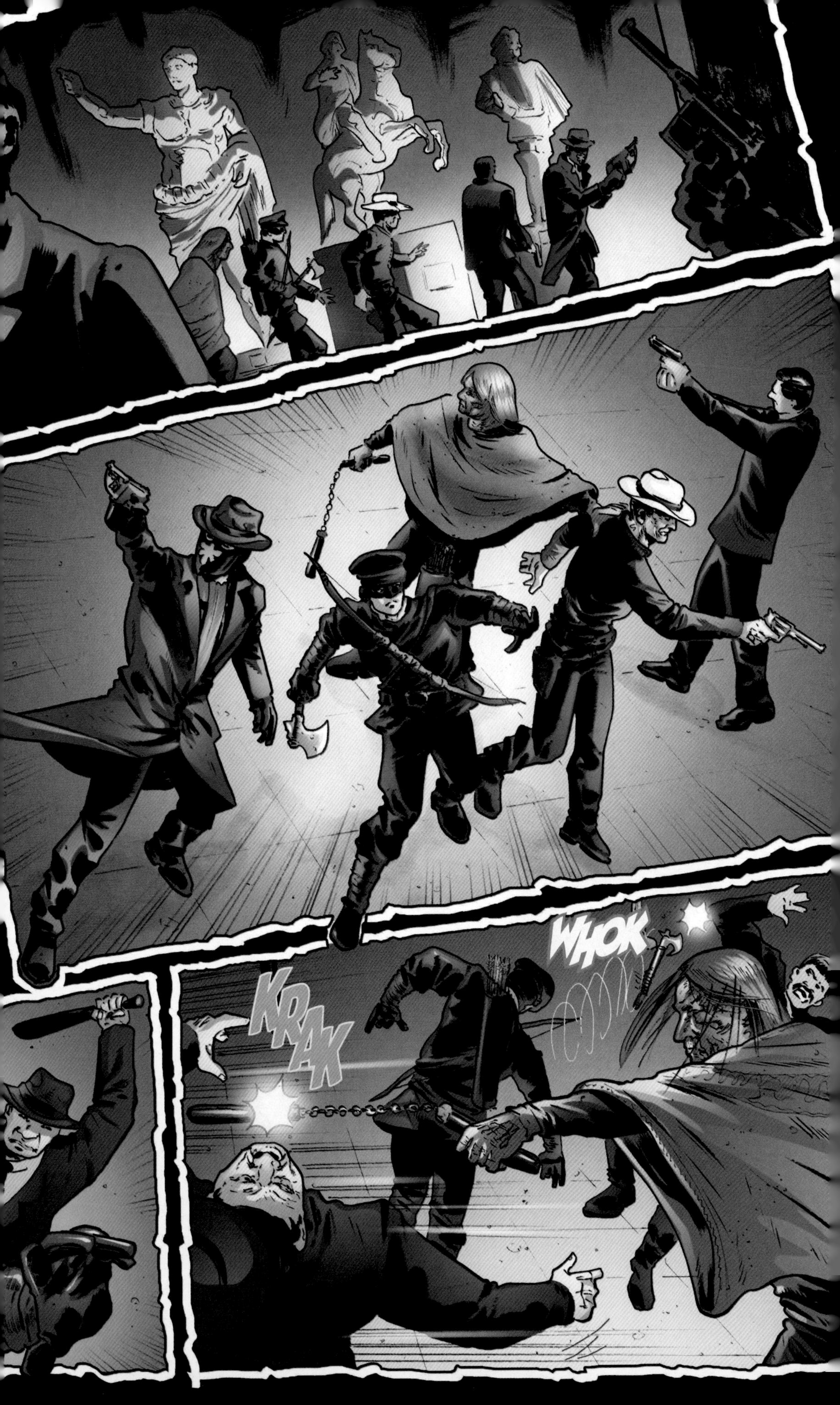

WHOK
KRAK

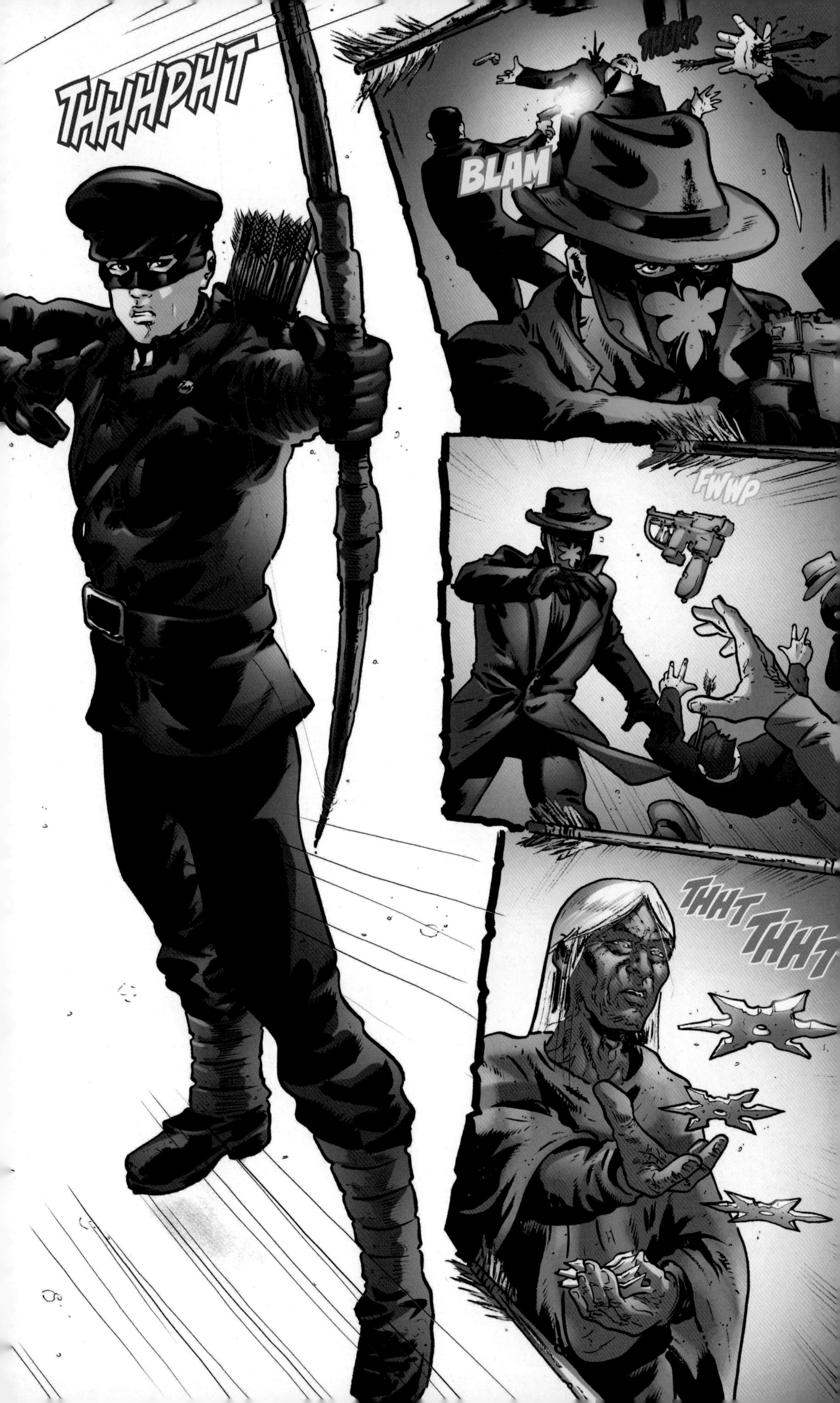

THHPHT
BLAM
FWWP
THHT
THHT

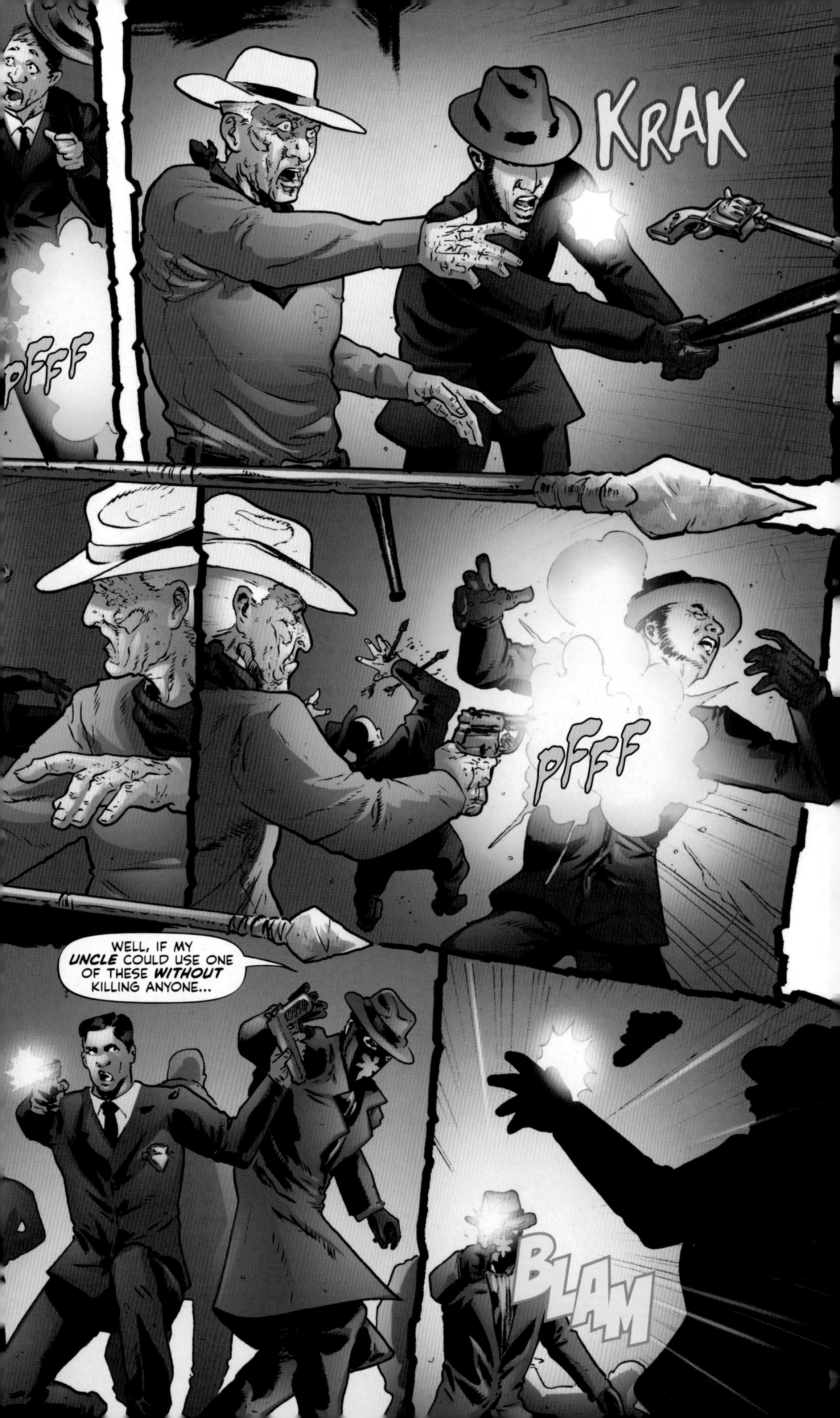

KRAK
pFFF
pFFF
WELL, IF MY UNCLE COULD USE ONE OF THESE WITHOUT KILLING ANYONE...
BLAM

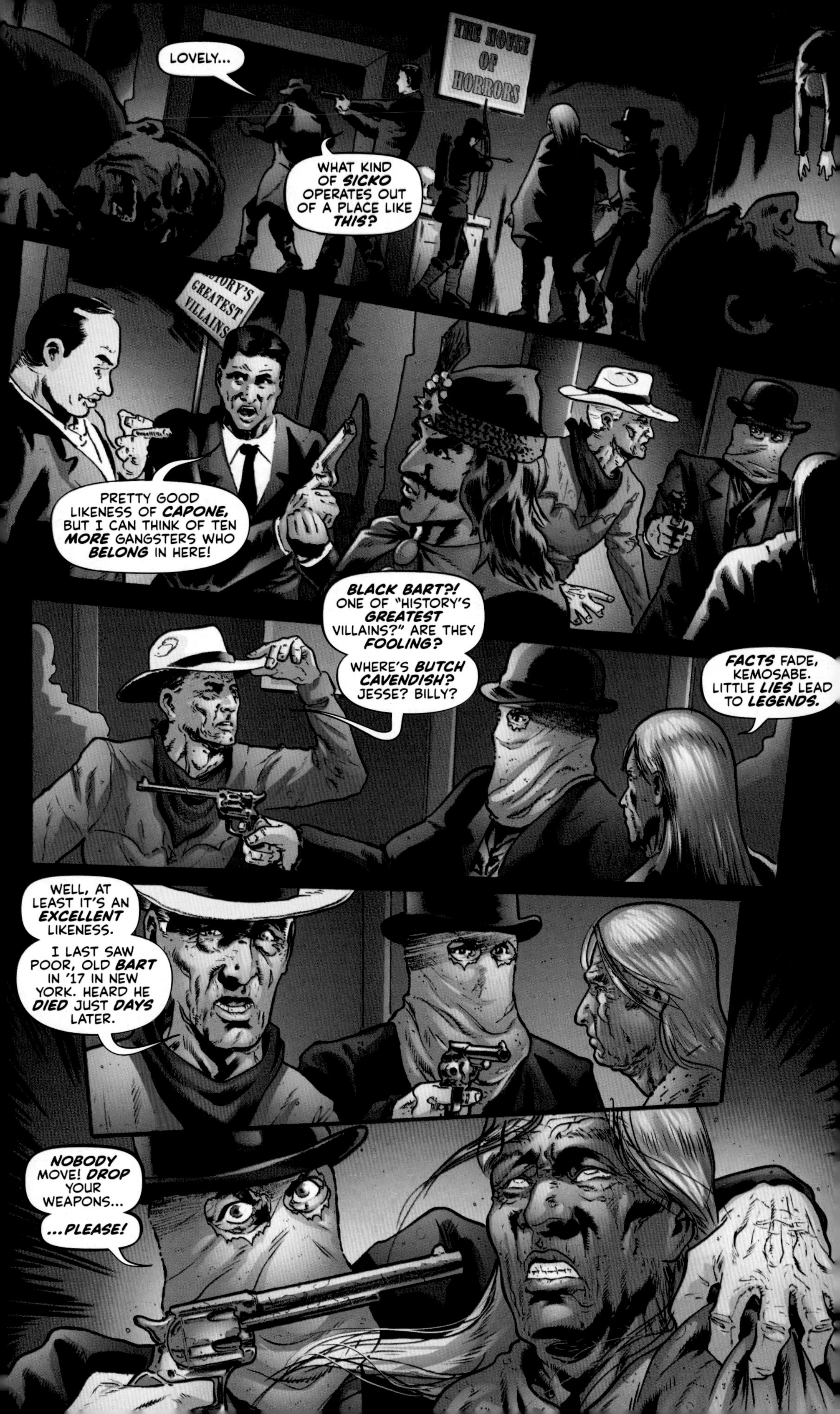
THE HOUSE OF HORRORS
LOVELY...
WHAT KIND OF SICKO OPERATES OUT OF A PLACE LIKE THIS?
HISTORY'S GREATEST VILLAINS
PRETTY GOOD LIKENESS OF CAPONE, BUT I CAN THINK OF TEN MORE GANGSTERS WHO BELONG IN HERE!
BLACK BART?! ONE OF "HISTORY'S GREATEST VILLAINS?" ARE THEY FOOLING?
WHERE'S BUTCH CAVENDISH? JESSE? BILLY?
FACTS FADE, KEMOSABE. LITTLE LIES LEAD TO LEGENDS.
WELL, AT LEAST IT'S AN EXCELLENT LIKENESS.
I LAST SAW POOR, OLD BART IN '17 IN NEW YORK. HEARD HE DIED JUST DAYS LATER.
NOBODY MOVE! DROP YOUR WEAPONS...
...PLEASE!

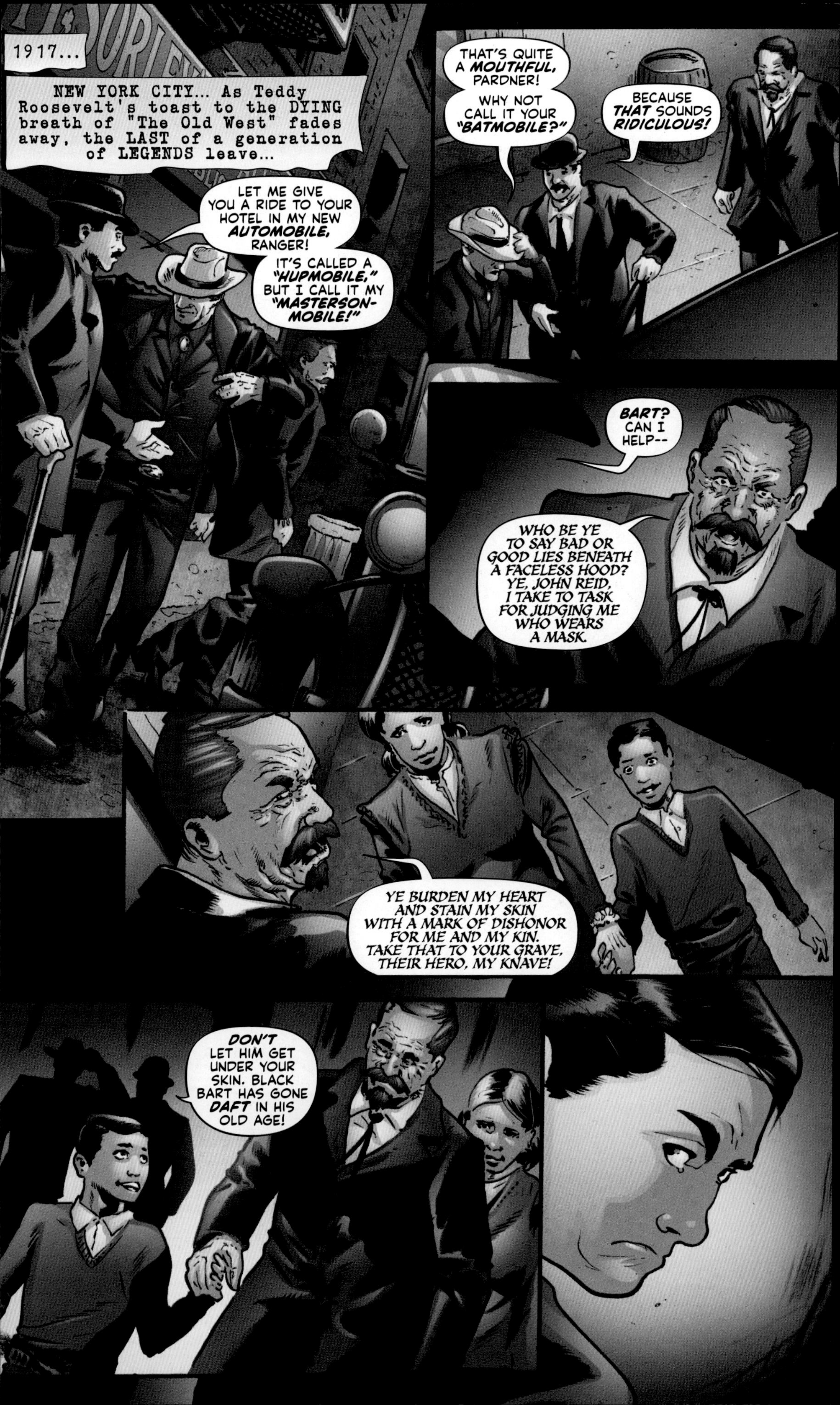
1917...
NEW YORK CITY... As Teddy Roosevelt's toast to the DYING breath of "The Old West" fades away, the LAST of a generation of LEGENDS leave...
LET ME GIVE YOU A RIDE TO YOUR HOTEL IN MY NEW AUTOMOBILE, RANGER!
IT'S CALLED A "HUPMOBILE," BUT I CALL IT MY "MASTERSON-MOBILE!"
THAT'S QUITE A MOUTHFUL, PARDNER!
WHY NOT CALL IT YOUR "BATMOBILE?"
BECAUSE THAT SOUNDS RIDICULOUS!
BART? CAN I HELP--
WHO BE YE TO SAY BAD OR GOOD LIES BENEATH A FACELESS HOOD? YE, JOHN REID, I TAKE TO TASK FOR JUDGING ME WHO WEARS A MASK.
YE BURDEN MY HEART AND STAIN MY SKIN WITH A MARK OF DISHONOR FOR ME AND MY KIN. TAKE THAT TO YOUR GRAVE, THEIR HERO, MY KNAVE!
DON'T LET HIM GET UNDER YOUR SKIN. BLACK BART HAS GONE DAFT IN HIS OLD AGE!

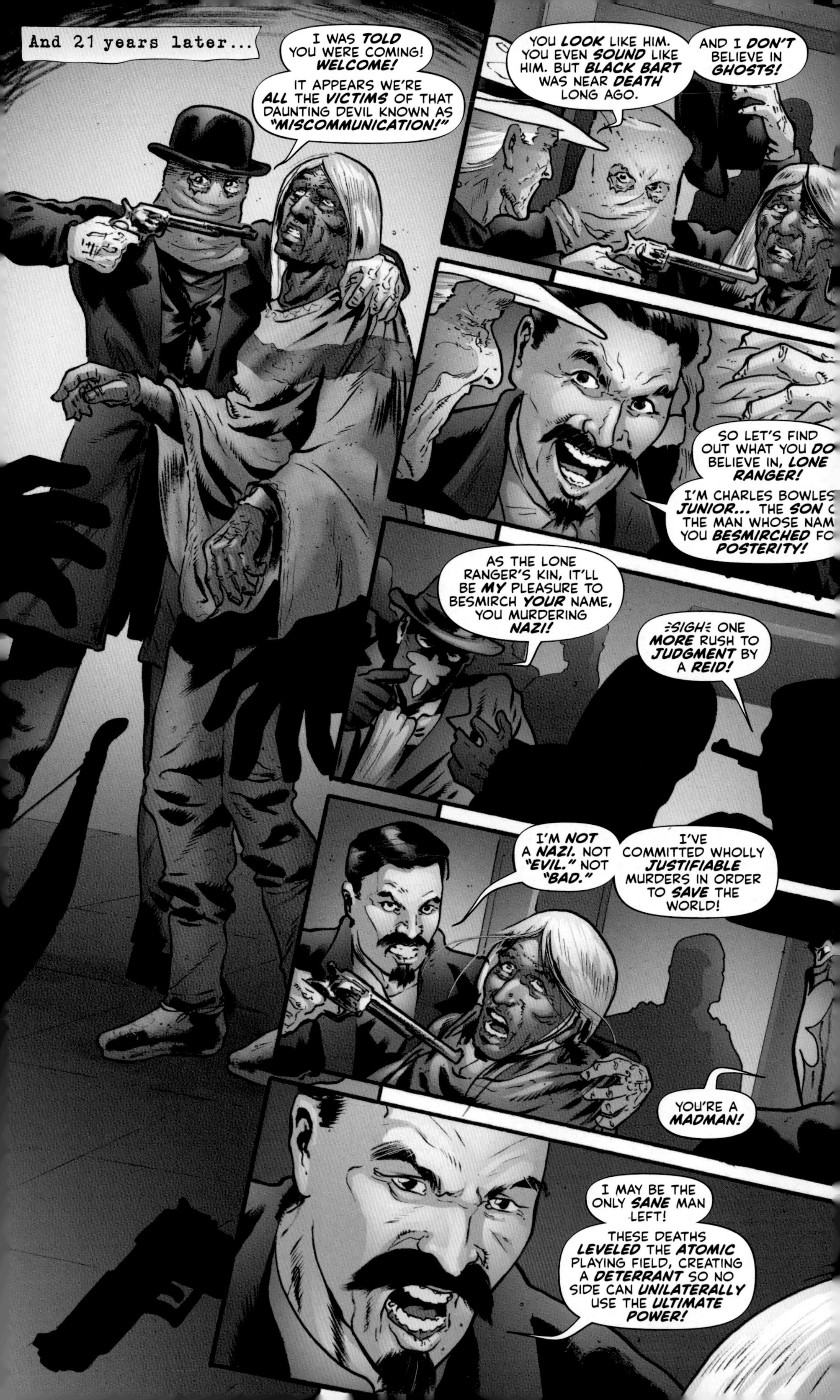

And 21 years later...
I WAS TOLD YOU WERE COMING! WELCOME!
IT APPEARS WE'RE ALL THE VICTIMS OF THAT DAUNTING DEVIL KNOWN AS "MISCOMMUNICATION!"
YOU LOOK LIKE HIM. YOU EVEN SOUND LIKE HIM. BUT BLACK BART WAS NEAR DEATH LONG AGO.
AND I DON'T BELIEVE IN GHOSTS!
SO LET'S FIND OUT WHAT YOU DO BELIEVE IN, LONE RANGER!
I'M CHARLES BOWLES JUNIOR... THE SON OF THE MAN WHOSE NAME YOU BESMIRCHED FOR POSTERITY!
AS THE LONE RANGER'S KIN, IT'LL BE MY PLEASURE TO BESMIRCH YOUR NAME, YOU MURDERING NAZI!
SIGH ONE MORE RUSH TO JUDGMENT BY A REID!
I'M NOT A NAZI. NOT "EVIL." NOT "BAD."
I'VE COMMITTED WHOLLY JUSTIFIABLE MURDERS IN ORDER TO SAVE THE WORLD!
YOU'RE A MADMAN!
I MAY BE THE ONLY SANE MAN LEFT!
THESE DEATHS LEVELED THE ATOMIC PLAYING FIELD, CREATING A DETERRANT SO NO SIDE CAN UNILATERALLY USE THE ULTIMATE POWER!

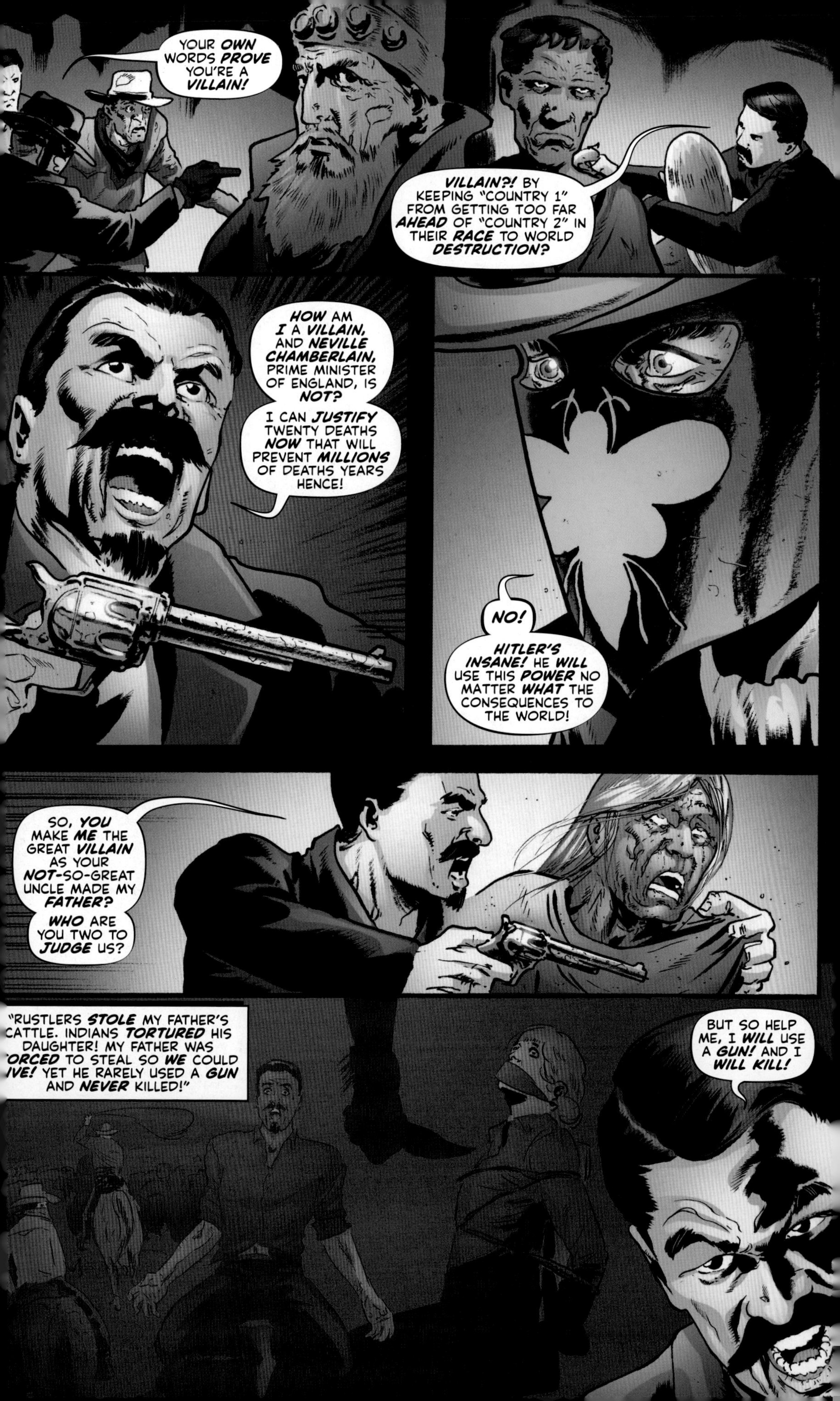
YOUR OWN WORDS PROVE YOU'RE A VILLAIN!
VILLAIN?! BY KEEPING "COUNTRY 1" FROM GETTING TOO FAR AHEAD OF "COUNTRY 2" IN THEIR RACE TO WORLD DESTRUCTION?
HOW AM I A VILLAIN, AND NEVILLE CHAMBERLAIN, PRIME MINISTER OF ENGLAND, IS NOT?
I CAN JUSTIFY TWENTY DEATHS NOW THAT WILL PREVENT MILLIONS OF DEATHS YEARS HENCE!
NO!
HITLER'S INSANE! HE WILL USE THIS POWER NO MATTER WHAT THE CONSEQUENCES TO THE WORLD!
SO, YOU MAKE ME THE GREAT VILLAIN AS YOUR NOT-SO-GREAT UNCLE MADE MY FATHER?
WHO ARE YOU TWO TO JUDGE US?
"RUSTLERS STOLE MY FATHER'S CATTLE. INDIANS TORTURED HIS DAUGHTER! MY FATHER WAS FORCED TO STEAL SO WE COULD LIVE! YET HE RARELY USED A GUN AND NEVER KILLED!"
BUT SO HELP ME, I WILL USE A GUN! AND I WILL KILL!

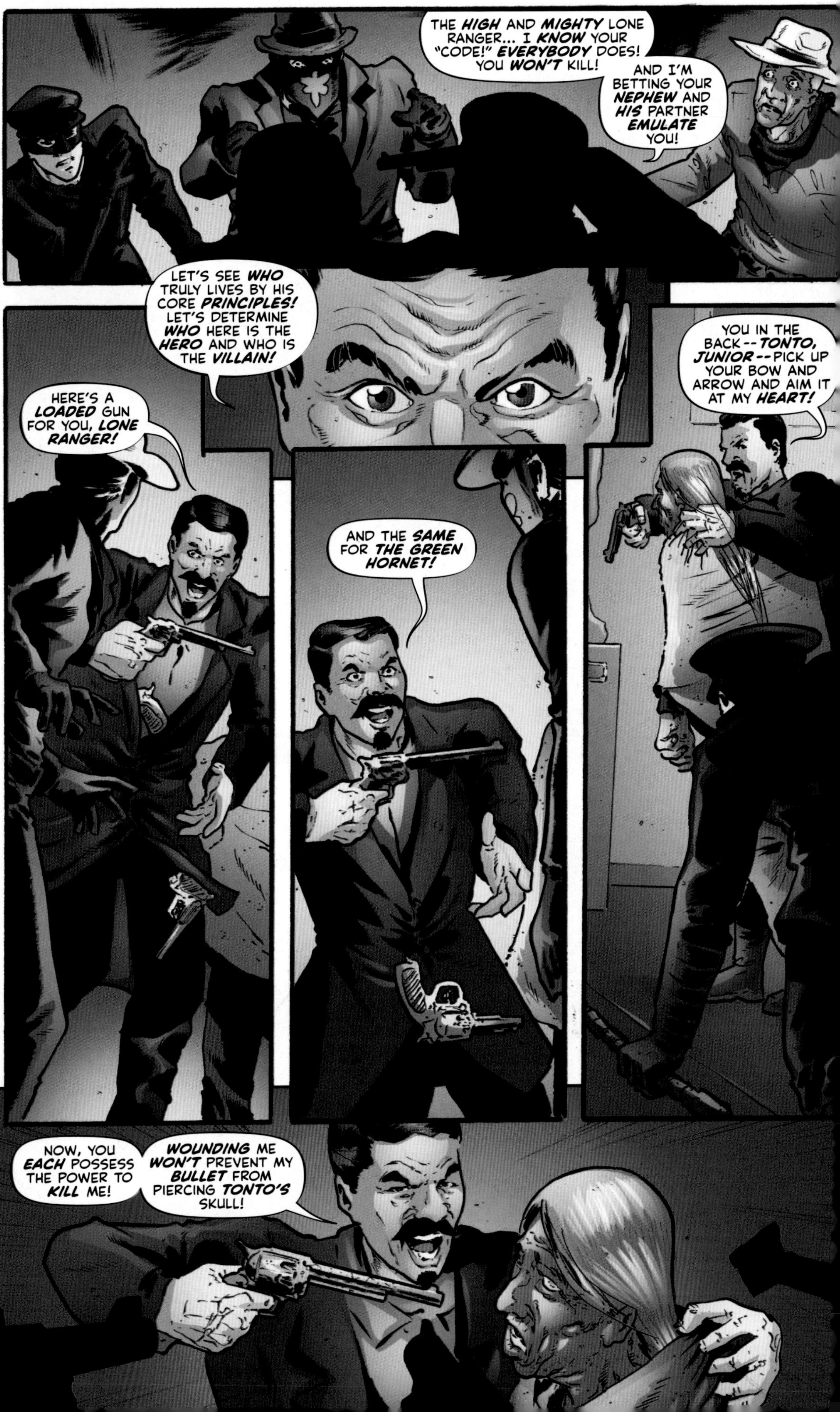
THE HIGH AND MIGHTY LONE RANGER... I KNOW YOUR "CODE!" EVERYBODY DOES! YOU WON'T KILL!
AND I'M BETTING YOUR NEPHEW AND HIS PARTNER EMULATE YOU!
LET'S SEE WHO TRULY LIVES BY HIS CORE PRINCIPLES! LET'S DETERMINE WHO HERE IS THE HERO AND WHO IS THE VILLAIN!
HERE'S A LOADED GUN FOR YOU, LONE RANGER!
AND THE SAME FOR THE GREEN HORNET!
YOU IN THE BACK--TONTO, JUNIOR--PICK UP YOUR BOW AND ARROW AND AIM IT AT MY HEART!
NOW, YOU EACH POSSESS THE POWER TO KILL ME!
WOUNDING ME WON'T PREVENT MY BULLET FROM PIERCING TONTO'S SKULL!

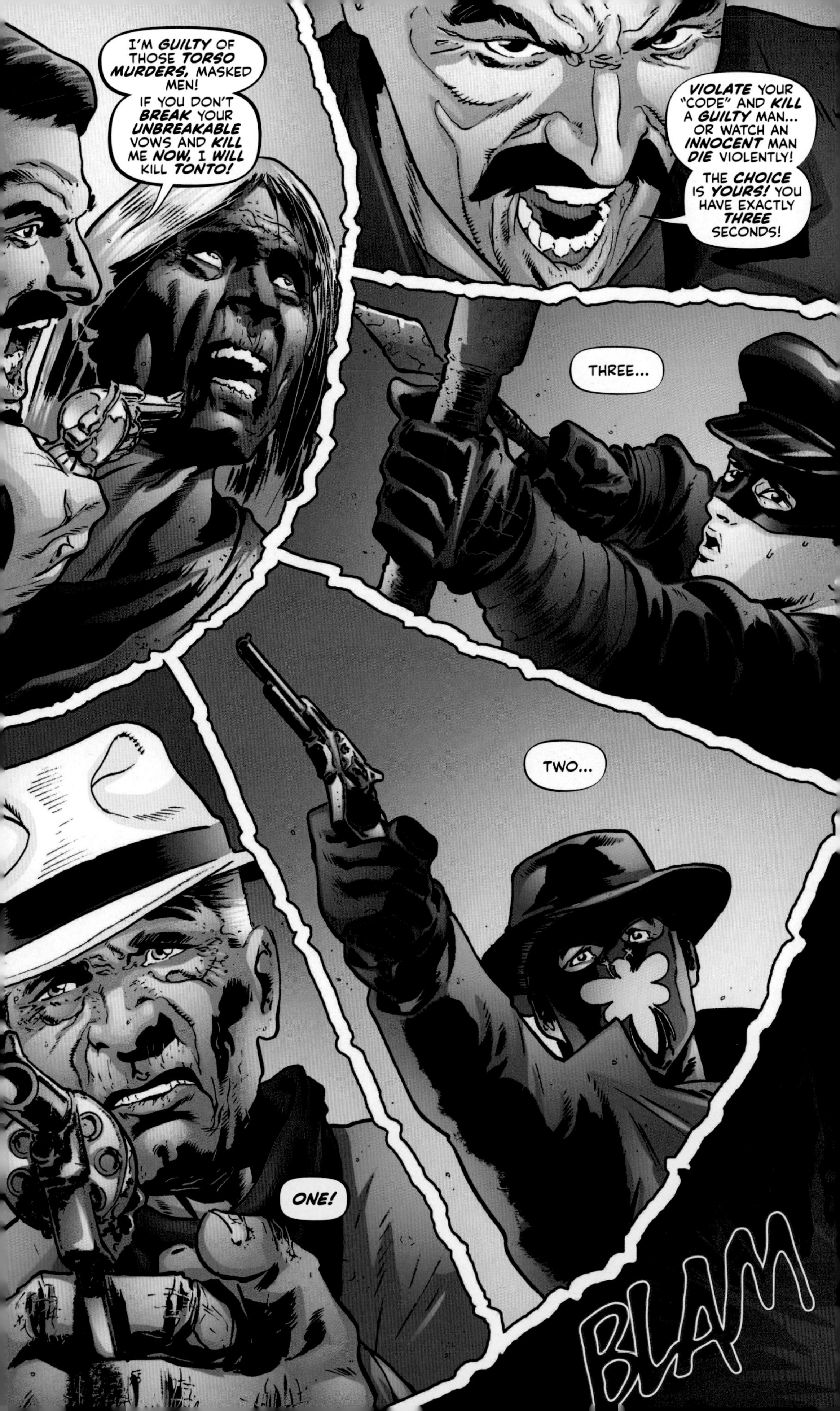

I'M GUILTY OF THOSE TORSO MURDERS, MASKED MEN!
IF YOU DON'T BREAK YOUR UNBREAKABLE VOWS AND KILL ME NOW, I WILL KILL TONTO!
VIOLATE YOUR "CODE" AND KILL A GUILTY MAN... OR WATCH AN INNOCENT MAN DIE VIOLENTLY!
THE CHOICE IS YOURS! YOU HAVE EXACTLY THREE SECONDS!
THREE...
TWO...
ONE!
BLAM

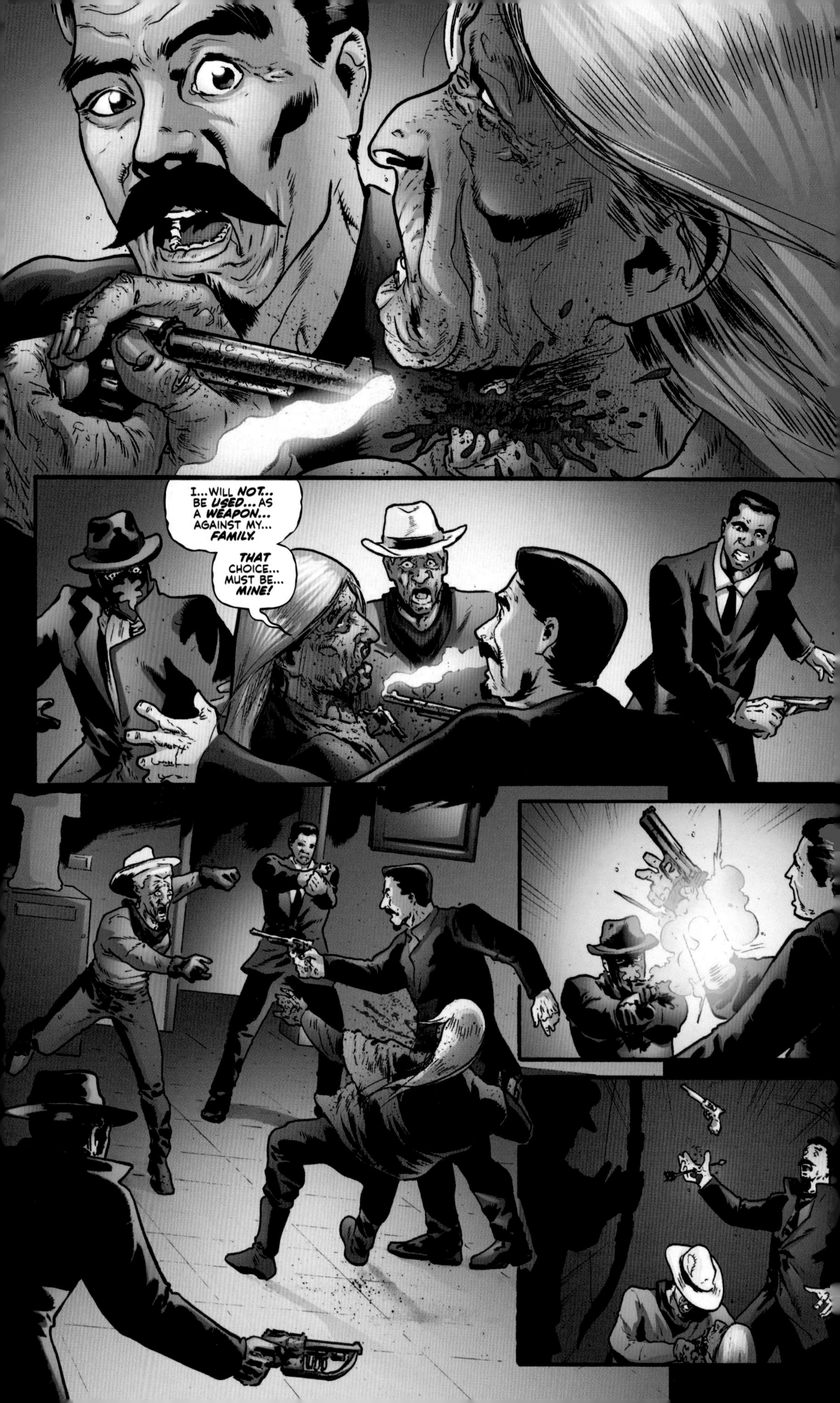
I...WILL NOT... BE USED... AS A WEAPON... AGAINST MY... FAMILY.
THAT CHOICE... MUST BE... MINE!

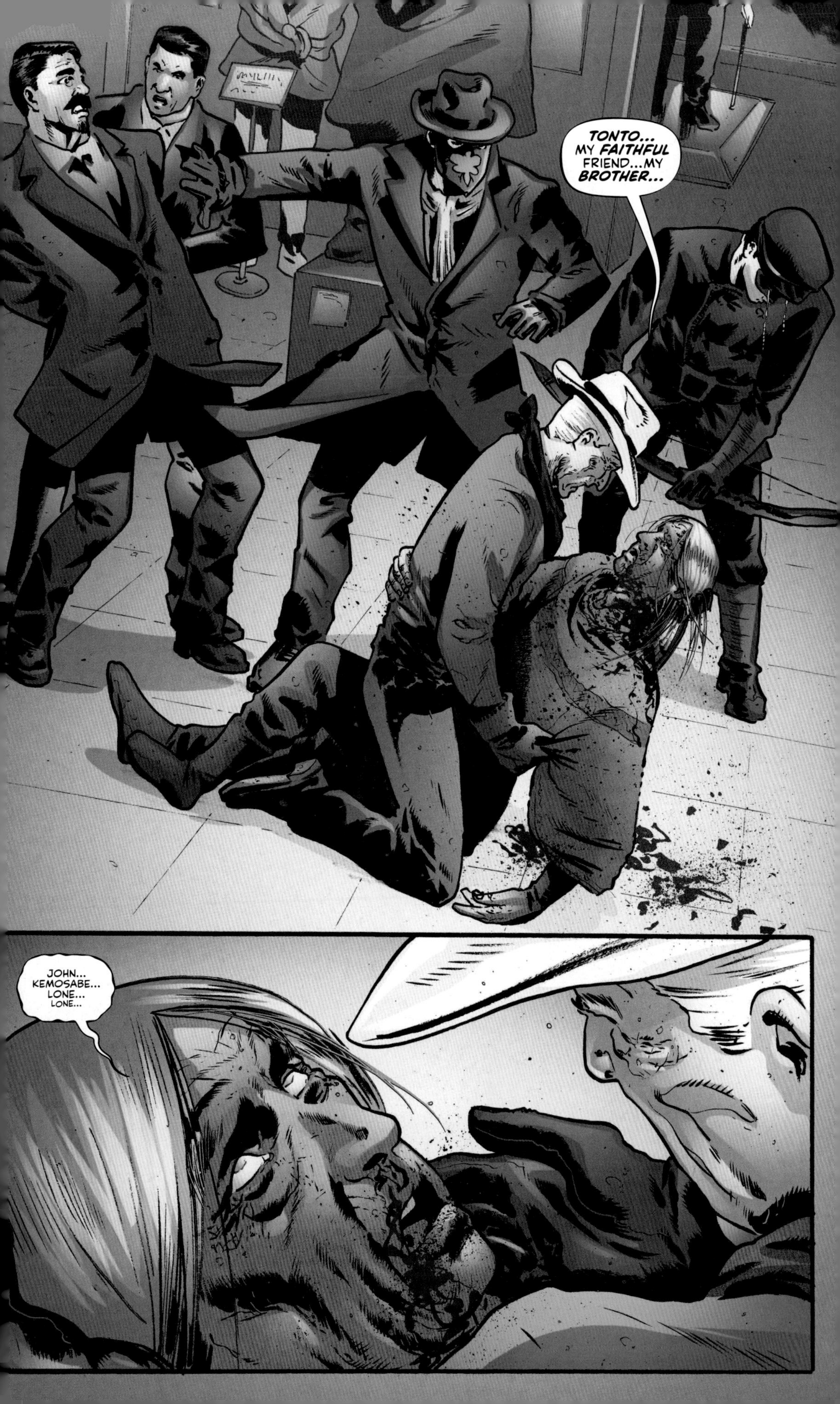
TONTO... MY FAITHFUL FRIEND...MY BROTHER...
JOHN... KEMOSABE... LONE... LONE...

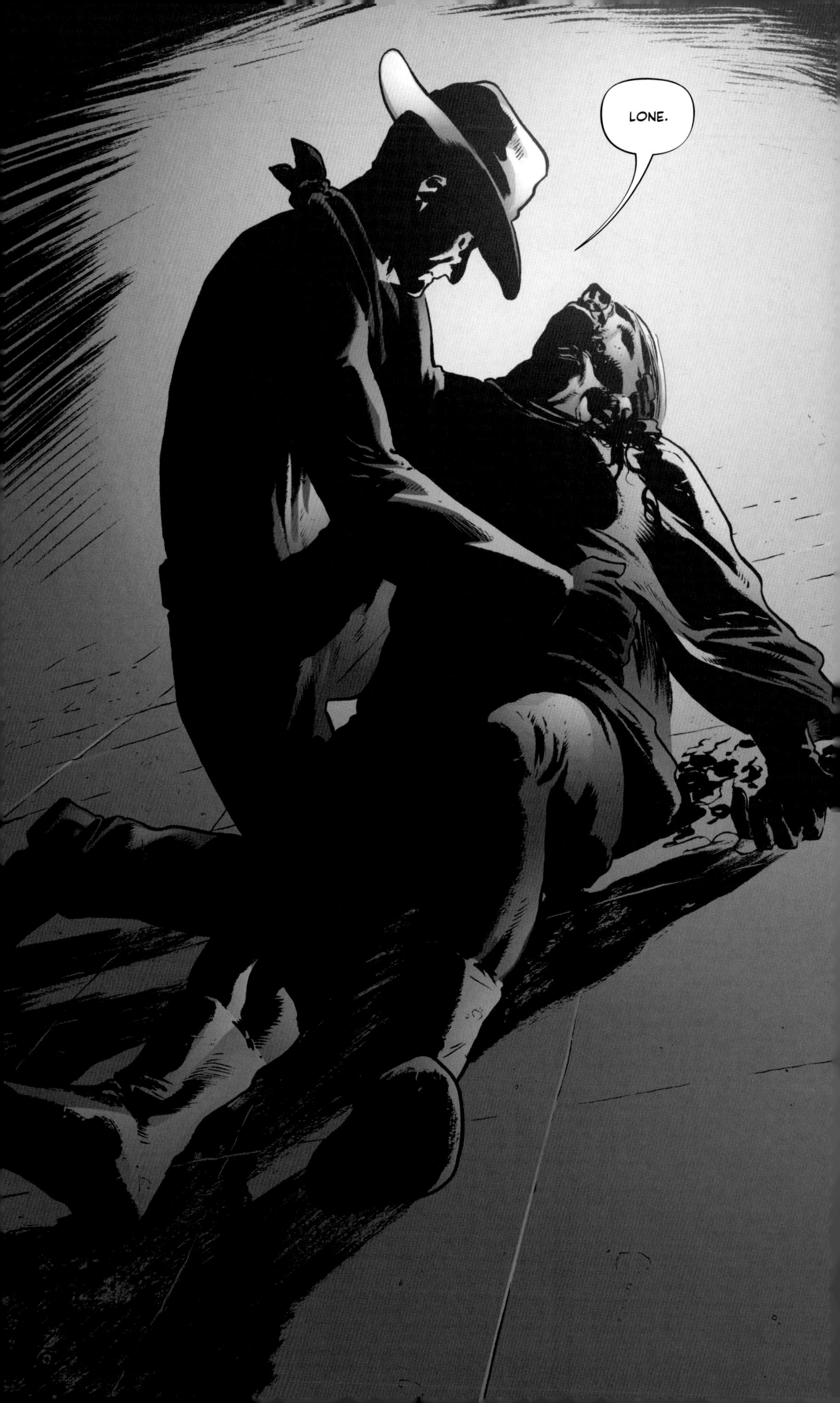
LONE.

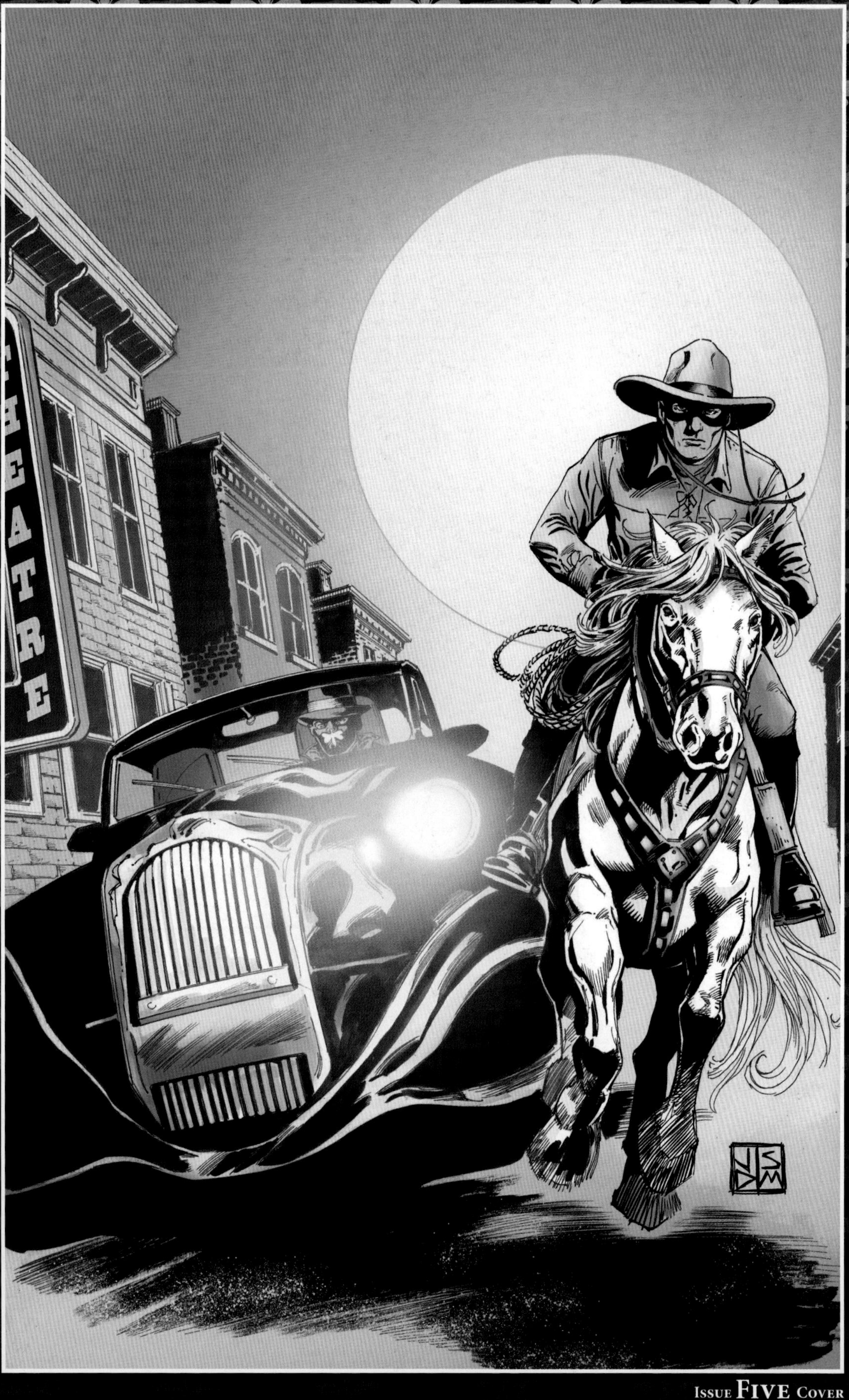
HEATRE

Issue **FIVE** Cover

Art by **JAN DUURSEMA** Colors by **SIAN MANDRAKE**

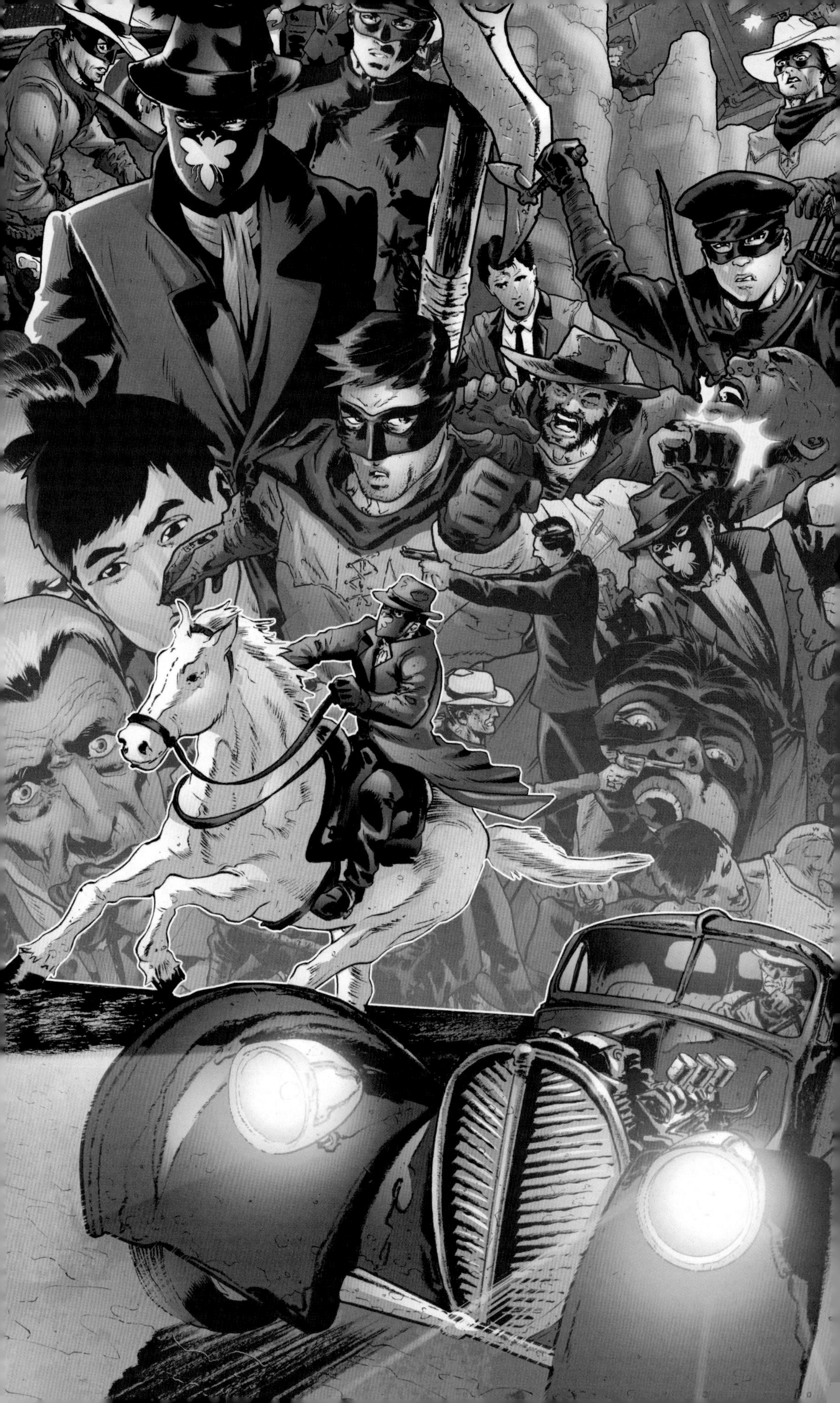

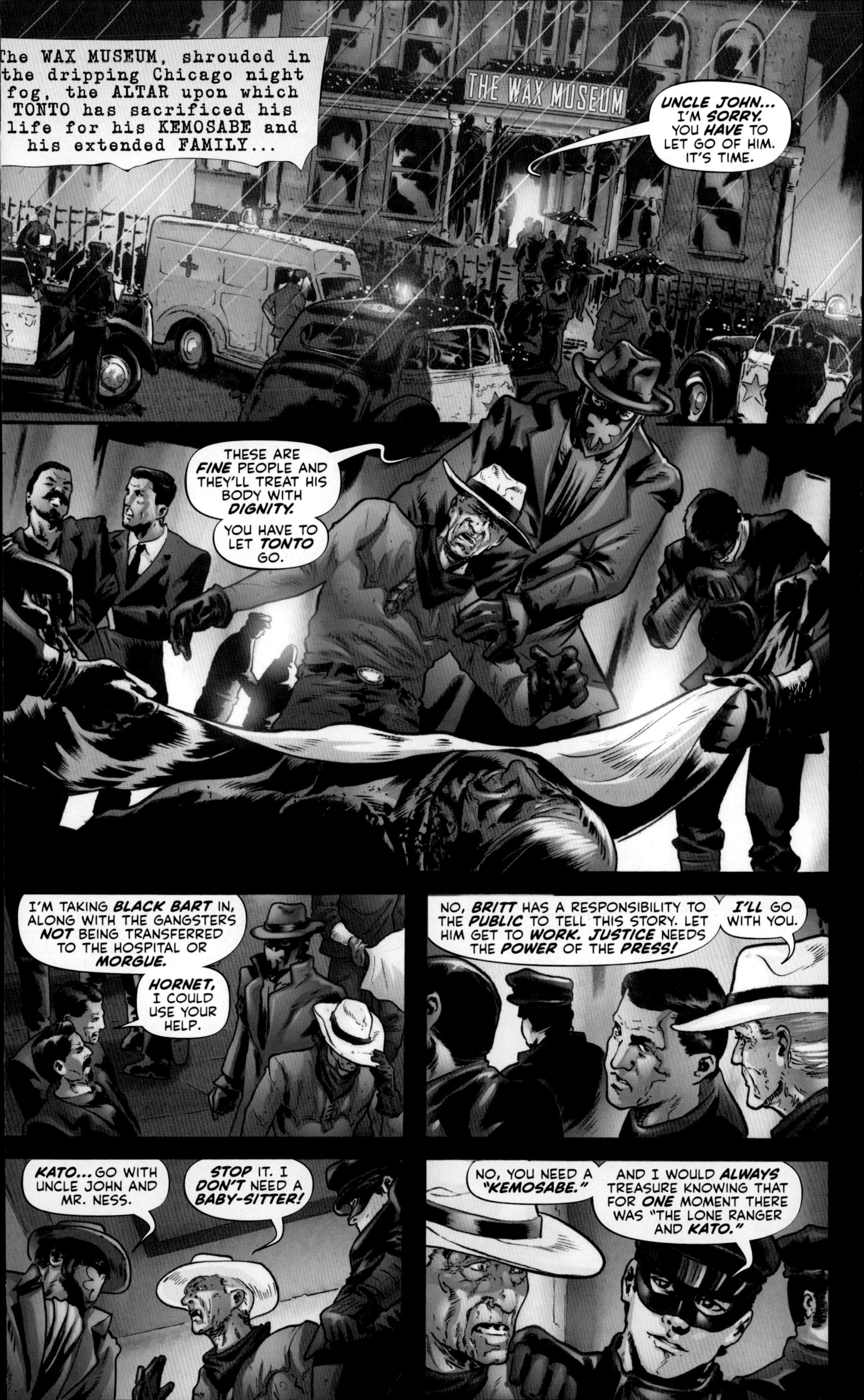
The WAX MUSEUM, shrouded in the dripping Chicago night fog, the ALTAR upon which TONTO has sacrificed his life for his KEMOSABE and his extended FAMILY...
THE WAX MUSEUM
UNCLE JOHN... I'M SORRY. YOU HAVE TO LET GO OF HIM. IT'S TIME.
THESE ARE FINE PEOPLE AND THEY'LL TREAT HIS BODY WITH DIGNITY.
YOU HAVE TO LET TONTO GO.
I'M TAKING BLACK BART IN, ALONG WITH THE GANGSTERS NOT BEING TRANSFERRED TO THE HOSPITAL OR MORGUE.
HORNET, I COULD USE YOUR HELP.
NO, BRITT HAS A RESPONSIBILITY TO THE PUBLIC TO TELL THIS STORY. LET HIM GET TO WORK. JUSTICE NEEDS THE POWER OF THE PRESS!
I'LL GO WITH YOU.
KATO... GO WITH UNCLE JOHN AND MR. NESS.
STOP IT. I DON'T NEED A BABY-SITTER!
NO, YOU NEED A "KEMOSABE."
AND I WOULD ALWAYS TREASURE KNOWING THAT FOR ONE MOMENT THERE WAS "THE LONE RANGER AND KATO."

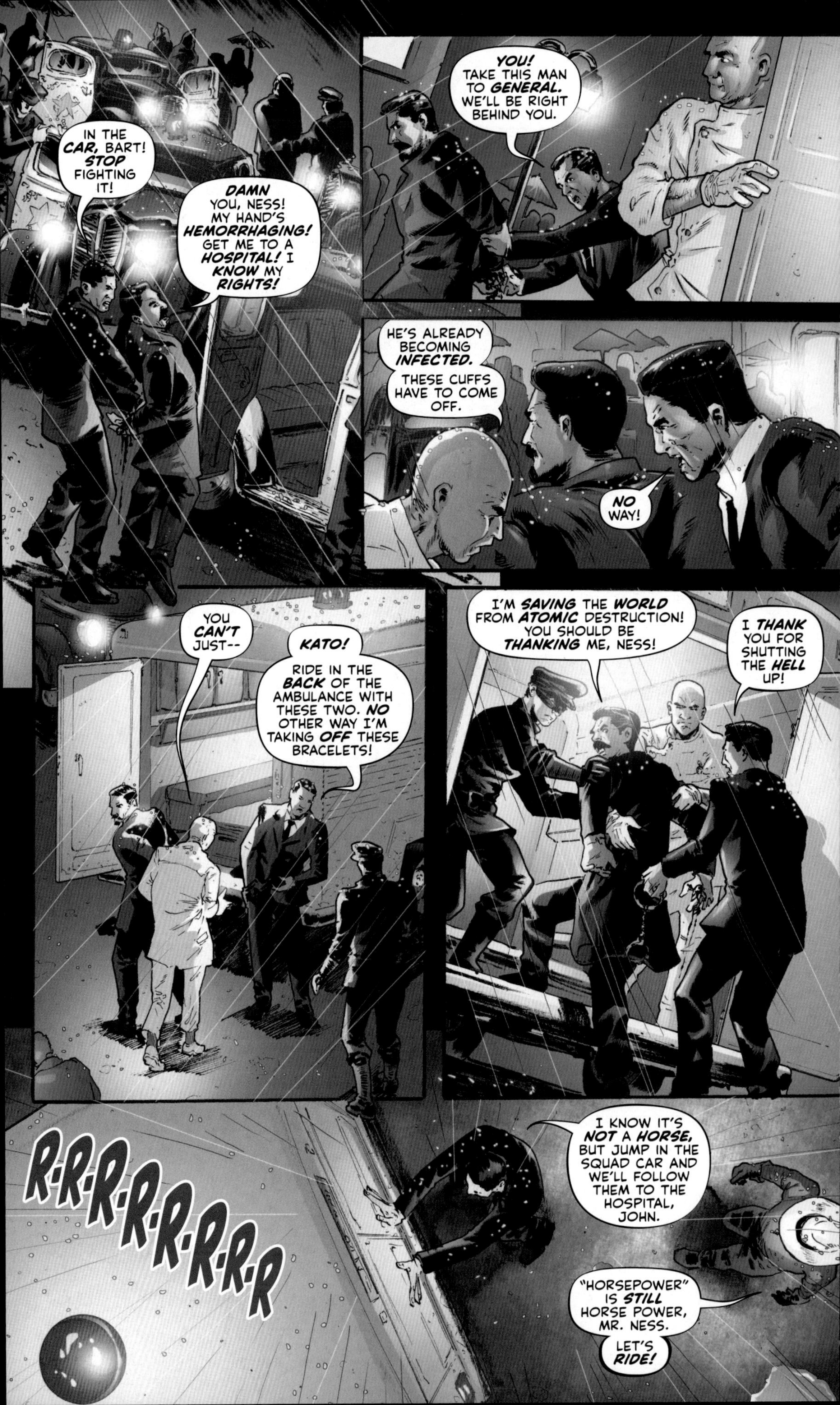
IN THE CAR, BART! STOP FIGHTING IT!
DAMN YOU, NESS! MY HAND'S HEMORRHAGING! GET ME TO A HOSPITAL! I KNOW MY RIGHTS!
YOU! TAKE THIS MAN TO GENERAL. WE'LL BE RIGHT BEHIND YOU.
HE'S ALREADY BECOMING INFECTED.
THESE CUFFS HAVE TO COME OFF.
NO WAY!
YOU CAN'T JUST--
KATO!
RIDE IN THE BACK OF THE AMBULANCE WITH THESE TWO. NO OTHER WAY I'M TAKING OFF THESE BRACELETS!
I'M SAVING THE WORLD FROM ATOMIC DESTRUCTION! YOU SHOULD BE THANKING ME, NESS!
I THANK YOU FOR SHUTTING THE HELL UP!
R-R-R-R-R-R-R-R-R-R
I KNOW IT'S NOT A HORSE, BUT JUMP IN THE SQUAD CAR AND WE'LL FOLLOW THEM TO THE HOSPITAL, JOHN.
"HORSEPOWER" IS STILL HORSE POWER, MR. NESS.
LET'S RIDE!

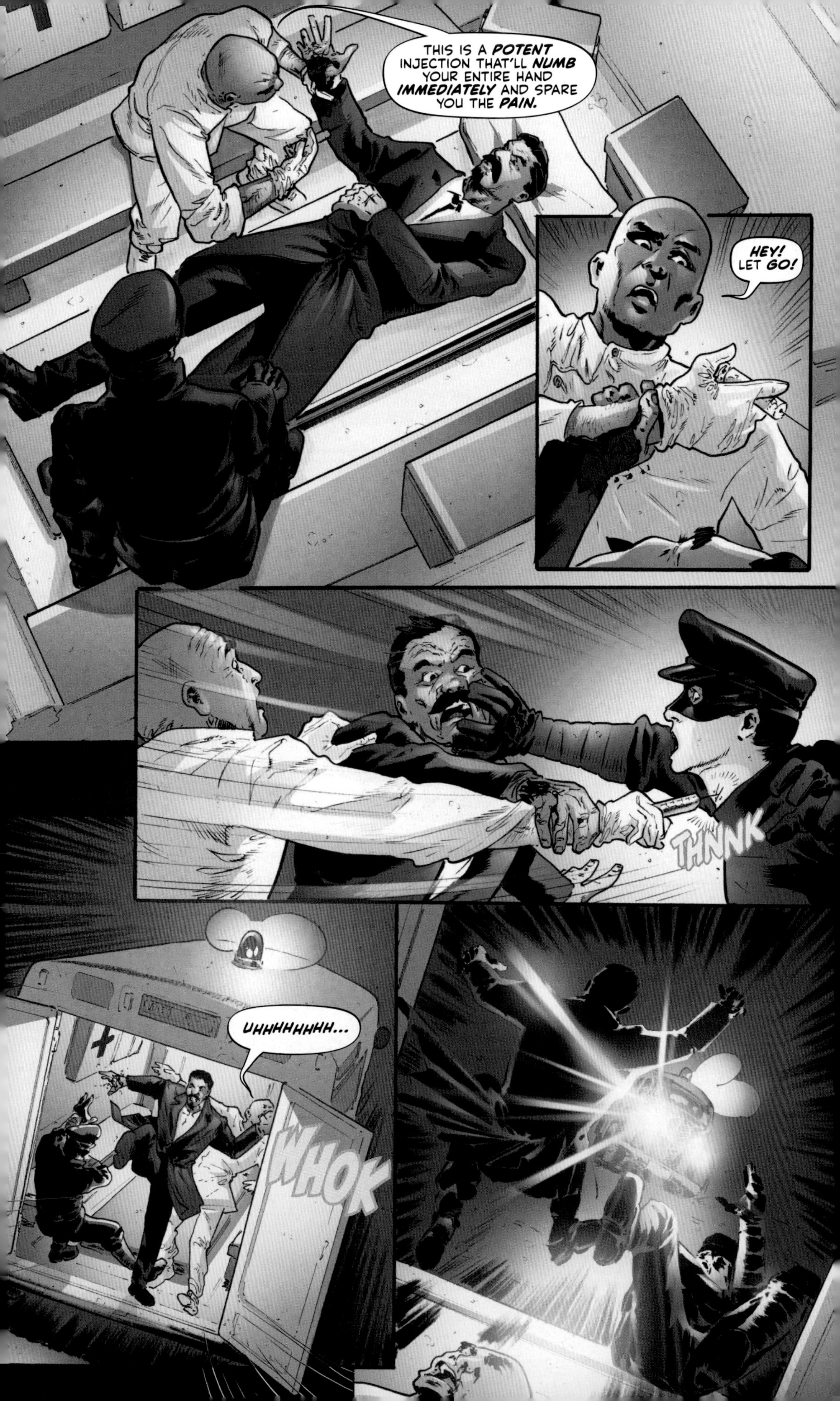
THIS IS A POTENT INJECTION THAT'LL NUMB YOUR ENTIRE HAND IMMEDIATELY AND SPARE YOU THE PAIN.
HEY! LET GO!
THNNK
UHHHHHHHH...
WHOK

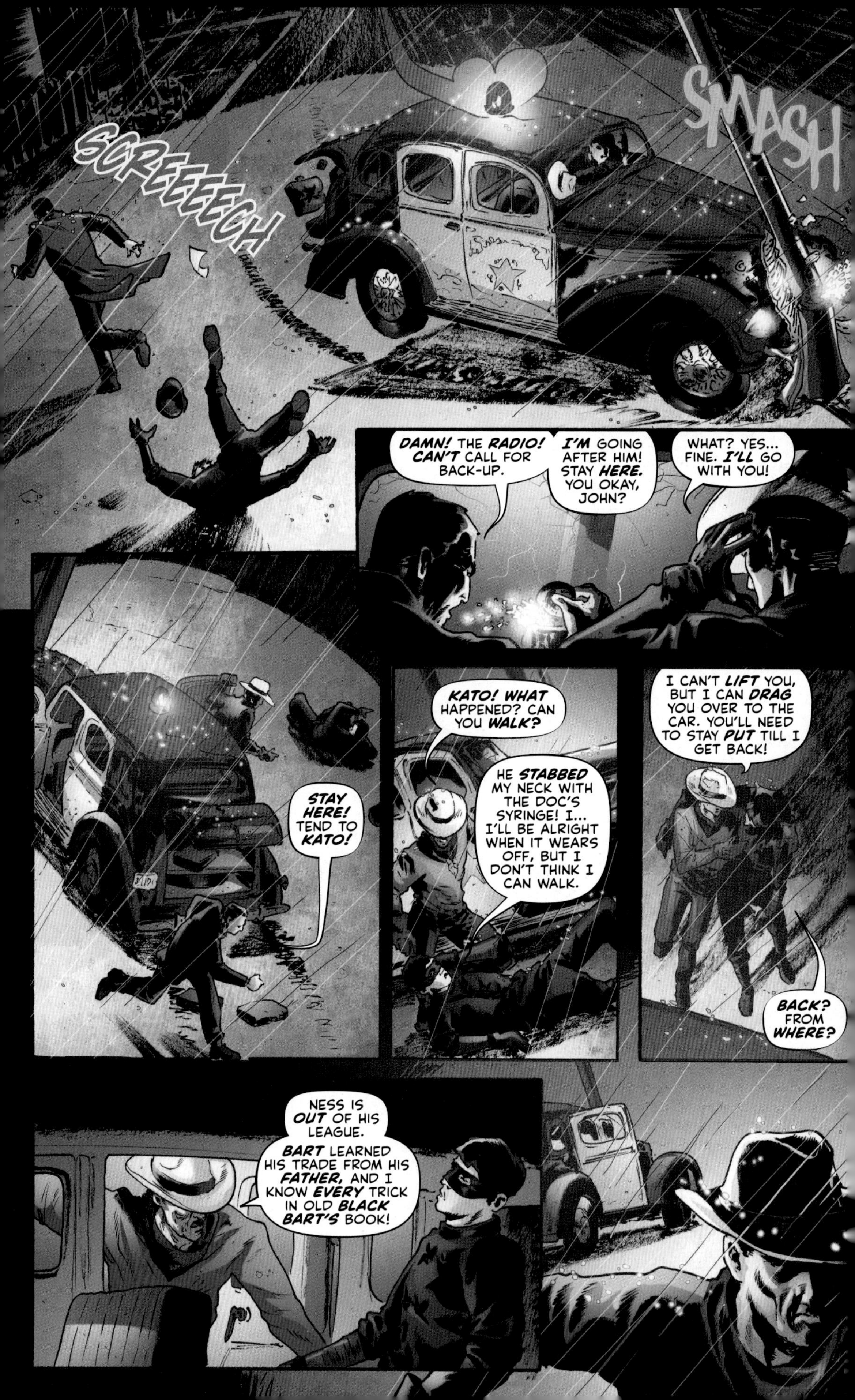
SCREEEEECH
SMASH
DAMN! THE RADIO! CAN'T CALL FOR BACK-UP.
I'M GOING AFTER HIM! STAY HERE. YOU OKAY, JOHN?
WHAT? YES... FINE. I'LL GO WITH YOU!
STAY HERE! TEND TO KATO!
KATO! WHAT HAPPENED? CAN YOU WALK?
HE STABBED MY NECK WITH THE DOC'S SYRINGE! I... I'LL BE ALRIGHT WHEN IT WEARS OFF, BUT I DON'T THINK I CAN WALK.
I CAN'T LIFT YOU, BUT I CAN DRAG YOU OVER TO THE CAR. YOU'LL NEED TO STAY PUT TILL I GET BACK!
BACK? FROM WHERE?
NESS IS OUT OF HIS LEAGUE. BART LEARNED HIS TRADE FROM HIS FATHER, AND I KNOW EVERY TRICK IN OLD BLACK BART'S BOOK!

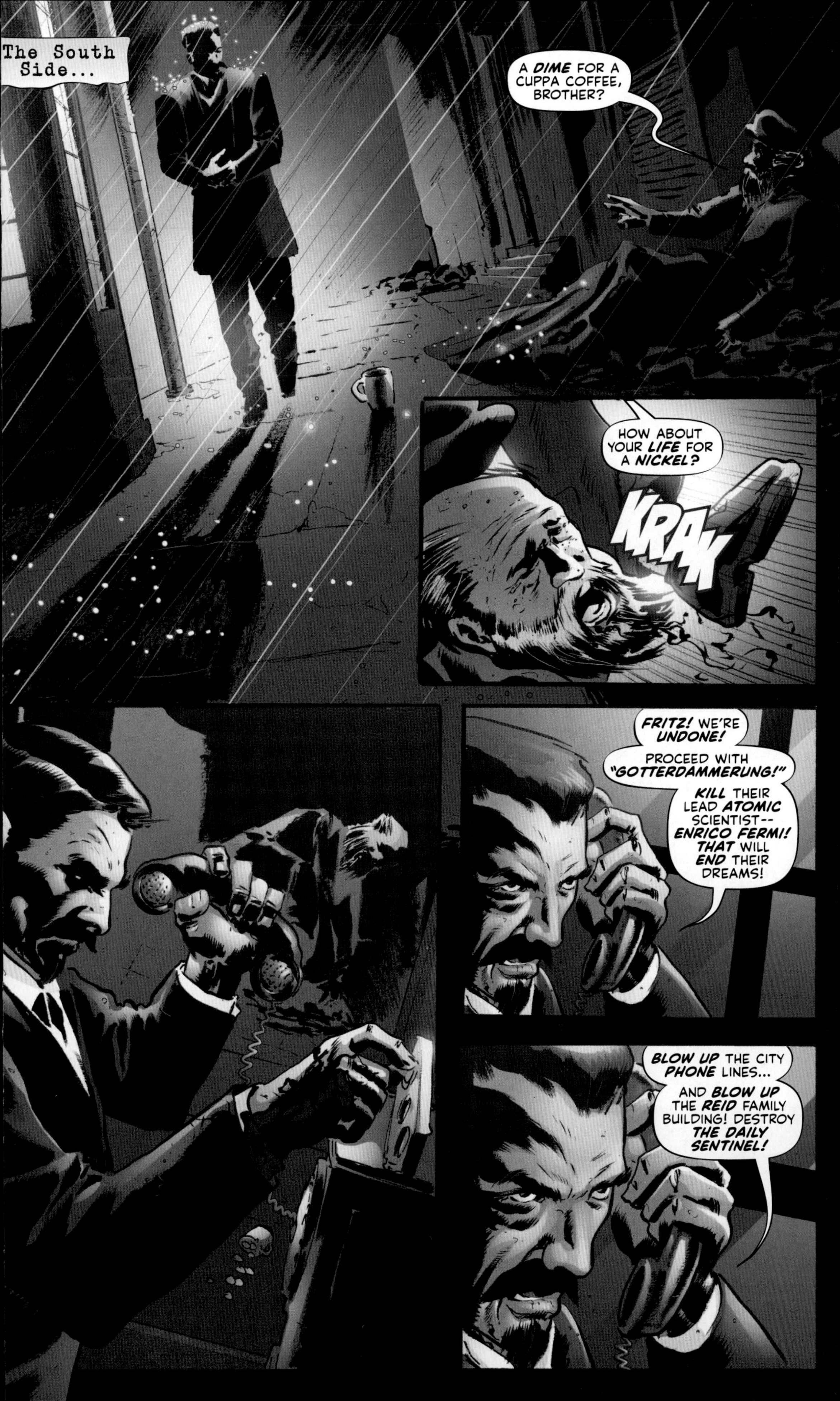

The South Side...
A DIME FOR A CUPPA COFFEE, BROTHER?
HOW ABOUT YOUR LIFE FOR A NICKEL?
KRAK
FRITZ! WE'RE UNDONE!
PROCEED WITH "GOTTERDAMMERUNG!"
KILL THEIR LEAD ATOMIC SCIENTIST-- ENRICO FERMI! THAT WILL END THEIR DREAMS!
BLOW UP THE CITY PHONE LINES...
AND BLOW UP THE REID FAMILY BUILDING! DESTROY THE DAILY SENTINEL!

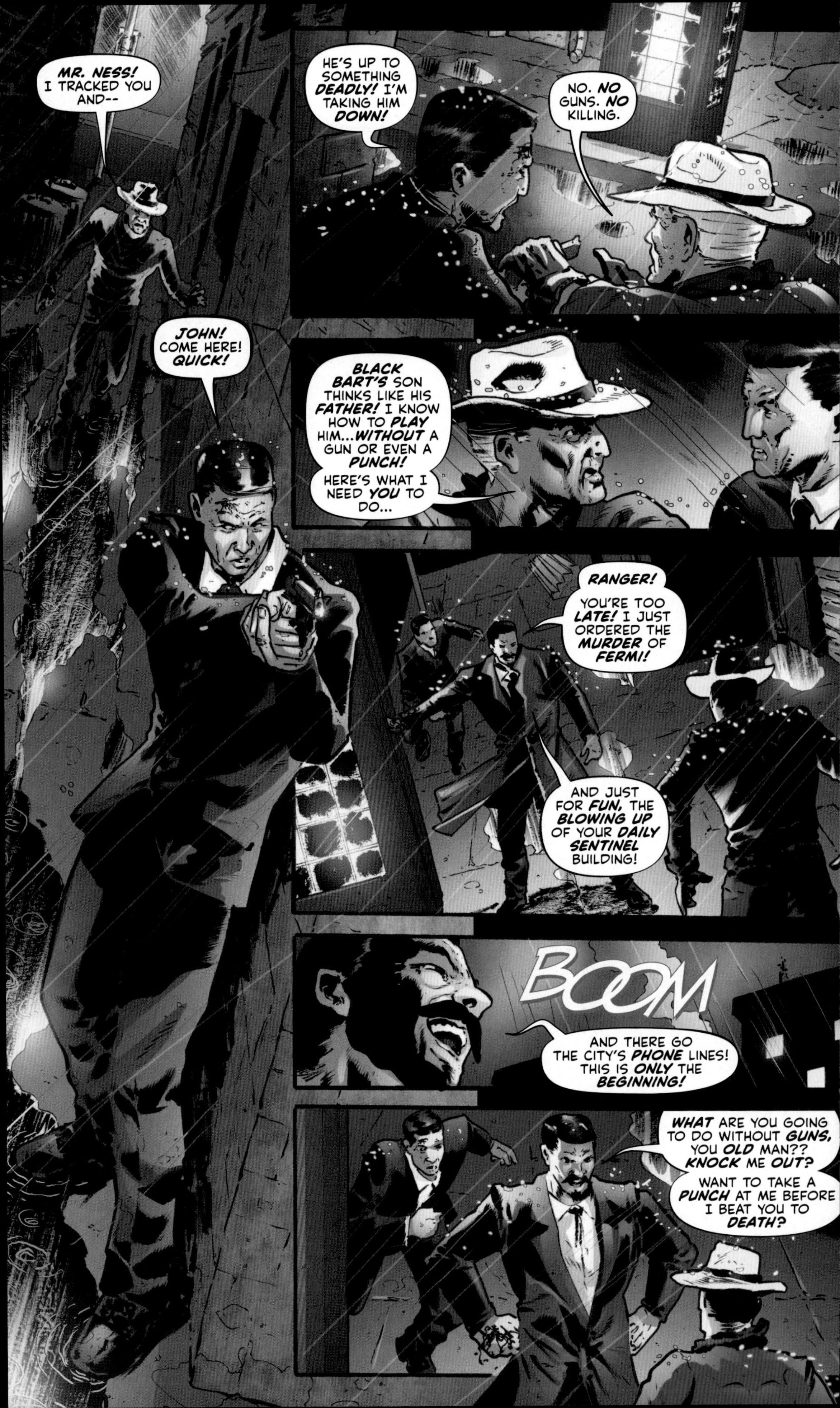
MR. NESS! I TRACKED YOU AND--
HE'S UP TO SOMETHING DEADLY! I'M TAKING HIM DOWN!
NO. NO GUNS. NO KILLING.
JOHN! COME HERE! QUICK!
BLACK BART'S SON THINKS LIKE HIS FATHER! I KNOW HOW TO PLAY HIM...WITHOUT A GUN OR EVEN A PUNCH!
HERE'S WHAT I NEED YOU TO DO...
RANGER!
YOU'RE TOO LATE! I JUST ORDERED THE MURDER OF FERMI!
AND JUST FOR FUN, THE BLOWING UP OF YOUR DAILY SENTINEL BUILDING!
BOOM
AND THERE GO THE CITY'S PHONE LINES! THIS IS ONLY THE BEGINNING!
WHAT ARE YOU GOING TO DO WITHOUT GUNS, YOU OLD MAN?? KNOCK ME OUT?
WANT TO TAKE A PUNCH AT ME BEFORE I BEAT YOU TO DEATH?

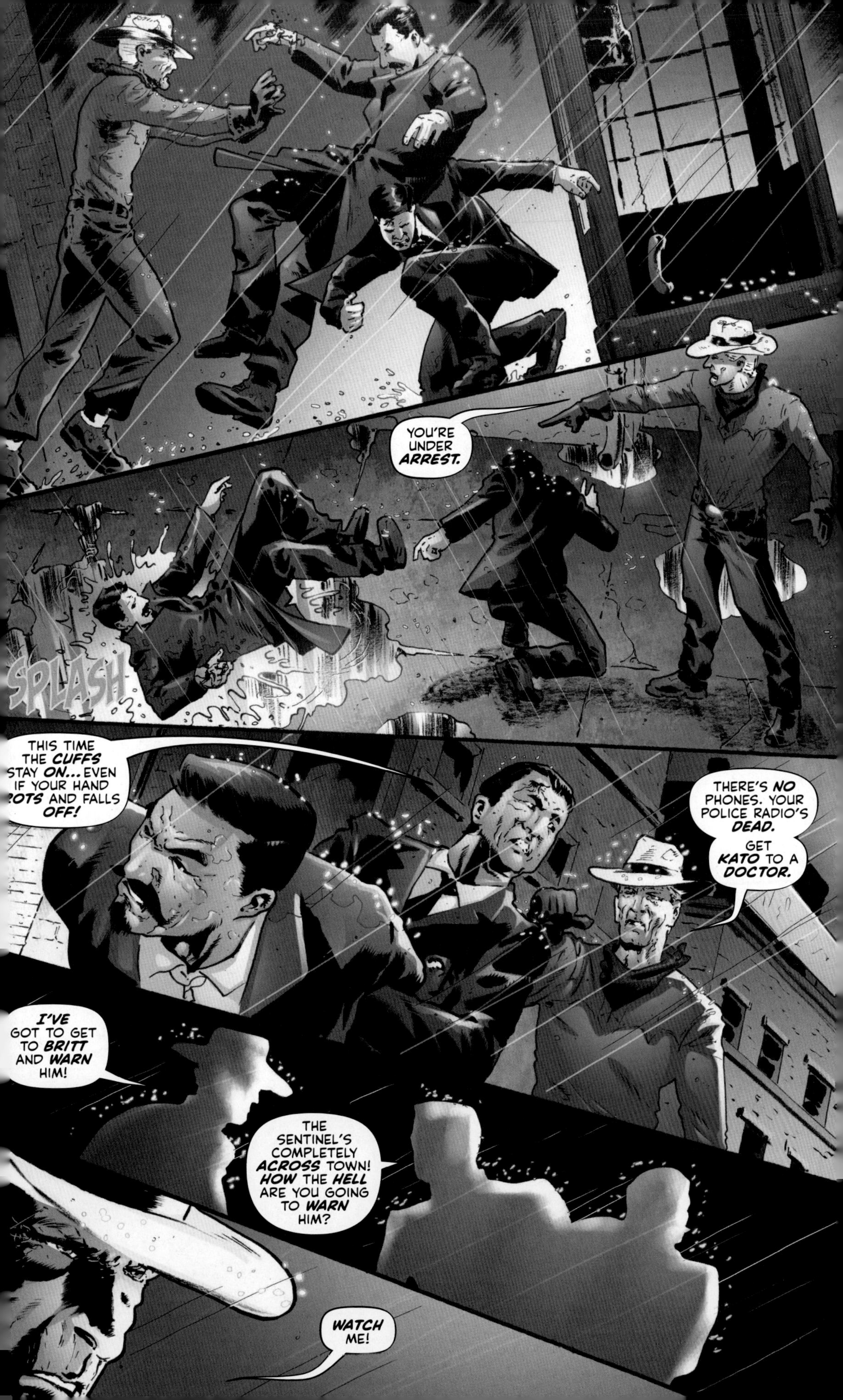

YOU'RE UNDER ARREST.
SPLASH
THIS TIME THE CUFFS STAY ON... EVEN IF YOUR HAND ROTS AND FALLS OFF!
THERE'S NO PHONES. YOUR POLICE RADIO'S DEAD.
GET KATO TO A DOCTOR.
I'VE GOT TO GET TO BRITT AND WARN HIM!
THE SENTINEL'S COMPLETELY ACROSS TOWN! HOW THE HELL ARE YOU GOING TO WARN HIM?
WATCH ME!

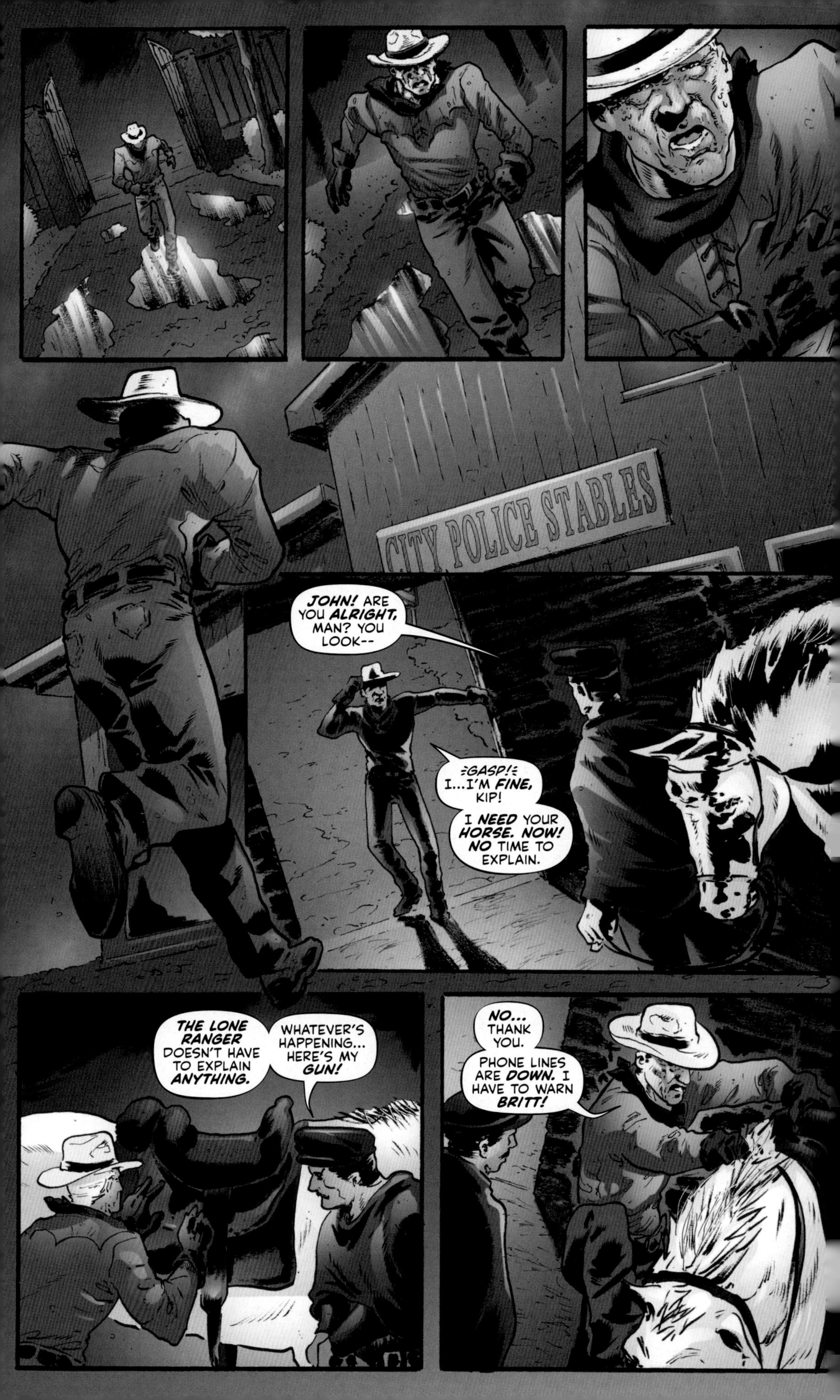
CITY POLICE STABLES
JOHN! ARE YOU ALRIGHT, MAN? YOU LOOK--
GASP! I...I'M FINE, KIP!
I NEED YOUR HORSE. NOW! NO TIME TO EXPLAIN.
THE LONE RANGER DOESN'T HAVE TO EXPLAIN ANYTHING.
WHATEVER'S HAPPENING... HERE'S MY GUN!
NO... THANK YOU.
PHONE LINES ARE DOWN. I HAVE TO WARN BRITT!

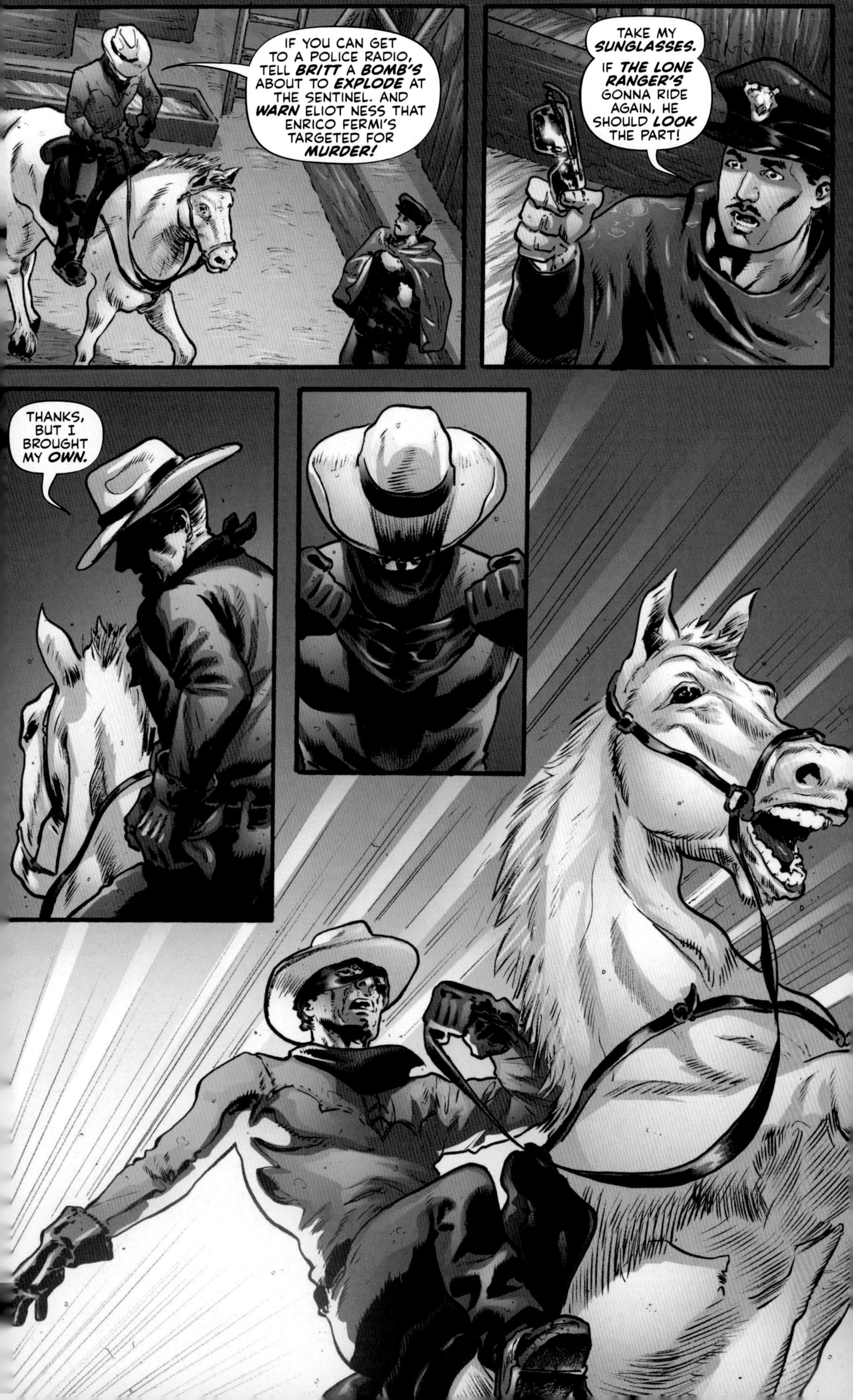
IF YOU CAN GET TO A POLICE RADIO, TELL BRITT A BOMB'S ABOUT TO EXPLODE AT THE SENTINEL. AND WARN ELIOT NESS THAT ENRICO FERMI'S TARGETED FOR MURDER!
TAKE MY SUNGLASSES.
IF THE LONE RANGER'S GONNA RIDE AGAIN, HE SHOULD LOOK THE PART!
THANKS, BUT I BROUGHT MY OWN.

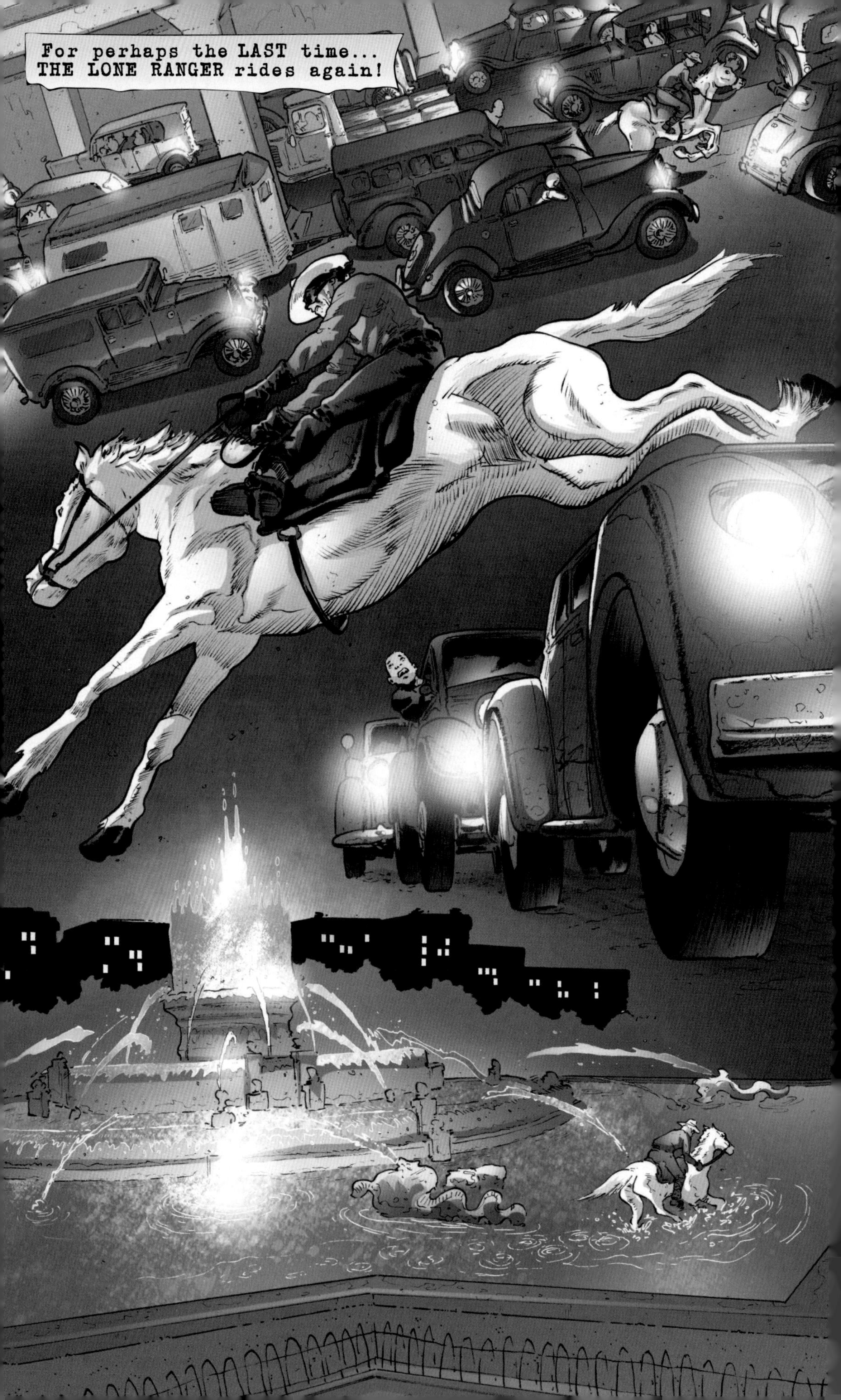
For perhaps the LAST time... THE LONE RANGER rides again!

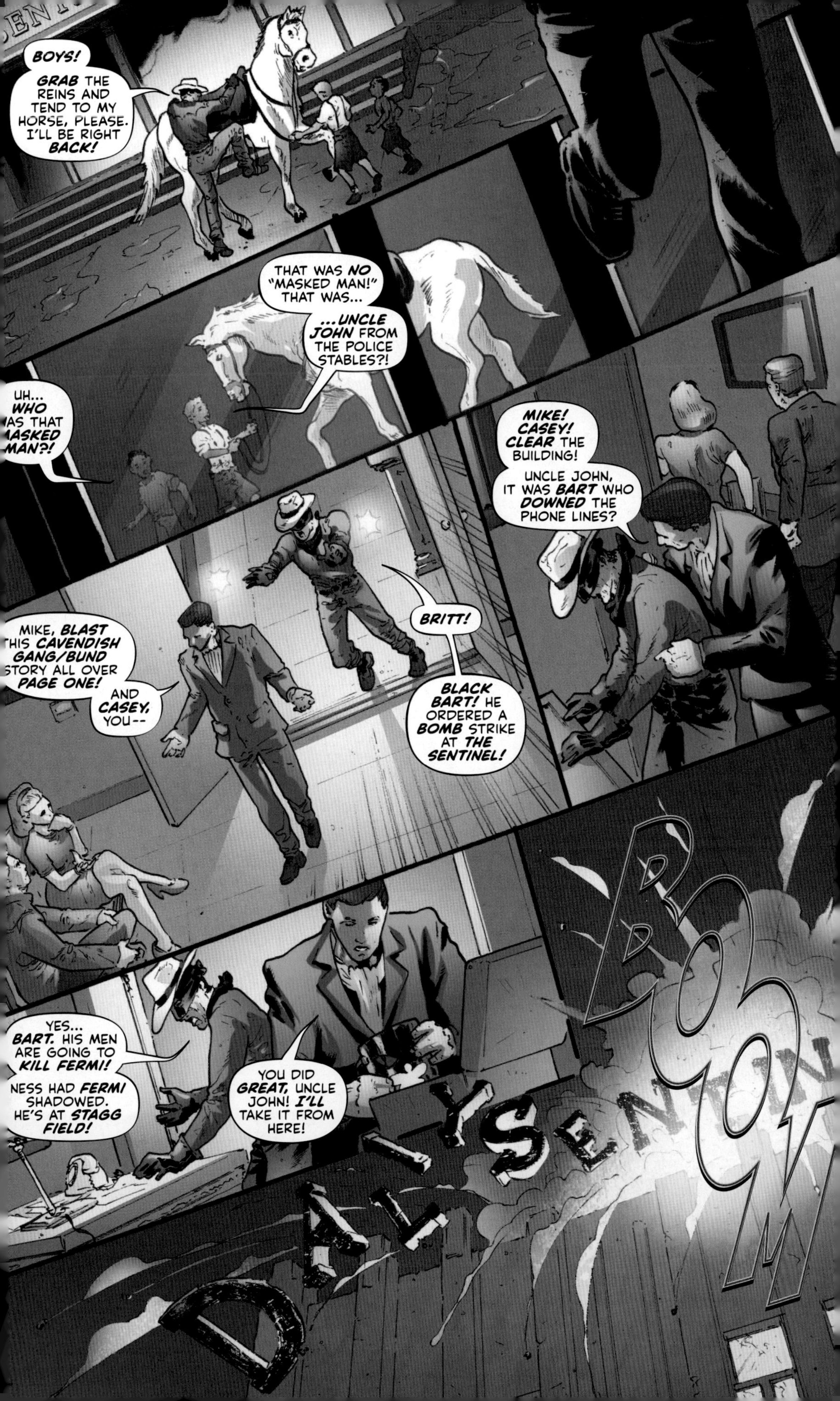

BOYS!
GRAB THE REINS AND TEND TO MY HORSE, PLEASE. I'LL BE RIGHT BACK!
THAT WAS NO "MASKED MAN!" THAT WAS...
...UNCLE JOHN FROM THE POLICE STABLES?!
UH... WHO WAS THAT MASKED MAN?!
MIKE! CASEY! CLEAR THE BUILDING!
UNCLE JOHN, IT WAS BART WHO DOWNED THE PHONE LINES?
BRITT!
BLACK BART! HE ORDERED A BOMB STRIKE AT THE SENTINEL!
MIKE, BLAST THIS CAVENDISH GANG/BUND STORY ALL OVER PAGE ONE!
AND CASEY, YOU--
YES... BART. HIS MEN ARE GOING TO KILL FERMI!
NESS HAD FERMI SHADOWED. HE'S AT STAGG FIELD!
YOU DID GREAT, UNCLE JOHN! I'LL TAKE IT FROM HERE!
BOOOM
DAILY SENTIN

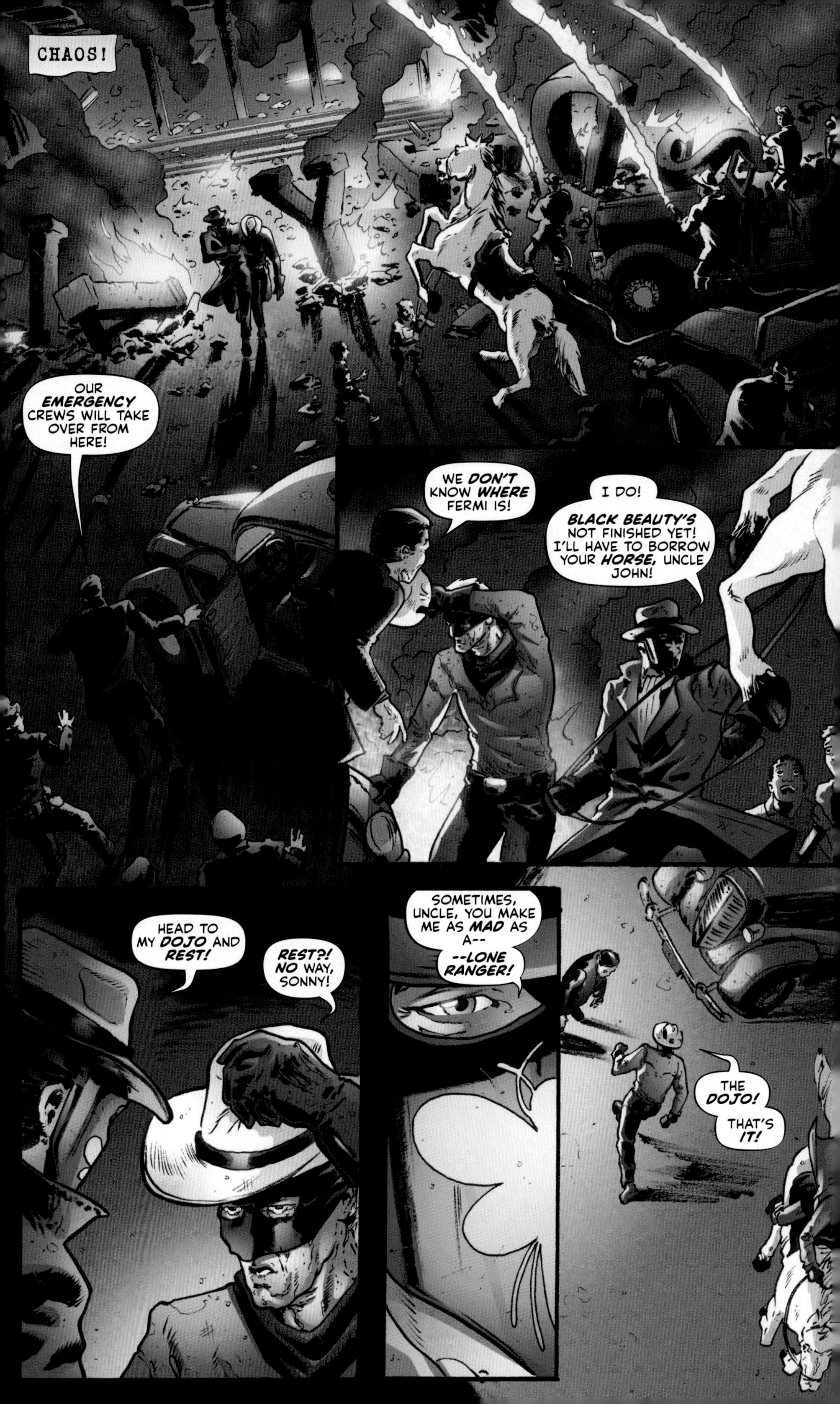
CHAOS!
OUR EMERGENCY CREWS WILL TAKE OVER FROM HERE!
WE DON'T KNOW WHERE FERMI IS!
I DO!
BLACK BEAUTY'S NOT FINISHED YET! I'LL HAVE TO BORROW YOUR HORSE, UNCLE JOHN!
HEAD TO MY DOJO AND REST!
REST?! NO WAY, SONNY!
SOMETIMES, UNCLE, YOU MAKE ME AS MAD AS A--
--LONE RANGER!
THE DOJO!
THAT'S IT!

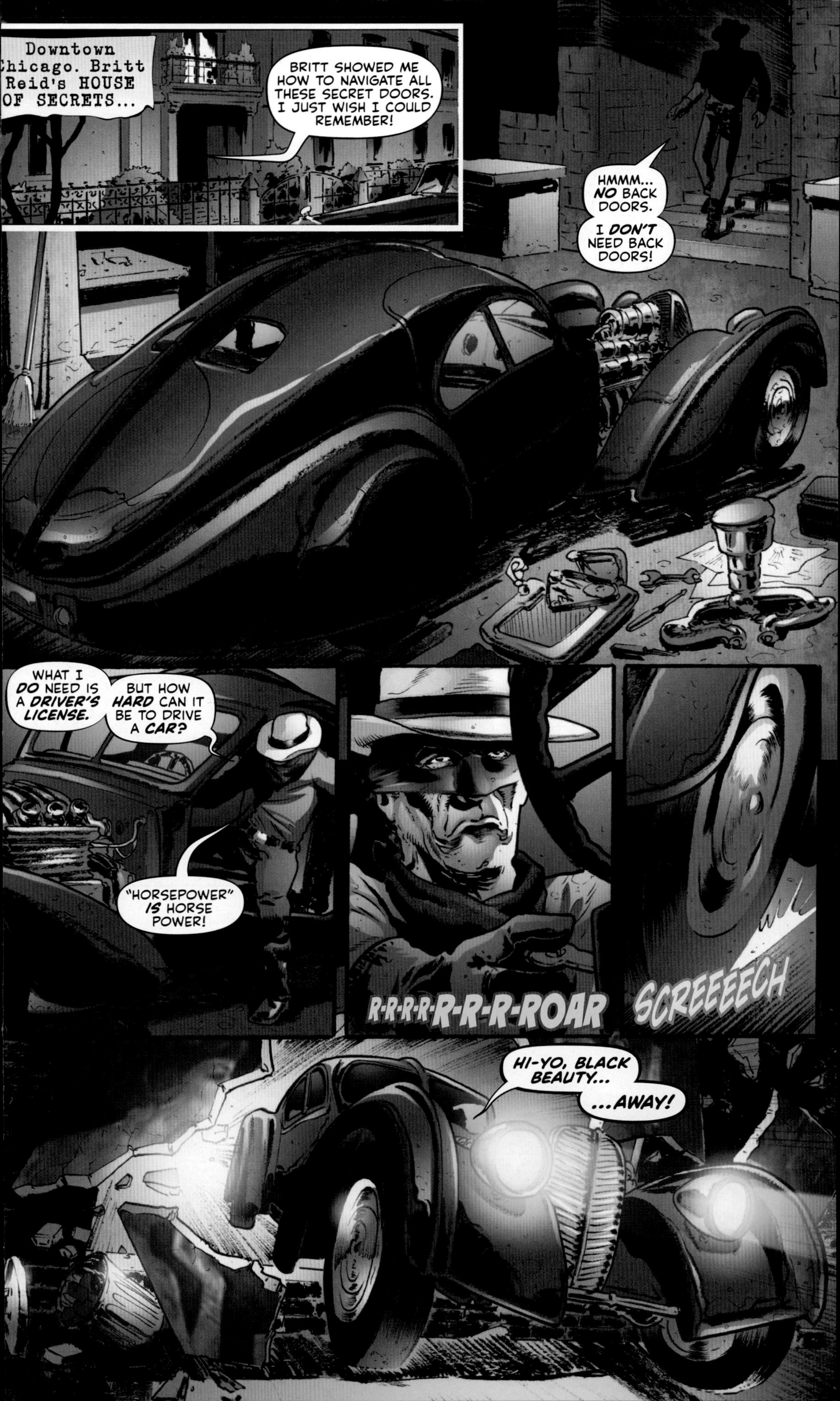
Downtown Chicago. Britt Reid's HOUSE OF SECRETS...
BRITT SHOWED ME HOW TO NAVIGATE ALL THESE SECRET DOORS. I JUST WISH I COULD REMEMBER!
HMMM... NO BACK DOORS.
I DON'T NEED BACK DOORS!
WHAT I DO NEED IS A DRIVER'S LICENSE.
BUT HOW HARD CAN IT BE TO DRIVE A CAR?
"HORSEPOWER" IS HORSE POWER!
R-R-R-R-R-R-R-ROAR
SCREEEECH
HI-YO, BLACK BEAUTY...
...AWAY!

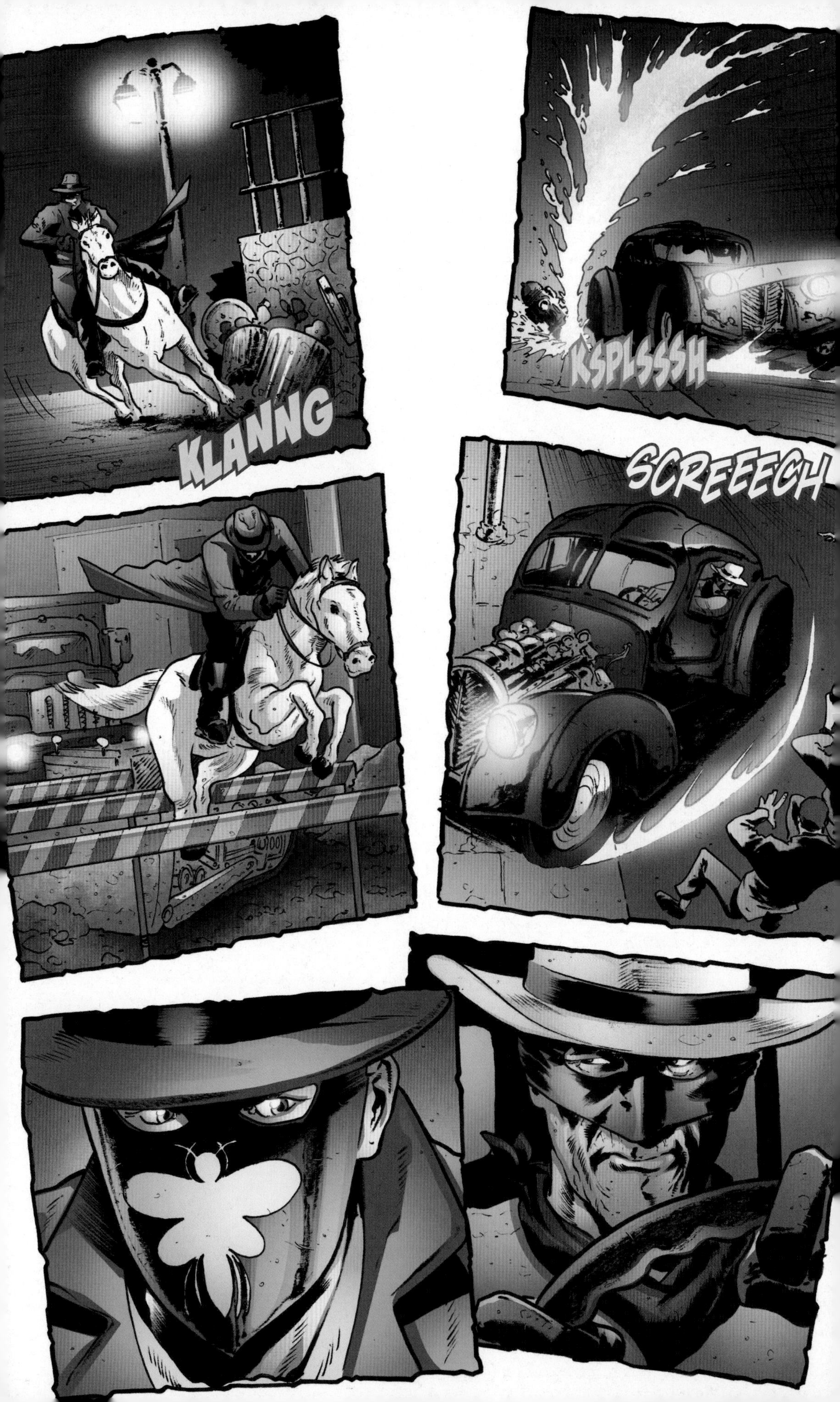
KLANNG
KSPLSSSH
SCREEECH

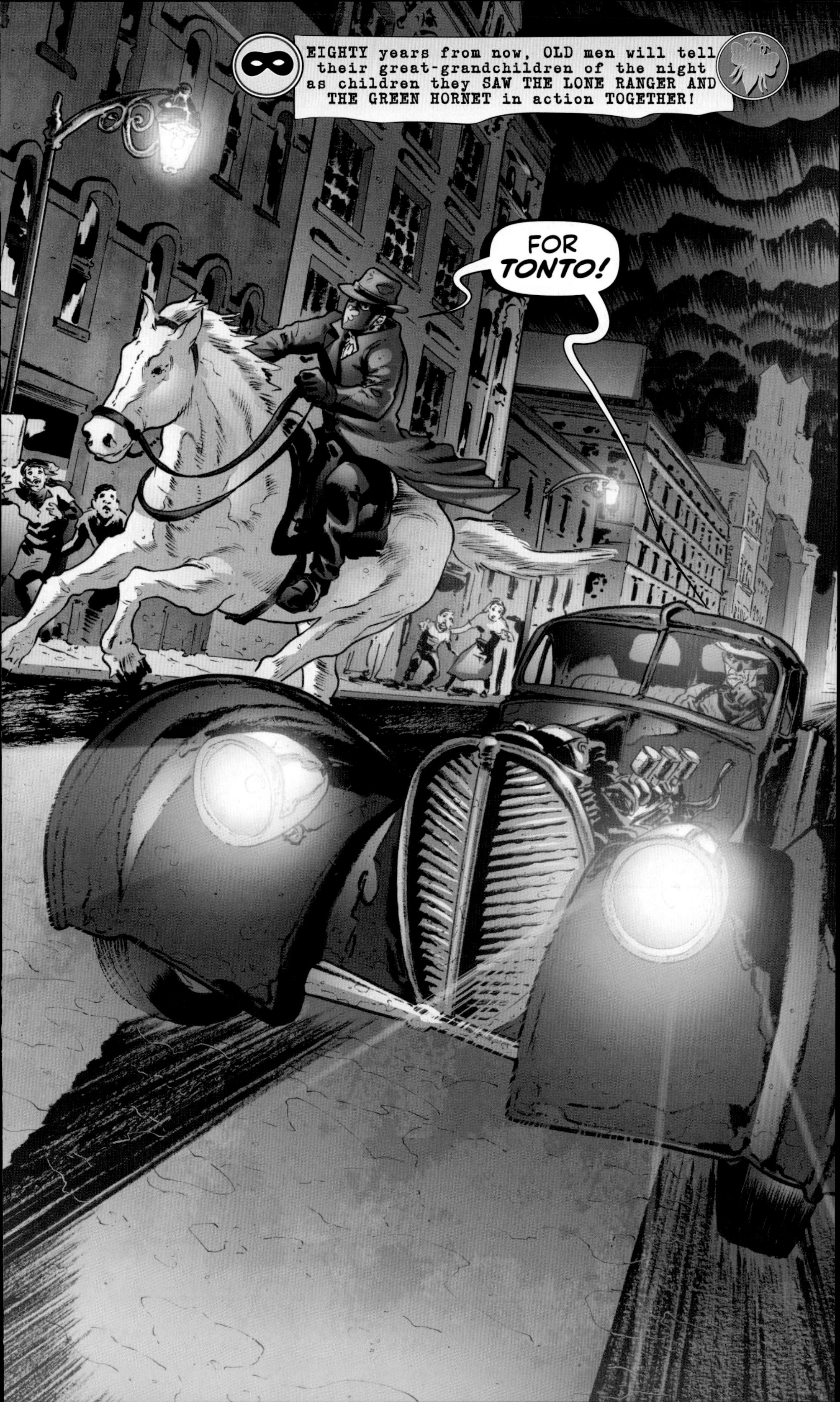
EIGHTY years from now, OLD men will tell their great-grandchildren of the night as children they SAW THE LONE RANGER AND THE GREEN HORNET in action TOGETHER!
FOR TONTO!

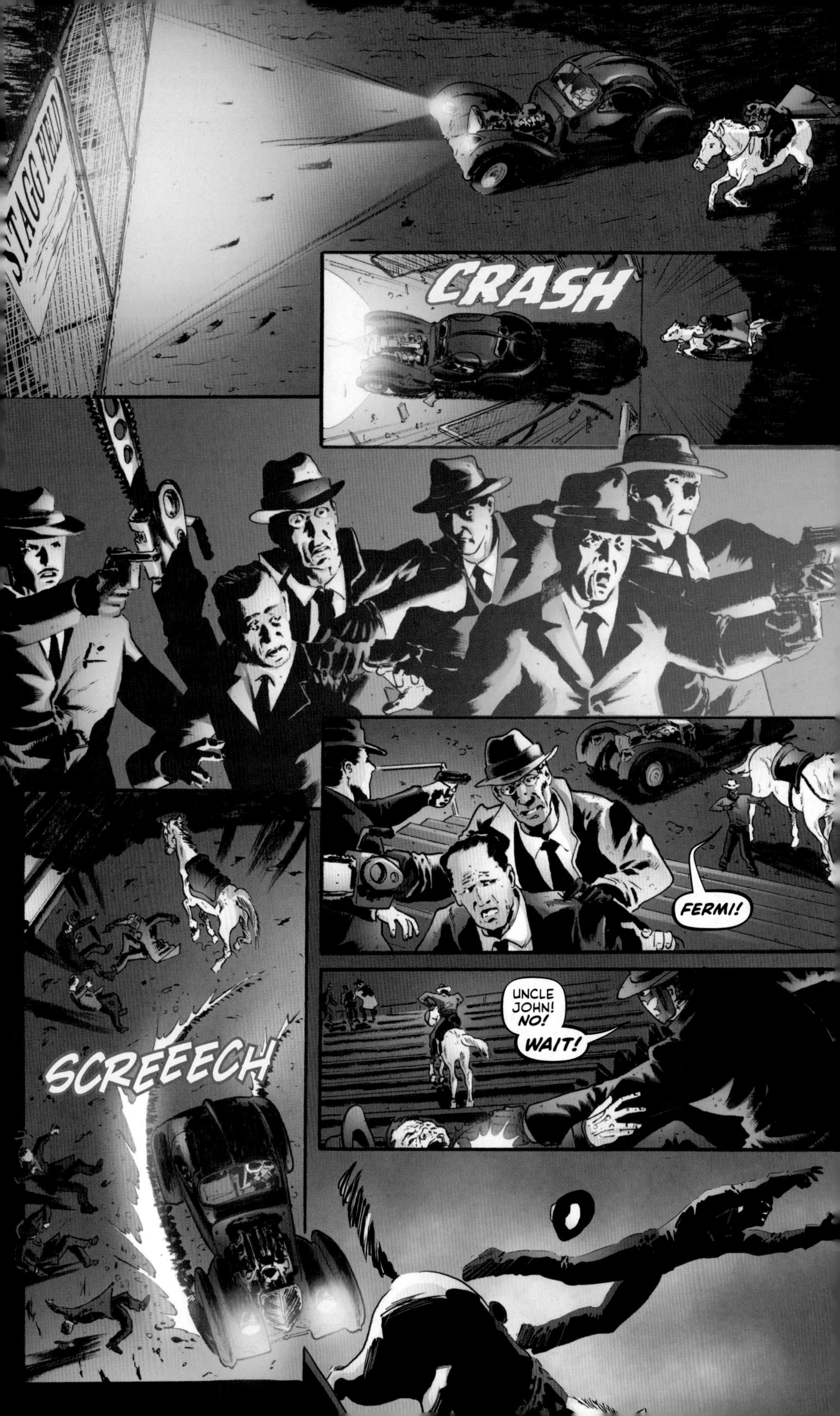
STAGG FIELD
CRASH
FERMI!
UNCLE JOHN! NO!
WAIT!
SCREEECH

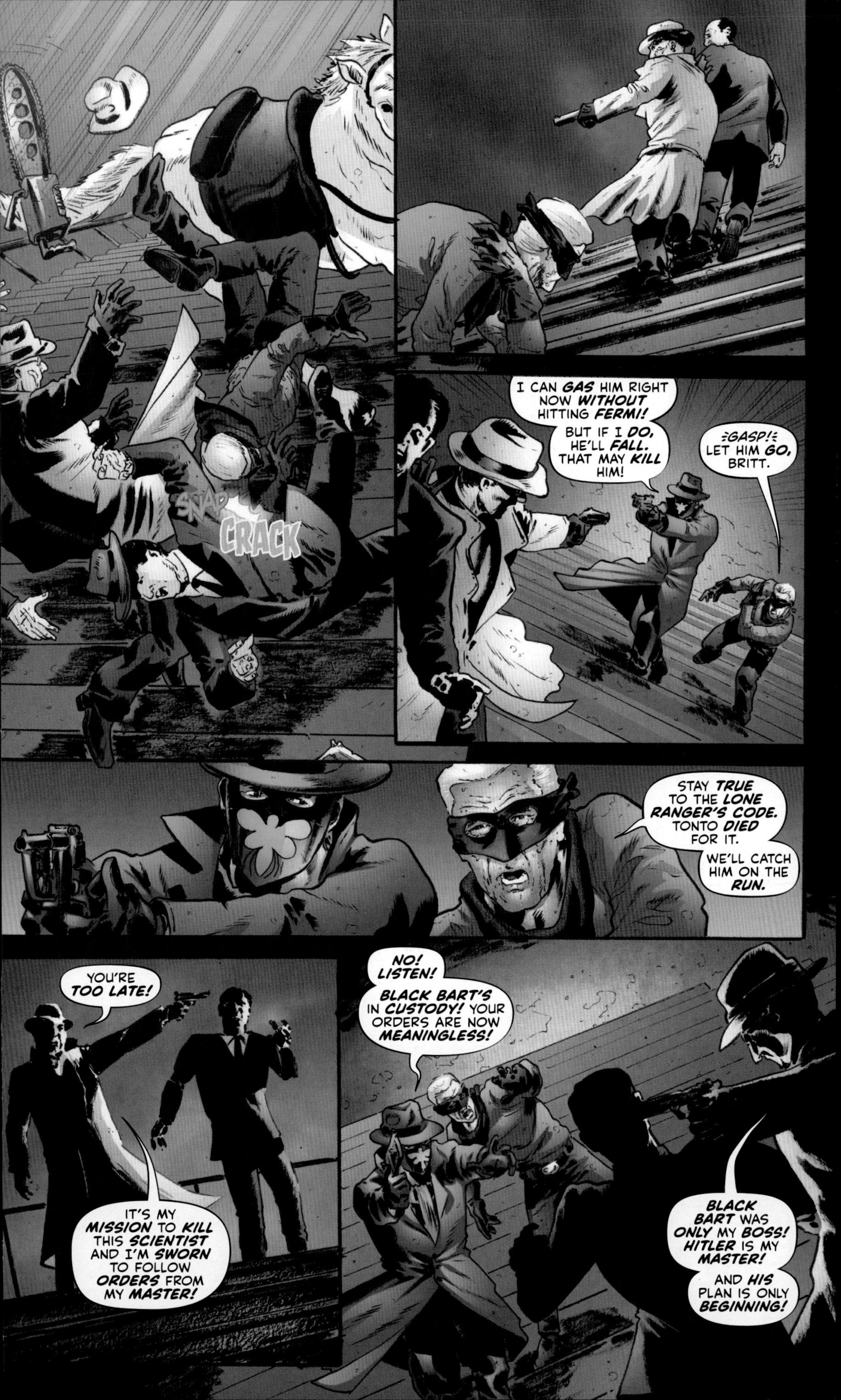
SNAP
CRACK
I CAN GAS HIM RIGHT NOW WITHOUT HITTING FERMI!
BUT IF I DO, HE'LL FALL. THAT MAY KILL HIM!
GASP! LET HIM GO, BRITT.
STAY TRUE TO THE LONE RANGER'S CODE. TONTO DIED FOR IT.
WE'LL CATCH HIM ON THE RUN.
YOU'RE TOO LATE!
IT'S MY MISSION TO KILL THIS SCIENTIST AND I'M SWORN TO FOLLOW ORDERS FROM MY MASTER!
NO! LISTEN!
BLACK BART'S IN CUSTODY! YOUR ORDERS ARE NOW MEANINGLESS!
BLACK BART WAS ONLY MY BOSS! HITLER IS MY MASTER!
AND HIS PLAN IS ONLY BEGINNING!

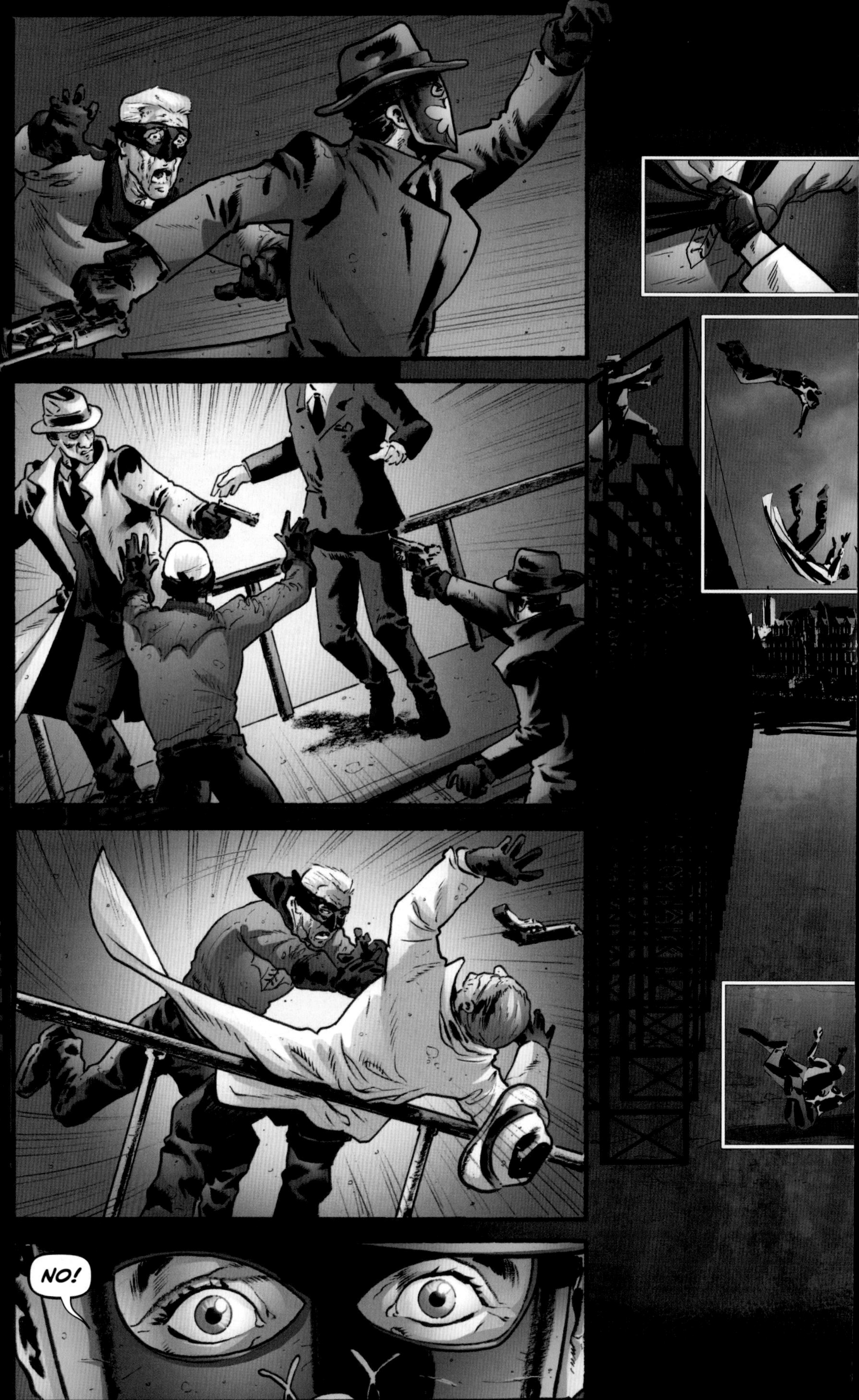
NO!

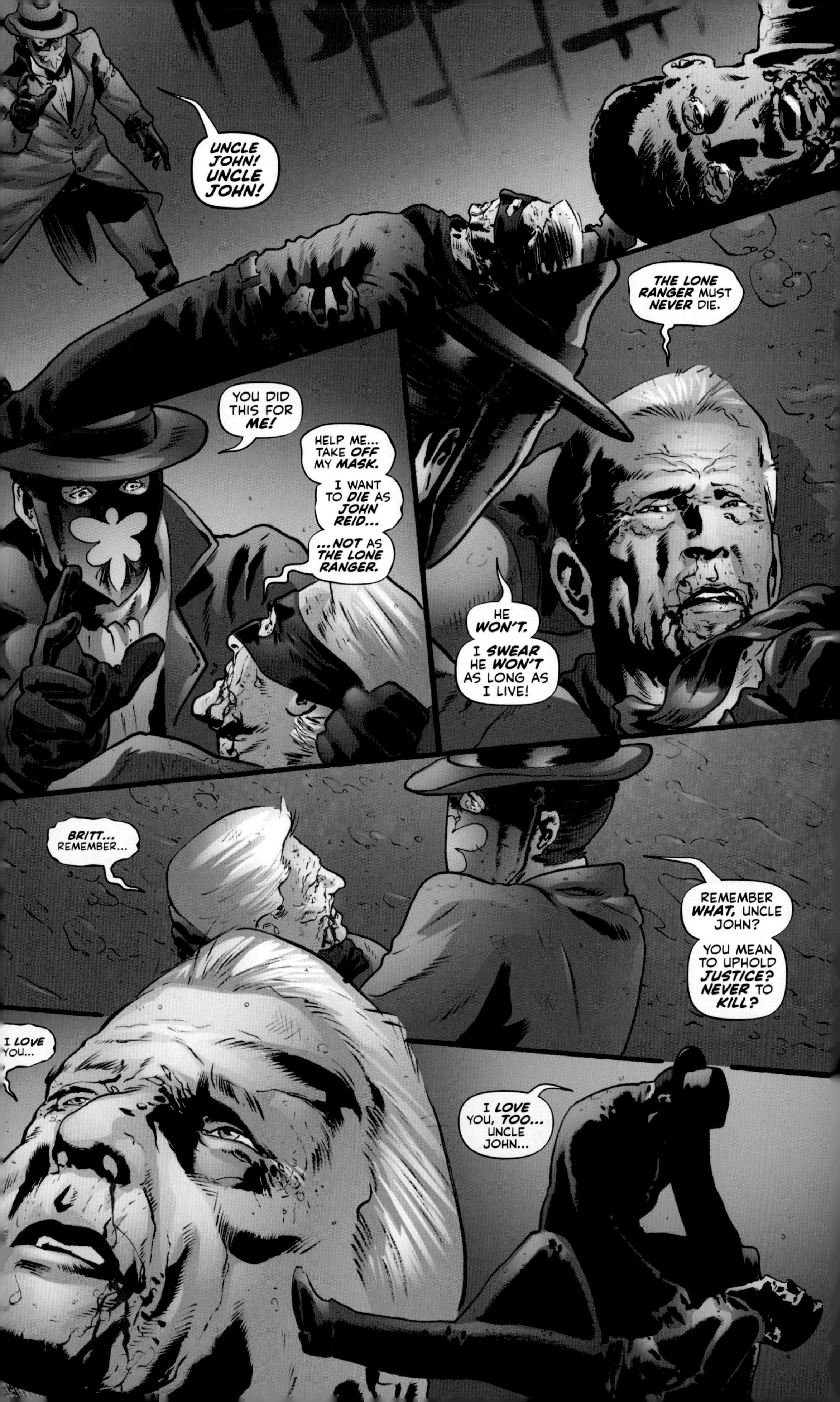
UNCLE JOHN! UNCLE JOHN!
THE LONE RANGER MUST NEVER DIE.
YOU DID THIS FOR ME!
HELP ME... TAKE OFF MY MASK.
I WANT TO DIE AS JOHN REID...
...NOT AS THE LONE RANGER.
HE WON'T.
I SWEAR HE WON'T AS LONG AS I LIVE!
BRITT... REMEMBER...
REMEMBER WHAT, UNCLE JOHN?
YOU MEAN TO UPHOLD JUSTICE? NEVER TO KILL?
I LOVE YOU...
I LOVE YOU, TOO... UNCLE JOHN...

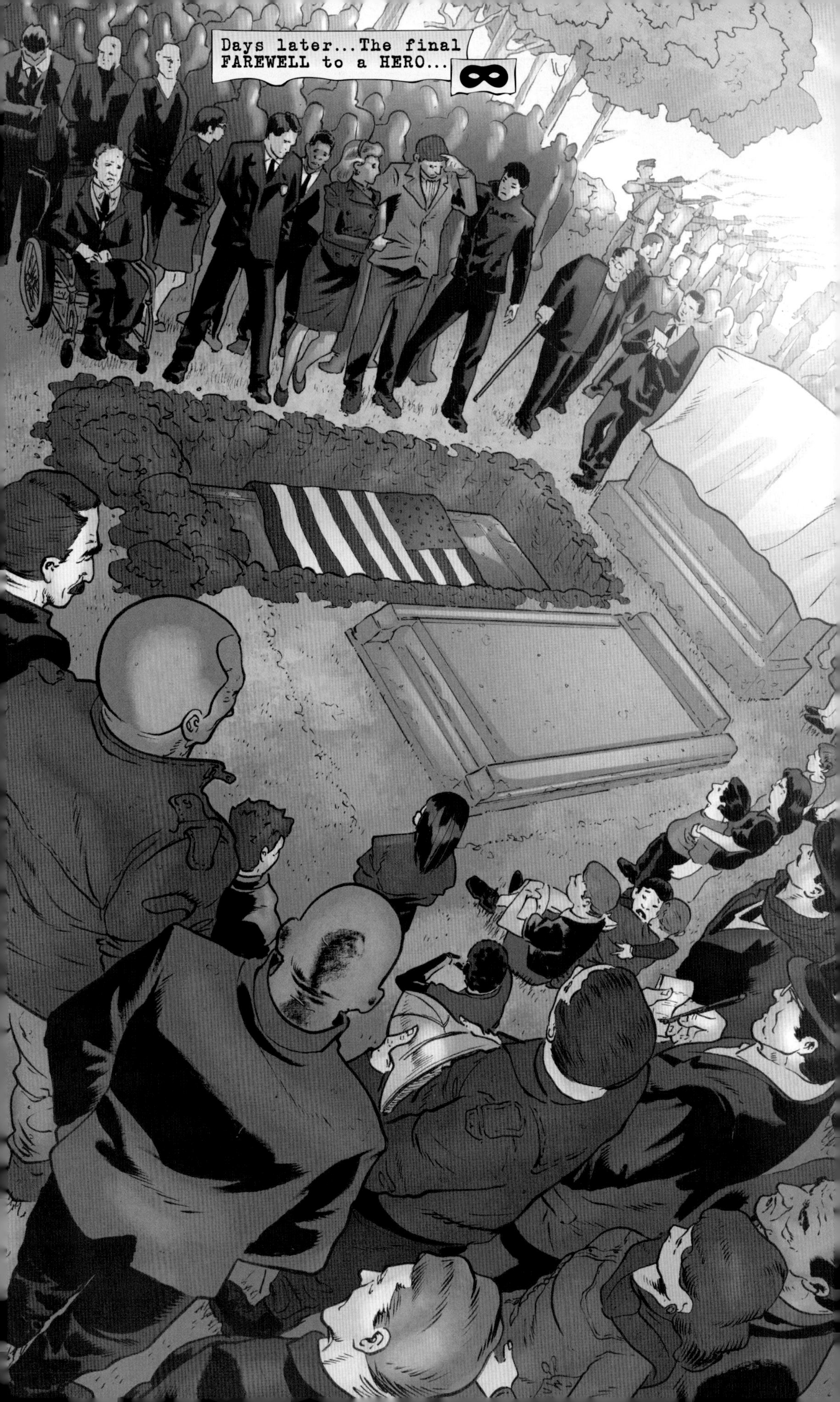
Days later...The final FAREWELL to a HERO...

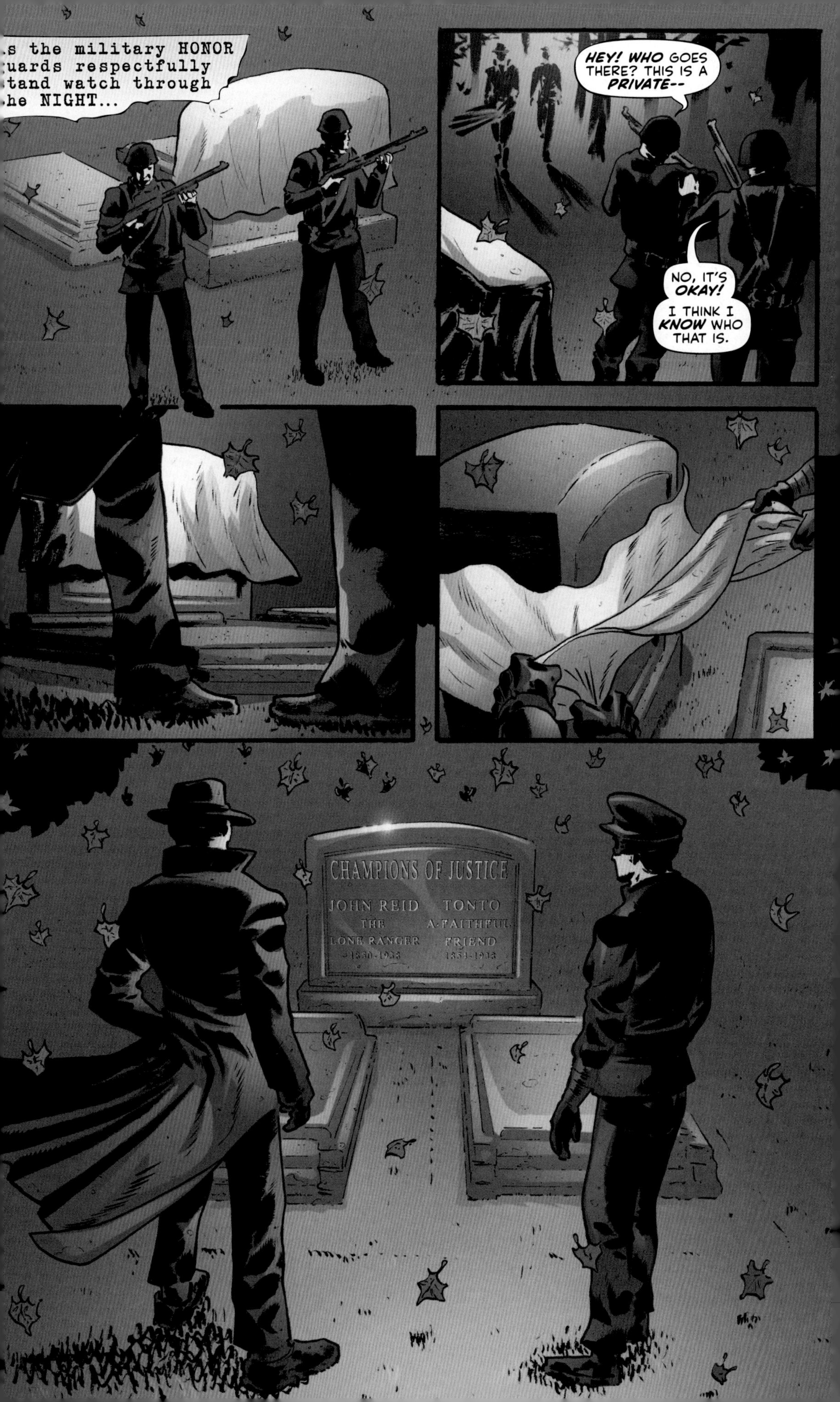

s the military HONOR uards respectfully tand watch through he NIGHT...
HEY! WHO GOES THERE? THIS IS A PRIVATE--
NO, IT'S OKAY!
I THINK I KNOW WHO THAT IS.
CHAMPIONS OF JUSTICE
JOHN REID THE LONE RANGER
TONTO A FAITHFUL FRIEND

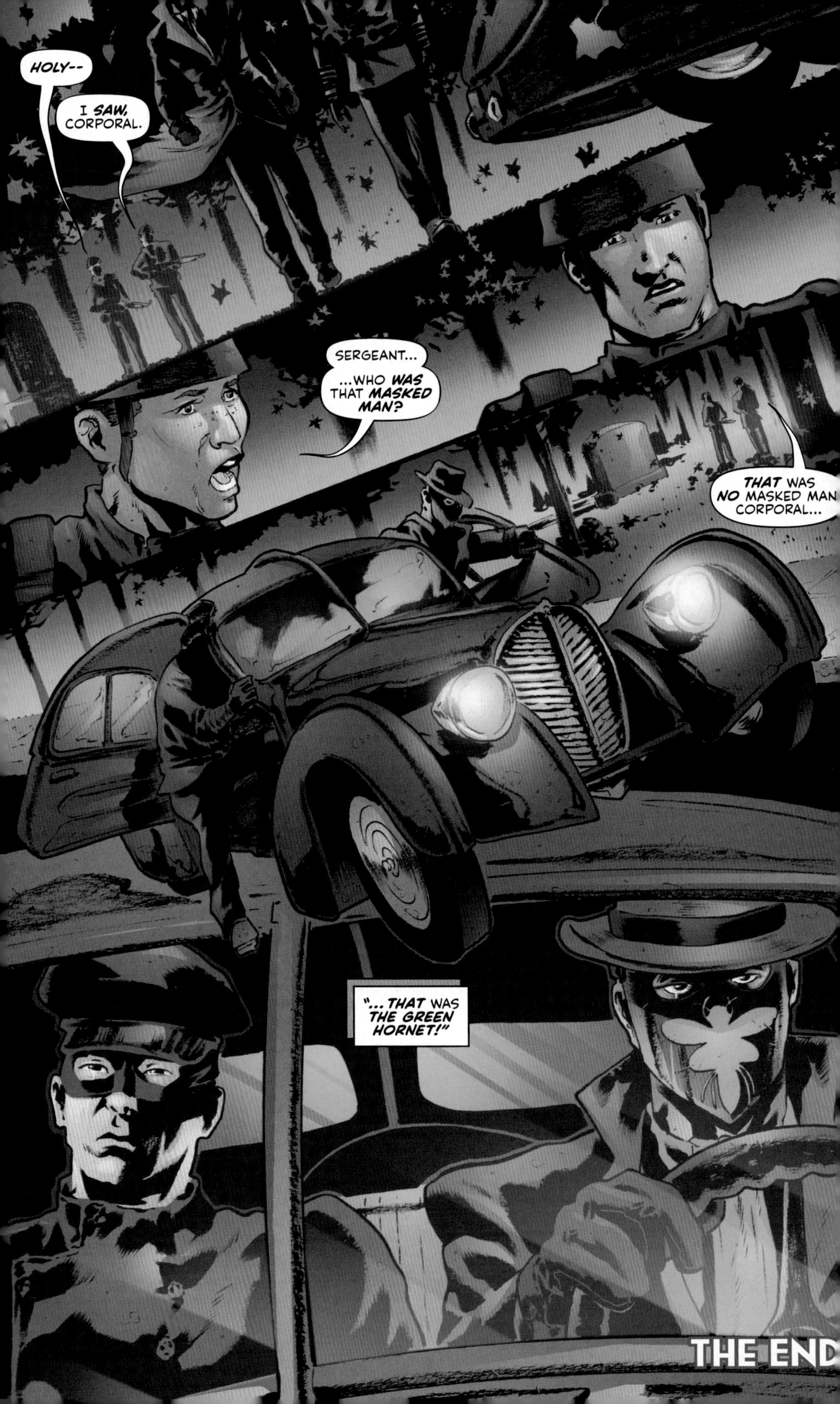
HOLY--
I SAW, CORPORAL.
SERGEANT...
...WHO WAS THAT MASKED MAN?
THAT WAS NO MASKED MAN CORPORAL...
"...THAT WAS THE GREEN HORNET!"
THE END

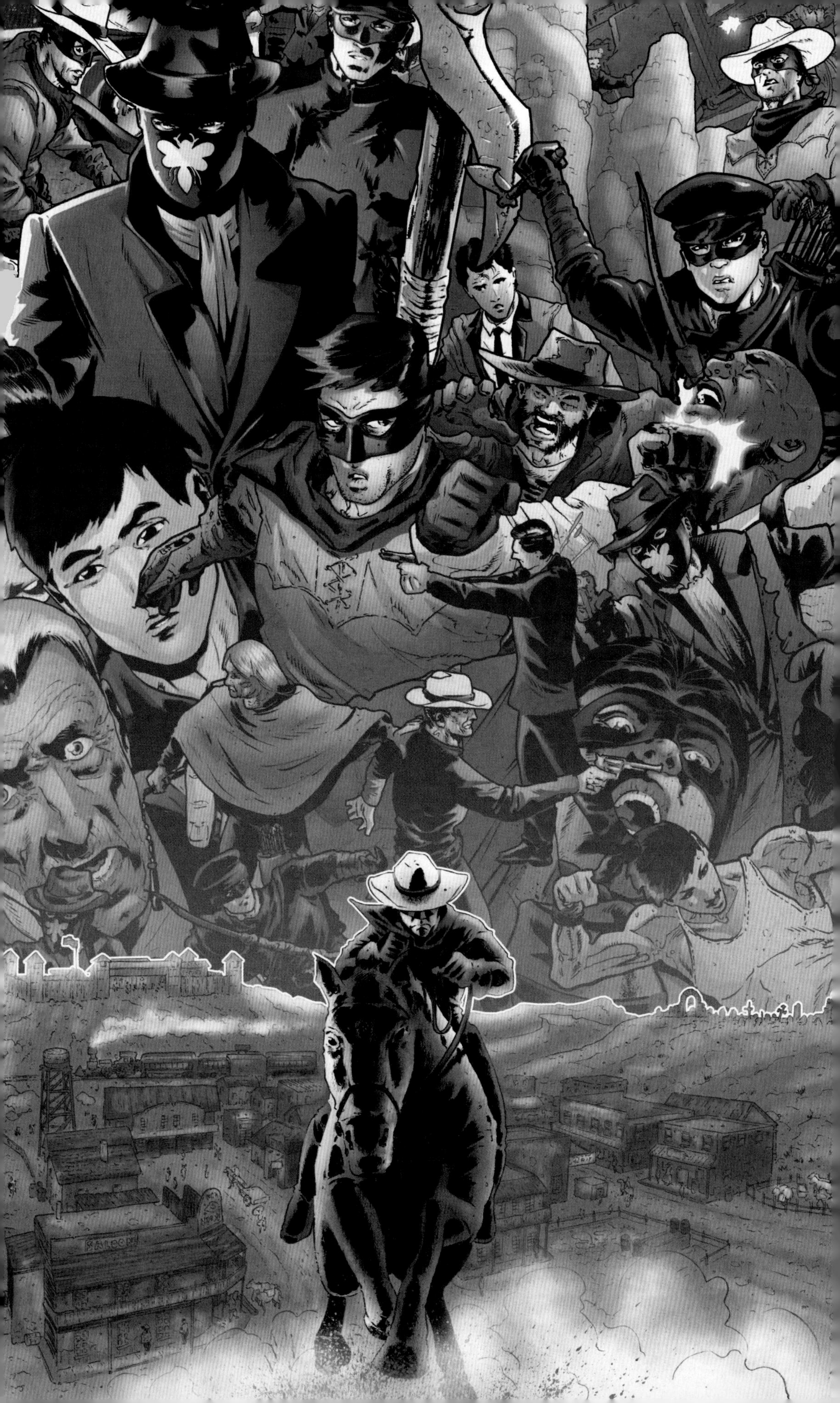

THE LONE RANGER GREEN HORNET

FOOTNOTES TO HISTORY
By Michael Uslan

Issue 1

Page 2: The posters are correct. The Presidential election of 1936 was between Franklin D. Roosevelt and Alf Landon, and those were their respective campaign slogans.

Page 2: How lucky for us that the Fireman's Brigade Band was starting their concert this day with Rossini's "William Tell Overture," which coincidentally happens to be the immortal theme song to "The Lone Ranger." That song was chosen by George W. Trendle, owner of the radio station WXYZ-Detroit and owner of "The Lone Ranger" because he didn't want to spend the money for an original theme and ordered classical music that was in the public domain.

Page 10: For the full story of Britt Reid's "meanderings" around the world on his journey of self-discovery, which led to his meeting Kato, read the fabulous *Green Hornet: Year One* Volumes 1 and 2. This very scene is right there on page 123 of Volume 1.

Page 18: Eliot Ness was one of the most famous law enforcement men of the 20th Century in America. In a time and place of great corruption (i.e. Chicago), he and his squad of eleven men were considered to be "Untouchables." Among many accomplishments, Ness helped put Mafia kingpin Al Capone in prison. After Chicago, Ness moved to Cleveland where, as its Director for Public Safety, he had to deal with the grisly, unsolved Cleveland Torso Murders involving decapitated and sometimes sawed-in-half torsos.

Page 20-22: Yes, the Nazi Bund was active and a real threat inside America beginning in 1936. Led by hate-monger, Fritz Kuhn, the Bund was based in New York City with secret "training camps" from New York and New Jersey to Pennsylvania and Wisconsin. Their primary targets were Jews and President Franklin D. Roosevelt and their socio-political poison culminated in a rally of 20,000 people at Madison Square Garden in 1939 that erupted in violence

between the Bund's storm-troopers and American protesters. According to Captain America's co-creator, Joe Simon, it was the Bund in New York that threatened him and Jack Kirby and Timely Comics when "Captain America" #1 was published showing Cap punching Adolf Hitler on the cover. The Bund organized Nazi protests in front of the McGraw-Hill Building on West 42nd Street where Timely had their offices.

Issue 2

PAGE 1, PANEL 1: McSorley's still stands in downtown New York City, having first done business there in the mid-1800's, and, yes, Teddy Roosevelt was a patron (the third U.S. President to drink there, following Abraham Lincoln and Ulysses Grant.)

PAGE 1, PANEL 2: Everyone here was a REAL person, with the possible exception of The Lone Ranger. This date in January 1917 is very important because all of these historical figures connected to the Old West were still alive. Former President and Rough Rider, Teddy Roosevelt was two years from his death. Bat Masterson was living in the City and actually writing for "The New York Telegraph," covering sporting events like boxing, politics, and more. At this moment, he was four years from his demise. He was the subject of an NBC TV series beginning in 1958. Buffalo Bill Cody had kept the good old days alive with his famous "Wild West Shows," featuring such legends as Annie Oakley and Chief Sitting Bull. By January 1917, the show was gone, and in ten days from this gathering, Buffalo Bill would be gone, too. Sheriff Wyatt Earp, hero of the infamous gunfight at the O.K. Corral, was twelve years from his death, and thirty-eight years from the TV series based on his life and legend. Annie Oakley, possibly the greatest sharp-shooter in history, was a star of Buffalo Bill's Wild West Show. By 1917, she had incurred a devastating leg injury and was forced to wear an archaic metal brace, and was nine years from her last breath, and thirty-seven years from being immortalized in a TV series. Texas John Slaughter was a Texas Ranger and later a Sheriff in Arizona who helped capture Geronimo, chief of the Apaches. He was the subject of a Walt Disney TV series starting in 1958. In 1917, he was five years from his end. Elfego Baca was a lawman and lawyer who single-handedly faced some forty to eighty attackers who fired 4,000 shots at him while he held them off inside an adobe house without wounding him. In 1958, Walt Disney hired actor Robert Loggia to star in TV's "The Nine Lives of Elfego Baca." Possibly the last survivor of The Old West, Baca perished twenty-eight years after this "final" meeting at McSorley's. There were only rumors that Charles "Black Bart" Bowles had cheated the law and death by making his way to New York City, dying there in 1917, probably right after this get together with some of his most illustrious one-time pursuers. He was the dapper and debonair Brit who robbed stagecoaches in the Wild West and sometimes did so with poetry. The poem he recites on Page 3, Panel 3 is actually one of his originals. Truth IS stranger than fiction!

PAGE 4, PANEL 1: Yes, Action Comics #1 introducing Superman hit the newsstands by June 1938. The boy buying ten of them is your and my fan-boy wish-fulfillment! As for ELIOT NESS, see last issue's Footnotes.

PAGE 4, PANEL 3: The Nazi Bund in America- See last issue's Footnotes.

PAGE 5, PANEL 1: Murder, Inc. was very real! Infamous gangsters associated with these Mafia enforcers included Bugsy Siegel, Meyer Lansky, The Mad Hatter. Lepke, and Lucky Luciano. NY DA Thomas Dewey built his national rep on his prosecution of this gang, leading him to become Governor of New York, and then the Presidential nominee of the Republican Party against FDR in 1944.

PAGE 6, PANEL 5: Forget "Blazing Saddles" and "A Christmas Story," there really was a Black Bart bad guy in the Old West. See the PAGE 1, PANEL 2 Footnote above for more information.

PAGE 10, PANEL 3: For the full story of the "more modern approach" developed by Britt, Kato and Rusty, read the excellent trade paperback books, *GREEN HORNET: YEAR ONE*, Volumes 1 and 2. Reading these two tomes will enhance your reading of this graphic novel/mini-series.

PAGE 10, PANEL 4: The Cleveland Torso Murders- See last issue's Footnotes.

PAGE 12, PANEL 1: Early theorists include Professor Max Bodenstein of Germany who, as early as 1913, posited the concept of chemical chain reactions, Dr. Leo Szilard of Hungary who advanced the concept of a nuclear chain reaction in 1933, Dr. Otto Hahn and Dr. Fritz Strassman of Germany who discovered nuclear fission in 1938, as expanded upon by Germany's Dr. Lise Meitner and Dr. Otto Frisch.

PAGE 12, PANELS 4 and 5: Indeed, Enrico Fermi won the 1938 Nobel Prize for his work on "induced radioactivity by neutron bombardment." He and his wife did emigrate to the U.S. in 1938 to escape religious persecution. He would go on to be one of the heads of The Manhattan Project during World War 2 which led to the creation of the Atom Bomb. Fermi did take a hard stance against any work on a Hydrogen Bomb, contemplating the moral consequences of a power so nearly unimaginable.

PAGE 13, PANEL S 2, 3, and 4: The 1936 Summer Olympics were held in Berlin, Germany with Hitler's intention being to use the games to advance Nazi propaganda. One of the attendees from America was Fritz Kuhn, head of the German-American Bund. Appalled by a black man beating Germany's best and

winning four Gold Medals in track and field, Hitler refused to meet or shake hands with Owens.

PAGE 14, PANEL 1: In 1942, Enrico Fermi's first nuclear reactor was, as part of The Manhattan Project, really finally built on this site underneath the bleachers of Stagg Field at the University of Chicago. With some scientists fearing it could set the earth's atmosphere on fire, why they decided to build this in the middle of Chicago is challenging to comprehend. As work progressed on the development of an A-Bomb, testing was eventually relocated to a more isolated part of New Mexico.

PAGE 16, PANEL 6: The Reid family wealth derives from a silver mine out west that was discovered by John and Dan Reid, Sr. It was the source of The Lone Ranger's silver bullets.

PAGE 21, PANEL 1: Look carefully at this edition of "The Daily Sentinel." It's true that years after the death of Buffalo Bill, his type of internationally famous, authentic "Wild West Show" was continued by Col. Tim McCoy, a well-known movie cowboy of the era. His last version of that show opened in Chicago in 1938 and while Sitting Bull was no longer around, his show did feature one legendary Indian as his headliner… a man who, though now reduced to an aging curiosity for the masses, was possibly the last of the generations of Native Americans who were once part of a great Indian Nation.

PAGE 21, PANEL 6: Now where have I seen this cab driver before? Could it have been in New York? Chicago? Hmmmm…

PAGE 22, PANEL 1: Jesse Owens, winner of four Gold Medals in the 1936 Berlin Olympics was America's hero for showing up Hitler! New York welcomed him back to our shores with a tremendous ticker-tape parade! Sitting next to him is the then Mayor of New York City, the popular Fiorello LaGuardia, who would later be honored by an airport named after him as well as, one day, a Broadway musical. Jesse's story was told in the 2016 movie, "*Race.*"

PAGE 22, PANELS 4-6: This is true. It was public knowledge at the time that due to Jesse being black, he was not reaping any benefits from being an Olympic super-star and the President completely ignored him. Someone, however, was determined that Jesse and his family would not financially suffer so, and approached his motorcade in the New York City parade and tossed him a brown paper bag that Jesse assumed were cookies. When he opened it, he found $10,000.00. Now you know the identity of the man who gave that to him!

Issue 3

PAGE 1: The 1936 Summer Olympics were held in Berlin, Germany under the cloud of war. In a globally spotlighted moment in time, Jesse Owens' winning of three Gold Medals became a repudiation of the Nazi claims of being "The Master Race" and was an international humiliation for Hitler, who did NOT shake the winner's hand. Other real life historical figures in this scene include Hitler's Minister of Propaganda, Joseph Goebbels, and the head of the American Nazi Bund, Fritz Kuhn, who, in fact, did attend these Olympic games.

PAGE 2: Yes, the reference is to Eliot Ness, one time leader of the famous Untouchables.

PAGE 4: Murder, Inc. was a real operation of the Mafia in this era. All the names mentioned were real gangsters associated in one way or another with Murder, Inc. For awhile, the notorious Frank Nitti was in its proverbial driver's seat. Other mobsters depicted in this scene are Tony Arcardo, Paul Ricci, driver Sam Giancana, and Sam's runty neighborhood pal, Jacob Rubenstein… who, as an adult Mob runner and lackey in Dallas, Texas, would be better known as Jack Ruby.

PAGE 5, PANEL 6: There is no known blood relation between Butch Cavendish and Henry Cavendish, the British scientist who discovered Hydrogen (1731-1810). And note that "Professor Striker" is named after writer Fran Striker, a creator of The *Lone Ranger* and *The Green Hornet*.

PAGE 13, PANEL 1: Matthew Brady put photography on the map in the United States with his early portraits of Abraham Lincoln, General Ulysses Grant, Civil War moments, and even a photo of John Quincy Adams. Take a moment and peruse the Matthew Brady collection and watch American history come to dramatic life.

PAGES 15-16: Here's my attempt to make Philip Jose Farmer proud, linking the Reid family with the Wayne family and the family of a certain Sergeant from the Yukon who is a famed member of The Royal Canadian Mounted Police.

PAGE 16, PANEL 4: This is the set-up for a pay-off that will occur in 1939 when then President Franklin D. Roosevelt will proudly show Britt Reid the Silver Bullet given to him as a child by The Lone Ranger, all as carefully chronicled in the Dynamite graphic novel, "*The Shadow/Green Hornet: Dark Nights*," written by yours truly.

PAGE 19: Uncle John Reid didn't get the last name of the RCMP Sergeant from the Yukon, but you did… right?

PAGE 20, PANEL 2: Elfego Baca was possibly the last famed name from The Wild West to pass, his death occurring in 1945.

PAGE 21: All real historic figures: Buffalo Bill Cody, Sitting Bull, Colonel Tim McCoy.

PAGE 20-22: Colonel Tim McCoy did, indeed, have the last Wild West Traveling Show in a changing America. Successor to Buffalo Bill's Wild West Show in earlier years, the Depression and the fading of the era of The Old West finally killed the show with McCoy calling it quits in 1938. A Colonel with the U.S. Army, he rose to Brigadier General. After World War I, he turned his talents to Hollywood, becoming a famous cowboy movie star until 1936. He also served in World War II. His second wife, Inga Arvad, was infamous for having been Hitler's companion at the 1936 Berlin Olympics and a lover to John F.Kennedy in the early 1940's. McCoy died in 1978.

Issue 4

PAGE 1: The Wild West Shows performed in the 1800's through early 1900's were led by the premiere show of Buffalo Bill Cody. Perhaps his star attraction, Annie Oakley aside, was famed Chief Sitting Bull, architect of the massacre at Little Big Horn. Clearly, The Lone Ranger was NOT happy about this fate of Sitting Bull! A willing paid performer or an abused minority exploited by the white man? This is for you and history to decide. Years later, it would be Hollywood's famed cowboy star and former cavalry officer Colonel Tim McCoy who owned the last Wild West Show, which did, indeed, go out of business in 1938, bringing the curtain down on this form of entertainment for the masses and, some say, on The Old West, itself.

PAGE 4: Bat Masterson was a real hero of the Old West. In 1875, he was, indeed, a deputy sheriff. He was immortalized in a TV series bearing his name and starring Gene Barry that lasted from 1958-61. And, yes, he wore a cane and derby hat.

PAGE 6: Watching "The Lone Ranger" TV series as a kid, I figured Tonto went into town alone ninety-six times and was beat up each time. I'm glad to see he warns Kato not to repeat his mistakes.

PAGE 8: As stated in previous FOOTNOTES TO HISTORY, Eliot Ness, The *Untouchables, Frank Nitti,* and *Murder, Inc.* were all very real. There are fascinating books and articles about all of them, plus a TV series and a movie on *"The Untouchables."* In the TV series from 1959-1963, Frank Nitti was regularly featured as the bad guy.

PAGE 15: In 1917, Bat Masterson was a New York City resident, working as a newspaper reporter covering the fights, sports in general, and eventually politics and corruption. The Hupmobile was a cool car first introduced in 1909. As a side-note to

history, the Hupmobile dealership in Canton, Ohio was where the National Football League was created in 1920.

PAGE 17: Neville Chamberlain was the Prime Minister of England who, in 1938, ignominiously chose to appease Hitler and sign the Munich Agreement, effectively ceding the Sudetenland to Germany and opening the door to Hitler's invasion of Poland in 1939 and the on-set of World War II.

PAGE 22, PANEL 3: I just have to say I admire Britt Reid here for sticking to his guns by... not sticking to his guns... and not allowing Eliot Ness to shoot down Black Bart, Jr. The Lone Ranger Code holds!

PAGE 24: This issue is dedicated to MY Tonto, Jay Silverheels, and to each actor who brought Tonto to life on radio, on TV, and in the movies.

Issue 5

PAGE 8, PANEL 4: Hmmm… A city cop circa 1938 who seems genuinely inspired by the man and the mask of The Lone Ranger? I wonder if this policeman named Kip might one day decide to follow in his shoes?

PAGE 9, PANEL 2: John Reid here did not have to suffer the indignity of wearing sunglasses to replace his mask. This scene is simply my personal "Thank You" to one of my childhood heroes, Clayton Moore.

PAGE 11, PANEL 5: See the Footnote in Issue #2 for the full story, but this site under the bleachers of Stagg Field at The University of Chicago was actually the chosen site by Enrico Fermi for his first nuclear reactor.

PAGE 20, PANEL 1: How many people at the burial can you identify? Can you find Britt Reid, Kato, Miss Case, Mike Axford, Rusty Schmidt, President Franklin D. Roosevelt, Jesse Owens, Eliot Ness, Police Officer Kip, and that Sergeant of the Royal Canadian Mounted Police who is related to the Reids? Then there are the kids from the Police Stables. You might also spy two famous movie and TV stars from Hollywood of that era who had to be there. Elfego Baca, perhaps the last surviving figure of The Old West is present. I also think I see an interesting man about town with a hawkish nose, a well know industrialist, an imposing man with what looks like a unique haircut, a mysterious man in a fedora who just may have a mask on under there, an erudite man seemingly over-dressed in a tux, a man holding a pith helmet, a sculpted man who somewhat resembles Olympic and Movie star Buster Crabbe, an intense man who attends because he has learned that his family is also related to the Reids and to that Mountie, and a reporter covering the burial not for "The Daily Sentinel" but rather for some other great metropolitan newspaper. Anybody else?

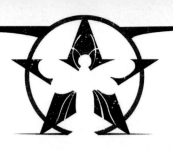

CLOSING FOOTNOTE: Regarding The Old West, I suggest you visit the captivating website for The Buffalo Bill Center of the West at: centerofthewest.org for more detailed history and true tales of the Wild West, Buffalo Bill, outlaws, and the greatest artist to ever capture that era and the faces of The Old West on canvas, Frederic Remington, the man The Lone Ranger claims painted his portrait in 1890. The museum in Cody, Wyoming has many of Remington's great works. Visitors as well as on-line visitors can read the actual letters of Buffalo Bill which have been digitized, see the Remington paintings, and look at photographs of all the real lawmen and Texas Rangers of the Plains. The Center welcomes comic book readers, fans and enthusiasts to its world of The Wild West along with the real-life supervillains of the era and the real-life super-heroes back then who "led the fight for law and order in the early West".

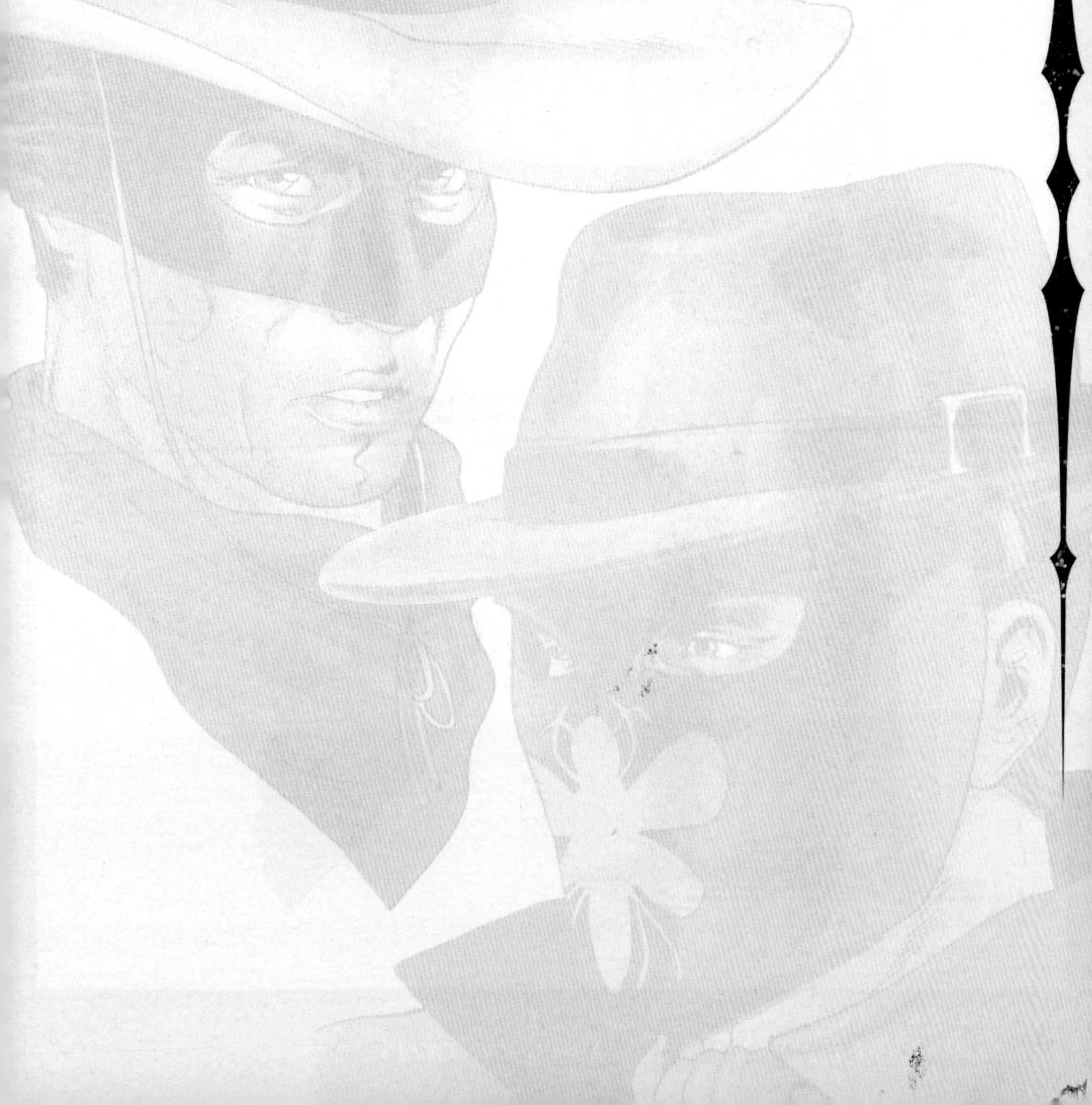

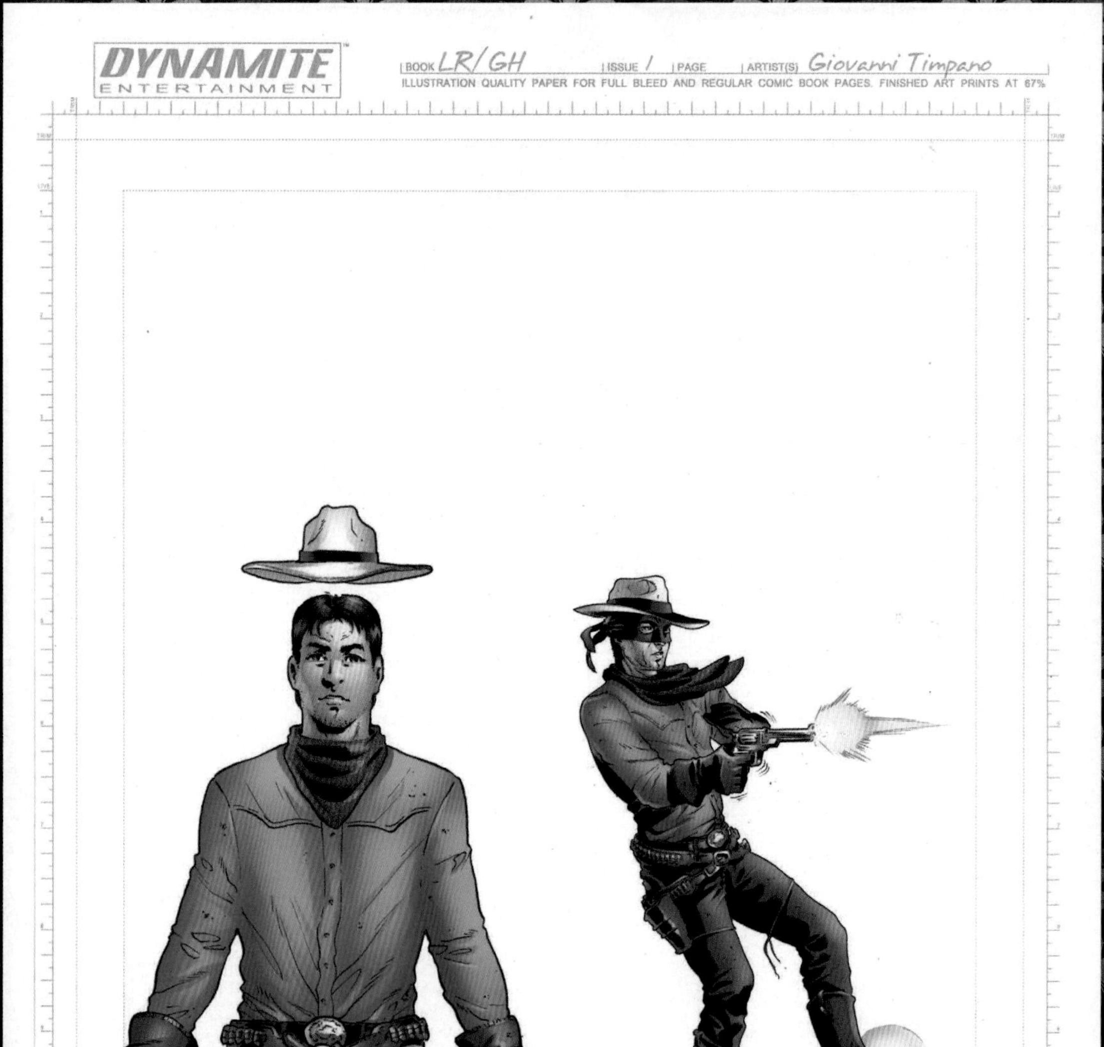
DYNAMITE ENTERTAINMENT
BOOK LR/GH ISSUE 1 PAGE ARTIST(S) Giovanni Timpano
ILLUSTRATION QUALITY PAPER FOR FULL BLEED AND REGULAR COMIC BOOK PAGES. FINISHED ART PRINTS AT 67%
◄ CUT RIGHT-HAND PAGE AT THIS LINE
FOR DOUBLE PAGE SPREAD: CUT AS SHOWN, ABUT PAGE EDGES, TAPE ON BACK. DO NOT OVERLAP.
ALL BLEED ART MUST EXTEND TO SOLID LINE. KEEP ALL LETTERING INSIDE BROKEN-LINE BOX (LIVE AREA).
CUT LEFT-HAND PAGE AT THIS LINE ►

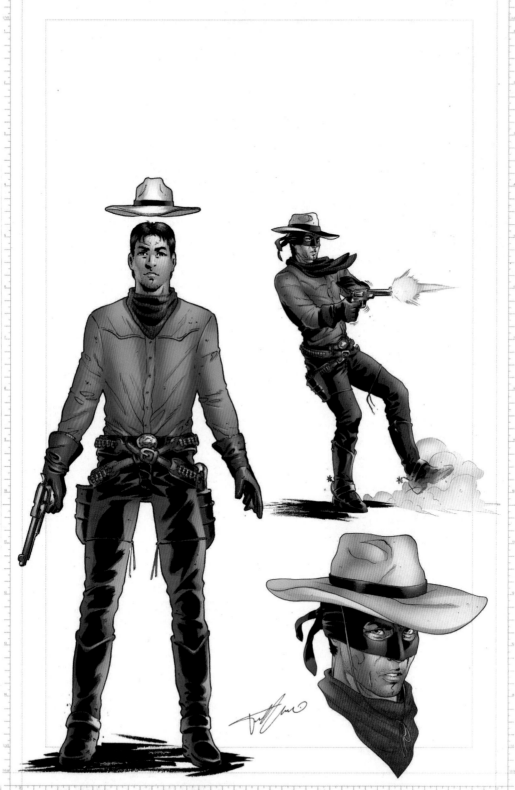

Issue ONE Variant Cover
Art by GIOVANNI TIMPANO Colors by PETE PANTAZIS

ISSUE ONE VARIANT COVER
ART BY GIOVANNI TIMPANO COLORS BY PETE PANTAZIS

"Worth its weight in hi-yo silver."

ENTERTAINMENT WEEKLY

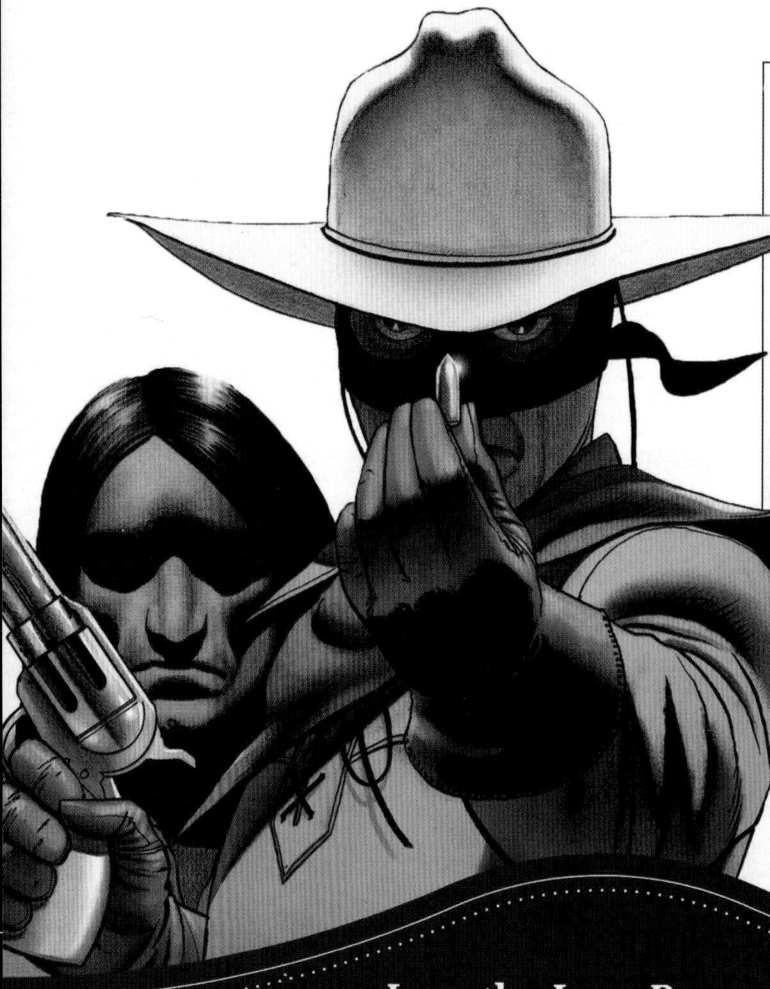

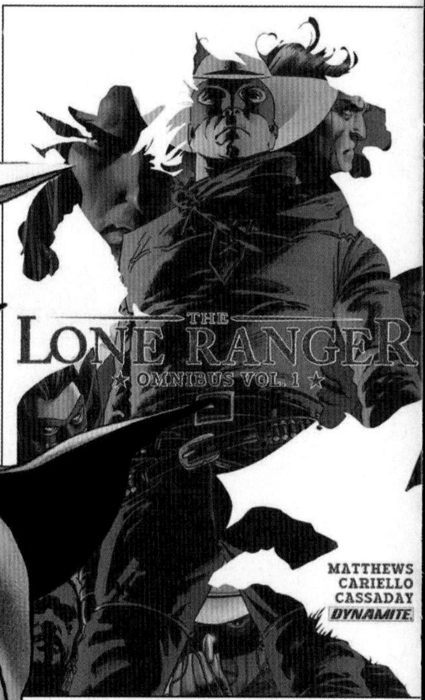
THE LONE RANGER
OMNIBUS VOL. 1
MATTHEWS
CARIELLO
CASSADAY
DYNAMITE

THE LONE RANGER OMNIBUS VOLUME 1
ISBN13: 978-1-60690-352-0

Love the Lone Ranger®?

Check out this fine round-up of Dynamite collections, Kemo sabe.

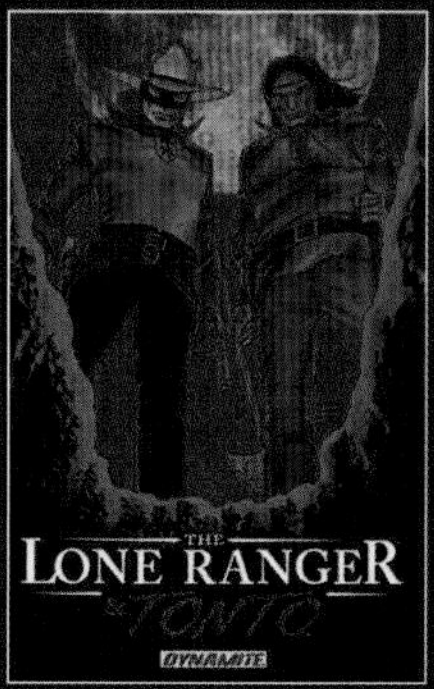
THE LONE RANGER & TONTO
DYNAMITE

THE LONE RANGER & TONTO
ISBN-13: 978-1-60690-123-6

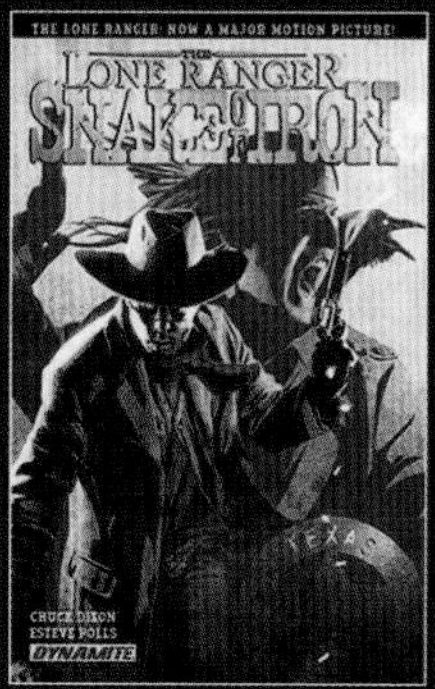
THE LONE RANGER: NOW A MAJOR MOTION PICTURE!
THE LONE RANGER
CHUCK DIXON
ESTEVE POLLS
DYNAMITE

VOLUME 5
ISBN-13: 978-1-60690-346-9

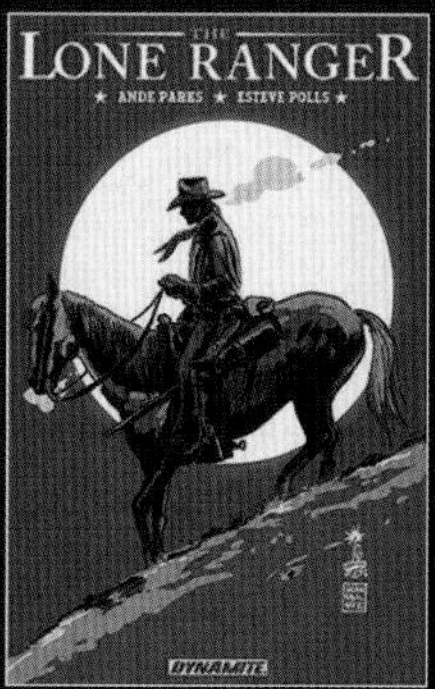
THE LONE RANGER
ANDE PARKS ★ ESTEVE POLLS
DYNAMITE

SNAKE OF IRON
ISBN13: 978-1-60690-396-4

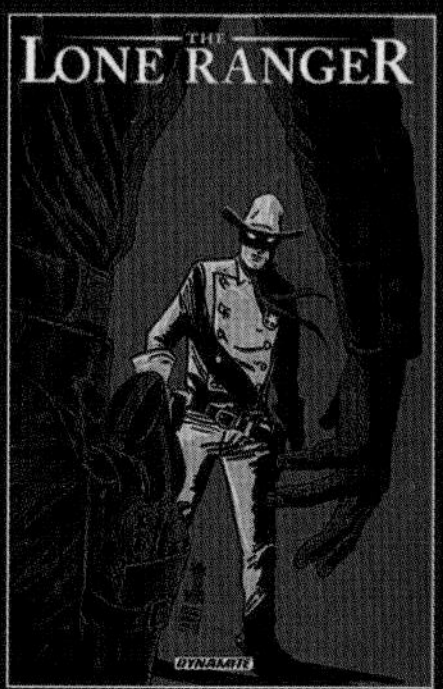
THE LONE RANGER
DYNAMITE

VINDICATED
ISBN13: 978-1-60690-699-6

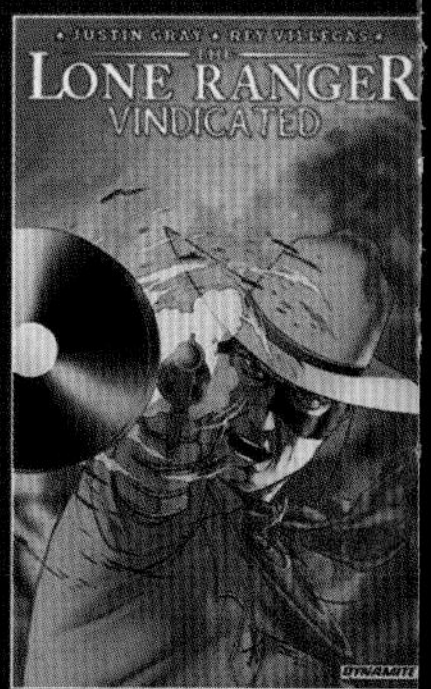
JUSTIN GRAY • REY VILLEGAS
THE LONE RANGER
VINDICATED
DYNAMITE

VOLUME 8
ISBN13: 978-1-60690-563-0

Read about these volumes and more at Dynamite.com.

DYNAMITE® YouTube
Online at www.DYNAMITE.com
Tumblr dynamitecomics.tumblr.com
Facebook /Dynamitecomics
Twitter @Dynamitecomics
Instagram /Dynamitecomics
YouTube /Dynamitecomics

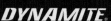

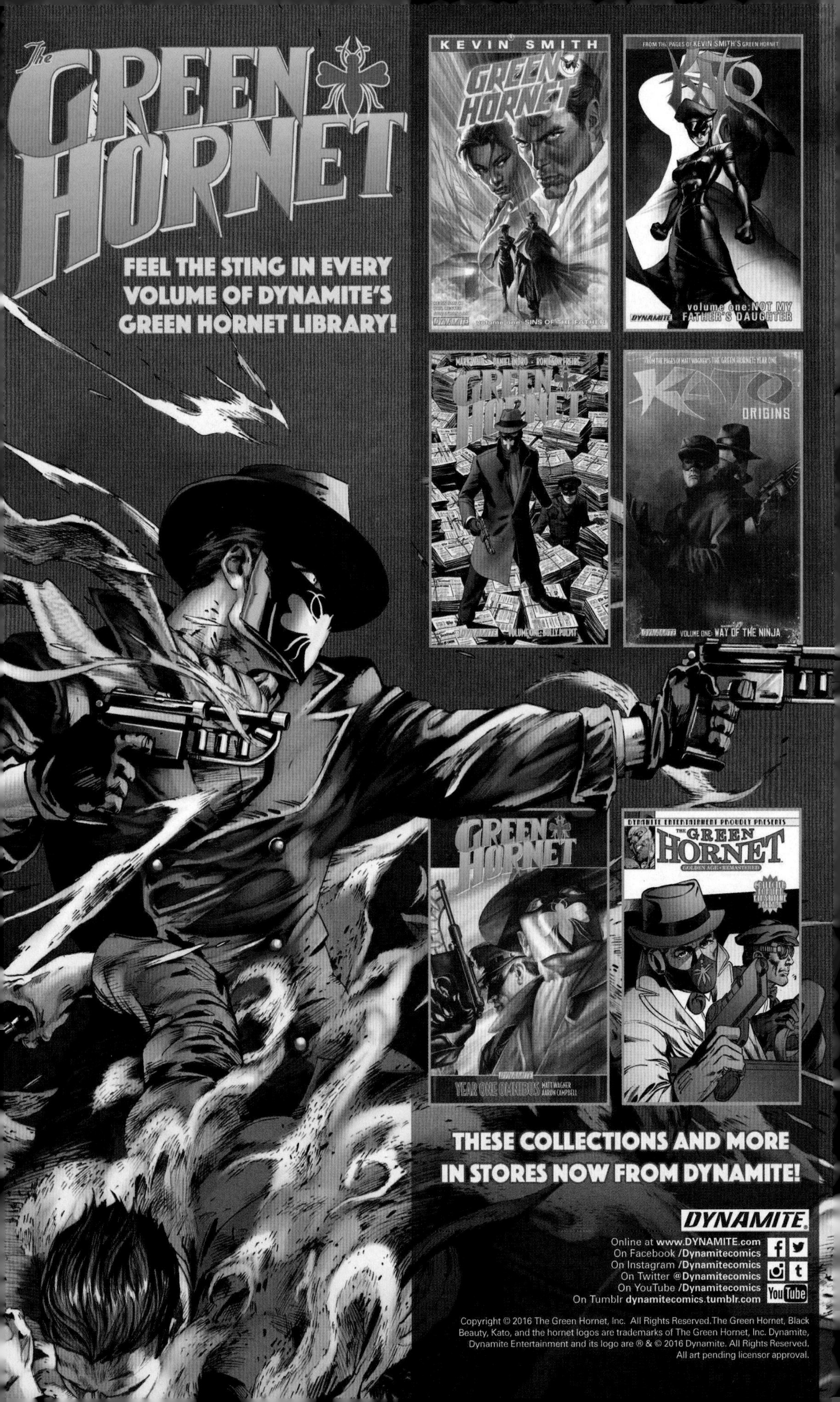
The GREEN HORNET
FEEL THE STING IN EVERY VOLUME OF DYNAMITE'S GREEN HORNET LIBRARY!
KEVIN SMITH
GREEN HORNET
volume one: SINS OF THE FATHER
FROM THE PAGES OF KEVIN SMITH'S GREEN HORNET
KATO
volume one: NOT MY FATHER'S DAUGHTER
GREEN HORNET
VOLUME ONE: BULLY PULPIT
FROM THE PAGES OF MATT WAGNER'S THE GREEN HORNET: YEAR ONE
KATO ORIGINS
VOLUME ONE: WAY OF THE NINJA
GREEN HORNET
YEAR ONE OMNIBUS
MATT WAGNER
AARON CAMPBELL
DYNAMITE ENTERTAINMENT PROUDLY PRESENTS
THE GREEN HORNET
GOLDEN AGE REMASTERED
THESE COLLECTIONS AND MORE IN STORES NOW FROM DYNAMITE!
DYNAMITE
Online at www.DYNAMITE.com
On Facebook /Dynamitecomics
On Instagram /Dynamitecomics
On Twitter @Dynamitecomics
On YouTube /Dynamitecomics
On Tumblr dynamitecomics.tumblr.com
Copyright © 2016 The Green Hornet, Inc. All Rights Reserved. The Green Hornet, Black Beauty, Kato, and the hornet logos are trademarks of The Green Hornet, Inc. Dynamite, Dynamite Entertainment and its logo are ® & © 2016 Dynamite. All Rights Reserved. All art pending licensor approval.

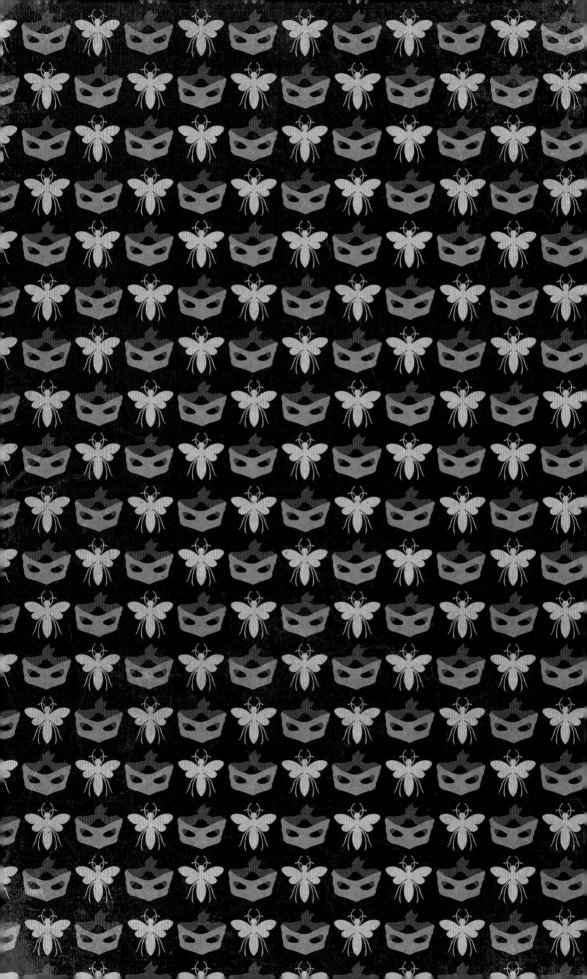